CROCHE'
MONSTERS

# CROCHET MONSTERS

## STACKPOLE BOOKS

Essex, Connecticut
Blue Ridge Summit, Pennsylvania

**MEGAN LAPP,**
**Creator of Crafty Intentions**

# STACKPOLE BOOKS

An imprint of Globe Pequot, the trade division of The Rowman & Littlefield Publishing Group, Inc.
4501 Forbes Blvd., Ste. 200
Lanham, MD 20706
www.rowman.com

Distributed by NATIONAL BOOK NETWORK
800-462-6420

British Library Cataloguing in Publication Information available

**Library of Congress Cataloging-in-Publication Data**
Names: Lapp, Megan, 1984– author.
Title: Crochet monsters / Megan Lapp.
Description: Essex, Connecticut ; Blue Ridge Summit, Pennsylvania :
    Stackpole Books, [2024] | Summary: "This book contains instructions for
    37 unique monster bodies and more than 15 teeth patterns, tongues and
    horns, hair and scales, tails and limbs, and more! Nearly everything is
    interchangeable, with over 30 limb options and so many more ways to
    customize your monster"— Provided by publisher.
Identifiers: LCCN 2023041413 (print) | LCCN 2023041414 (ebook) | ISBN
    9780811771627 (paperback) | ISBN 9780811771634 (epub)
Subjects: LCSH: Crocheting—Patterns. | Soft toy making—Patterns. |
    Monsters.
Classification: LCC TT825 .L3645 2024  (print) | LCC TT825  (ebook) | DDC
    746.43/4041—dc23/eng/20231207
LC record available at https://lccn.loc.gov/2023041413
LC ebook record available at https://lccn.loc.gov/2023041414

 The paper used in this publication meets the minimum requirements of American National Standard for Information Sciences—Permanence of Paper for Printed Library Materials, ANSI/NISO Z39.48-1992.

First Edition

# CONTENTS

# HAIR/HAIRSTYLE OPTIONS . . . . . . . 309

# TEETH OPTIONS . . . .314

# BELLY OPTIONS . . . .330

# CLAW OPTIONS . . . .334

# TONGUE OPTIONS. . .337

# EXTRAS/FACE OPTIONS . . . . . . . . 346

# INTRODUCTION

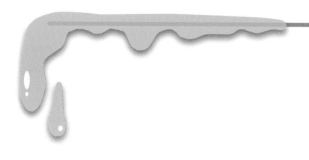

## Where to Begin

Each Monster is truly a unique individual. Throughout this book, you'll find many examples of Monster options pieced together in a variety of ways. Your yarn texture and color choices will further customize your creations. Use these examples as a jumping-off point for your own creativity. Do not be afraid to try new combinations!

Many factors will impact the size of finished Monsters, including your choice of yarn, your tension, how tightly your Monster is stuffed, and the options you ultimately select for body, limbs, horns, and more. Approximate sizing has been added to all sections. Monster bodies are generally sized between 4 and 9 inches tall for most selections created with the suggested materials. It is important to use the same weight yarn for all parts of your Monster. Using a different weight yarn for one piece may result in that piece being a different scale than what is shown in the book.

To help you plan, each section, such as "Body Options" on page 9, includes a photo gallery with all the available options for that attribute. Look through the book and note the options you'd like for your Monster. Use the Planning Sheet on page 3 to design your Monster and track your progress as you complete each piece.

Familiarize yourself with the Glossary of Terms and Stitches on page 4 to note any stitches or techniques that may be new to you, and refer to it as needed while you work.

## MATERIALS

*NOTE: All yarn amounts and sizing measurements are approximate.*

* Worsted weight #4 medium yarn
* Sport weight #2 light yarn for optionally smaller-scale teeth
* Crochet hooks, size G (4 mm) and size D (3.25 mm)
* Safety eyes: Sizing ranges from 24 mm and 30 mm to 40 mm with colored irises for use with bodies or eye accessories. Placement and details about sizing are included in the body instructions. I purchase safety eyes from two sources: Darkside Crochet and Suncatcher Craft Eyes. Darkside Crochet is UK based and Suncatcher is US based, but both ship worldwide. Both are also women-owned businesses.
  * You can find Darkside here: https://darksidecrochet.bigcartel.com
  * You can find Suncatcher here: https://suncatchercrafteyes.com
* Wire cutters
* Pliers
* Scissors

* Pet brush/small wire brush (for brushing out/fuzzing up yarn)
* Stitch markers
* Fiberfill
* Strong wire for armature for some Monsters
* Optional:
  * Hemostats/forceps (for stuffing small places with fiberfill)
  * Something to add weight to the bottom of the body, like glass gems (a.k.a. flat marbles), clean stones, pellets in nylon stockings, etc.
  * Screw-back metal rivets, studs, or spikes to use as claws, spikes, or general decoration (for tips on how to add these, go to page 172)
  * Plastic canvas
  * Bottle caps and/or felt furniture pads to reinforce bottoms of feet

*NOTE: Adding metal claws, safety eyes, weights, or wire will make the Monster unsafe for small children. If the Monster is meant for a child, avoid weights, wire, and metal claws. If the Monster is meant for children under the age of three, you should also avoid safety eyes and opt for crocheted eyes instead—crochet eye instructions are included in this book.*

## Tips and Tricks

**1.** Make sure as you work that you are crocheting right-side out versus inside out. This point is explained in the Glossary.

**2.** While worsted weight yarn with a G (4 mm) hook is recommended for these patterns, you can use any weight yarn you prefer so long as the fabric you are creating with a corresponding hook size has a tight-enough weave to hide the fiberfill inside the crochet work. If you change the yarn weight you are using, you will also need to adjust the crochet hook size and the safety eye size to be proportional to your work. The same weight yarn should be used for all Monster pieces.

**3.** Make sure you are working the "Sl St, Ch 1" join stitch correctly; check the Glossary for an explanation and YouTube tutorial link.

**4.** Hemostats are an excellent tool for stuffing hard-to-reach places inside your amigurumi. Consider using a pair as needed!

**5.** If you have any issues following a YouTube video link, you can go to the Crafty Intentions YouTube Channel here: https://www.youtube.com/c/CraftyIntentions

**6.** Stitch count is shown at the end of each row in brackets like this: [6]

The "Sl St to beginning stitch, Ch 1" join is NOT counted in the stitch count.

Chain stitches are not counted in the stitch count unless specified.

Sub-rows (like 6A, 6B, 6C, etc.) feature a stitch count like this [-6] for each sub-row step, and they also include a final stitch count to show how many stitches are available to work into once all the sub-rows are complete.

**7.** Use a sport weight yarn and a size D (3.25 mm) hook for smaller-scale teeth or other accessories.

**8.** Optional: You may add metal spikes that screw in place as claws on the ends of limbs. Place the screws through the limb in the desired locations, and twist the spike (claw) onto the end of the screw. Tighten it as much as possible. Once it is fully placed, you can cement it in place by putting some craft glue inside the toe on top of the screw head to fasten it more permanently. If the screw won't stay in place because the stitches are too open, you can use a washer, or you can fashion a washer from a small piece of plastic canvas, to prevent the screw from slipping through the stitches. Please note that adding metal spikes makes the piece unsafe for children.

# Monster Planning Sheet

Here's an easy-to-use planning guide to copy, photograph, or scan and to use as a template for noting the styles and options you want for each Monster you make.

**Body/Mouth Style(s)** _____

_____

**Eyes** _____

**Feet** _____

**Limbs** _____

_____

**Back Scales** _____

**Tail** _____

**Ears** _____

**Antennae** _____

**Horn(s)** _____

**Hairstyle** _____

**Teeth** _____

**Belly** _____

**Claws** _____

**Tongue** _____

**Extras** _____

_____

# Glossary of Terms and Stitches

To create the creatures in this book, you will need to learn a few possibly new-to-you stitches, particularly increases and decreases. The processes will be familiar, but where you work the stitches is important to note. Below is a list of terms and abbreviations for stitches that you should become familiar with and refer to as needed as you work the patterns.

| | |
|---|---|
| **[Brackets]** | Brackets that come after BLO or FLO indicate that these stitches are back loop only or front loop only. Ex.: "BLO [SC 6]"<br><br>Brackets at the end of the row indicate the stitch count for the row. Ex.: [6]; this means there are 6 stitches in the row. |
| **Underlined Stitches** | Underlined stitches are stitches worked around slip stitches, into the same stitch a slip stitch was worked into.<br><br>Go here for video demonstration: https://www.youtube.com/watch?v=khed-Ni_AjM&t=6s |
| **&** | Located between 2 stitches, the "&" indicates that both stitches are made into the same stitch, as an increase, but with two different types of stitches.<br><br>Go here for video demonstration: www.youtube.com/watch?v=jGA2nAzL2cU&t=16s |
| **< or >** | Indicates the stitch will start (<) or finish (>) in the same stitch as the last stitch or the next stitch. |
| **<Dec>** | Beginning in the *same* stitch as your last stitch, make a decrease stitch into that and the next stitch, and then, into the same stitch that the decrease stitch ends in, begin your next stitch. This technique can apply to a regular Dec, a HDC Dec, or any kind of decrease.<br><br>Go here for video demonstration: www.youtube.com/watch?v=Ni2ZM1cXJI4 |
| **2 Dec in 3 SC** | Make one decrease as normal, and then make the second decrease starting in the *same* stitch as the first decrease and ending in the next stitch.<br><br>Go here for video demonstration: www.youtube.com/watch?v=vWRuWd689KQ&t=4s |
| **BLO [ ]** | Back Loop Only<br><br>--------<br><br>*NOTE: The rows with FLO or BLO stitches will be structured with brackets [ ]. The brackets will enclose any and all stitches that the FLO or BLO instruction should apply to. Ex: "BLO [SC 3], SC 3" means 3 SC in the BLO and then 3 normal SC.* |
| **Ch** | Chain |
| **Colorwork** | For a seamless color change, switch to the new color during the final stitch before the color change. To switch colors at the end of a row, switch to the new color when you make the slip stitch join. When you make the final yarn over to complete the last stitch before the new color (or the slip stitch join at the end of the row), use the new color for that final yarn over, and pull up. Doing so will produce a seamless transition to that new color. As you work the next stitches, hold the unused color on top of the previous row of stitches and crochet around it as you work.<br><br>Go here for a video demonstration: https://www.youtube.com/watch?v=1XReLVEjZCo |

| DC | Double Crochet |
|---|---|
| **DC Dec** | YO, insert into next stitch, YO, pull up, YO, pull through 2 loops, YO, insert into next stitch, YO, pull up, YO, pull through 2 loops, YO, pull through all 3 loops |
| **DC/HDC Dec** | YO, insert into next stitch, YO, pull up, YO, pull through 2 loops, YO, insert into next stitch, YO, pull up, YO, pull through all 4 loops |
| **Dec** | Decrease: One stitch combining 2 spaces<br><br>Insert hook into the next stitch, YO, pull up<br><br>Insert hook into the next stitch, YO, pull up, YO, pull through all remaining loops<br><br>All decreases are single crochet decreases unless otherwise specified. |
| **FLO [ ]** | Front Loop Only<br><br>*NOTE: The rows with FLO or BLO stitches will be structured with brackets [ ]. The brackets will enclose any and all stitches that the FLO or BLO instruction should apply to. Ex: "FLO [SC 3], SC 3" would mean 3 SC in the FLO and then 3 SC.* |
| **FP HDC** | Front Post Half Double Crochet<br><br>YO, insert hook from front to back to front around post of corresponding stitch below, YO, pull up, YO, pull through all remaining loops |
| **Half Trip** | Half Triple Crochet<br><br>YO twice, insert into next stitch, YO, pull up, YO, pull through 2 loops, YO, pull through all remaining loops |
| **Half Trip Dec** | Half Triple Crochet Decrease<br><br>YO twice, insert into next stitch, YO, pull up, YO, pull through 2 loops, YO, insert into next stitch, YO, pull up, YO, pull through all remaining loops |
| **Half Trip Inc** | Half Triple Crochet Increase<br><br>Two half triple crochet stitches worked into the same stitch |
| **HDC** | Half Double Crochet<br><br>YO, insert hook into next stitch, YO, pull up, YO, pull through all 3 loops |
| **HDC Dec** | Half Double Crochet Decrease<br><br>YO, insert into next stitch, YO, pull up, YO, pull through 2 loops, YO, insert into next stitch, YO, pull up, YO, pull through all 4 loops |
| **HDC Inc** | Half Double Crochet Increase<br><br>Two half double crochet stitches worked into the same stitch |
| **HDC Triple Inc** | Half Double Crochet Triple Increase<br><br>Three half double crochet stitches worked into the same stitch |

| | |
|---|---|
| **HDC/SC Dec** | Half Double Crochet and Single Crochet Decrease<br><br>YO, insert into next stitch, YO, pull up, YO, pull through 2 loops, insert into next stitch, YO, pull up, YO, pull through all 3 loops |
| **Inc** | Increase: Create 2 stitches in 1 space<br><br>Assume all increases are single crochet increases unless otherwise specified. |
| **Invisible Triple SC Decrease** | Invisible Triple Single Crochet Decrease: single crochet decrease across 3 stitches FLO.<br><br>Insert hook into the FLO of the first stitch, do not YO, insert hook into the FLO of the second stitch, do not YO, insert hook into the FLO of the third stitch, YO, pull through 3 loops, YO, pull through remaining loops |
| **Joining Toes, Knees, Fingers, etc.** | Here is a video on this technique: www.youtube.com/watch?v=paLzIAi--vk |
| **Lark's Head Knot** | Fold a cut length of yarn in half, insert the hook into or around a stitch, insert the hook into the fold of the length of cut yarn, pull through, YO both pieces of the folded yarn length, pull through the loop, tighten the loop |
| **OC** | Original Chain<br><br>This refers to the very first set of chain stitches you made to start the piece you're working on. |
| **Picot** | Chain 3, slip stitch in the third chain from hook |
| **Right side/ Outside vs. Wrong side/ Inside** | To crochet right-side out, insert your hook from the outside/right side of the work to the inside/wrong side of the work; if you are right-handed, you will be working in a clockwise direction.<br><br>Here is a video on this technique: www.youtube.com/watch?v=beReNFWQPAs |
| **SC** | Single Crochet |
| **SC/HDC Dec** | Single Crochet/Half Double Crochet Decrease<br><br>Insert hook into next stitch, YO, pull up, YO, insert hook into next stitch, YO, pull up, YO, pull through all loops on hook<br><br>Here is a video on this stitch: www.youtube.com/watch?v=h4wkxMOMqXg&t=12s |
| **Sk St** | Skip Stitch |

| | |
|---|---|
| **Sl St to beginning stitch, Ch 1** | Most of the patterns are written with a "Slip Stitch, Chain 1" joining method for each row. This *does* affect the shape of each piece but in a minor way, as the piece was written with the seam shift in mind. If you prefer to crochet in spiral/in the round, you are welcome to try it, but I do not guarantee that all asymmetrical sections will come out exactly as shown. The "Sl St, Ch 1" join is not counted in the stitch count.<br><br>To end the row, after you have worked the entire row, you will slip stitch into the first stitch you worked in the row, and then chain 1. Begin the next row by crocheting into the same stitch you slip stitched into.<br><br>For video demonstration, go here: www.youtube.com/watch?v=Qqu5N7TCt3U |
| **Spike Stitch SC** | Work a single crochet by inserting your hook into the same space you worked your stitch in the previous row. This stitch will be worked around the single crochet in the previous row, completely encasing it. |
| **St** | Stitch |
| **Triple SC Dec** | Triple Single Crochet Decrease: one stitch combining 3 spaces using single crochet<br>(Insert hook in next stitch space, YO, pull up) x 3, YO, pull through all 4 loops |
| **Triple Crochet** | YO twice, insert into next stitch, YO, pull up, YO, pull through 2 loops, YO, pull through 2 loops, YO, pull through all remaining loops |
| **Triple SC Inc** | Triple Single Crochet Increase: 3 single crochet worked into 1 stitch |
| **YO** | Yarn Over |

# BODIES

There are more than 35 options for Monster Bodies. If you select an Open Mouth Monster Body, you will first need to make the Open Mouth. There are 7 options for Open Mouths, which are presented first.

If you select any other style of Monster Body, you may skip the Open Mouth options and go straight to the instructions for your Body choice.

## Open Mouths (make to use with Open Mouth body styles)

Open Mouth with
No Teeth...15

Open Mouth with No
Teeth Black Hole...15

Open Mouth with
Humanlike Teeth...16

Open Mouth with
Pointy Teeth...18

Open Mouth with Short Row of
Small Teeth...19

Open Mouth with
Buck Teeth...21

Open Mouth with Four
Pointed Teeth...24

## Blob Style Bodies

Blob Body with
Underbite...27

Blob Body with Deep
Pocket Underbite...29

Blob Body with
Overbite...33

Blob Body with
Open Mouth...35

Blob Body with
No Mouth...38

# Cylinder Bodies

Cylinder with Underbite and No Legs...41

Cylinder with Underbite and Legs...44

Cylinder with Deep Pocket Underbite and No Legs...46

Cylinder with Deep Pocket Underbite and Legs...49

Cylinder with Overbite and No Legs...52

Cylinder with Overbite and Legs...55

Cylinder with Open Mouth and No Legs...58

Cylinder with Open Mouth and Legs...60

Cylinder with No Mouth and No Legs...64

Cylinder with No Mouth and Legs...66

# Egg-shaped Bodies

Egg Shape with Underbite and No Legs...67

Egg Shape with Underbite and Legs...69

Egg Shape with Overbite and No Legs...75

Egg Shape with Overbite and Legs...76

Egg Shape with Open Mouth and No Legs...79

Egg Shape with Open Mouth and Legs...82

Egg Shape with No Mouth and No Legs...87

Egg Shape with No Mouth and Legs...89

# Sphere Bodies

Sphere with Underbite...92

Sphere with Overbite...94

Sphere with Open Mouth...95

Sphere with No Mouth...98

# Square Bodies

Square with Underbite and No Legs...99

Square with Underbite and Legs...105

Square with Deep Pocket Underbite and No Legs...108

Square with Deep Pocket Underbite and Legs...112

Square with Overbite and No Legs...118

Square with Overbite and Legs...120

Square with No Mouth and No Legs...126

Square with No Mouth and Legs...128

# Eyeball Monster Bodies

Eyeball Monster Main Body/ Eye with Crocheted Iris and Pupil...132

Eyeball Monster Main Body/ Eye with Safety Eye...134

Eyeball Monster Eyelid...135

Blob Body with Open Mouth, Open Mouth with No Teeth, Axolotl Flaps, Big Long Tongue

Cylinder Body with Open Mouth and No Legs, Open Mouth with No Teeth Black Hole, Three-toed Dangling Limbs for Legs and Arms, Skinny Curved Horns

# Open Mouths

Open Mouths are for use with any of the "Open Mouth" Monster Bodies.

## OPEN MOUTH WITH NO TEETH (MAKE 1)

*Approximately 4 in/10 cm wide*

*Mouth Color Yarn: Approximately 12 yd/11 m worsted/medium weight yarn*

1. SC 6 in Magic Circle, Sl St to beginning stitch, Ch 1 [6]

2. Inc x 6, Sl St to beginning stitch, Ch 1 [12]

3. (SC, Inc) x 6, Sl St to beginning stitch, Ch 1 [18]

4. (SC, Inc, SC) x 6, Sl St to beginning stitch, Ch 1 [24]

5. (SC 3, Inc) x 6, Sl St to beginning stitch, Ch 1 [30]

6. (SC 2, Inc, SC 2) x 6, Sl St to beginning stitch, Ch 1 [36]

7. (SC 5, Inc) x 6, Sl St to beginning stitch, Ch 1 [42]

8. (SC 3, Inc, SC 3) x 6, Sl St to beginning stitch [48]

Fasten off with a short yarn tail.

## OPEN MOUTH WITH NO TEETH BLACK HOLE (MAKE 1)

*Approximately 4 in/10 cm wide*

*Mouth Color Yarn: Approximately 34 yd/31 m worsted/medium weight yarn (Black recommended)*

*Monster Body Color Yarn: Approximately 12 yd/11 m worsted/medium weight yarn*

Starting with Mouth Color Yarn:

1. SC 6 in Magic Circle, Sl St to beginning stitch, Ch 1 [6]

2. Inc x 6, Sl St to beginning stitch, Ch 1 [12]

3. (SC, Inc) x 6, Sl St to beginning stitch, Ch 1 [18]

4. (SC, Inc, SC) x 6, Sl St to beginning stitch, Ch 1 [24]

5. (SC 3, Inc) x 6, Sl St to beginning stitch, Ch 1 [30]

6. (SC 2, Inc, SC 2) x 6, Sl St to beginning stitch, Ch 1 [36]

7. (SC 5, Inc) x 6, Sl St to beginning stitch, Ch 1 [42]

8. (SC 3, Inc, SC 3) x 3, switch to the Monster Body Color Yarn and carry the Mouth Color Yarn under your stitches as you continue: (SC 3, Inc, SC 3) x 3, switch to the Mouth Color Yarn, Sl St to beginning stitch, Ch 1 [48]

Keep the Mouth Color Yarn attached, and fasten off the Monster Body Color Yarn with a short yarn tail.

Row 8 contains some minor colorwork; for more information on colorwork technique, see the Colorwork Glossary entry.

9. SC 24, Ch 24, Skip 24 stitches, Sl St to the beginning stitch, Ch 1 [48]

The stitch count for Row 9 includes the chain stitches, as you will work into them in Row 10. In Row 10, you will work 24 SC in the SC stitches of Row 9, and then you will work SC stitches in each of the 24 Ch stitches from Row 9. Insert a stitch marker into the chain (on the chain side) that you will work the 25th SC of this row into for reference in where to begin to attach this mouth to any Open Mouth Monster Body.

10. SC 48, Sl St to beginning stitch, Ch 1 [48]

11. (SC 3, Dec, SC 3) x 6, Sl St to beginning stitch, Ch 1 [42]

12. (SC 5, Dec) x 6, Sl St to beginning stitch, Ch 1 [36]

13. (SC 2, Dec, SC 2) x 6, Sl St to beginning stitch, Ch 1 [30]

14. (SC 3, Dec) x 6, Sl St to beginning stitch, Ch 1 [24]

15. (SC, Dec, SC) x 6, Sl St to beginning stitch, Ch 1 [18]

16. (SC, Dec) x 6, Sl St to beginning stitch, Ch 1 [12]

17. Dec x 6, Sl St to beginning stitch [6]

Fasten off with a 12 in/30.5 cm yarn tail.

Use the yarn tail to sew the hole shut and then weave in the end.

Turn the Mouth inside out, as the right side/outside of the work will be visible inside the Mouth.

# OPEN MOUTH WITH HUMANLIKE TEETH (MAKE 1)

*Approximately 4 in/10 cm wide*

*Mouth Color Yarn: 15 yd/13.75 m medium/worsted weight yarn*

*Tooth Color Yarn: 5 yd/4.5 m lighter/sport weight yarn (White recommended)*

1. Starting with Mouth Color Yarn, SC 6 in Magic Circle, Sl St to beginning stitch, Ch 1 [6]

2. Inc x 6, Sl St to beginning stitch, Ch 1 [12]

3. (SC, Inc) x 6, Sl St to beginning stitch, Ch 1 [18]

4. (SC, Inc, SC) x 6, Sl St to beginning stitch, Ch 1 [24]

5. (SC 3, Inc) x 6, Sl St to beginning stitch, Ch 1 [30]

6. (SC 2, Inc, SC 2) x 6, Sl St to beginning stitch, Ch 1 [36]

7. (SC 5, Inc) x 6, Sl St to beginning stitch, Ch 1 [42]

8. Leave the Mouth Color Yarn attached and remove your hook at the end of Row 7. Attach Tooth Color Yarn to the FLO of the first stitch of Row 7 with a "Sl St, Ch 1," FLO [SC in the same stitch, Ch 1, Sl St in the same stitch, Sl St, (Sl St, Ch 1, SC in the same stitch, Ch 1, Sl St in the same stitch, Sl St) x 9, Sl St, (Sl St, Ch 1, SC in the same Stitch, Ch 1, Sl St in the same stitch, Sl St) x 10, Sl St] (for a total of 20 teeth)

Fasten off the Tooth Color Yarn with a short yarn tail.

For a video demonstration of how to work around a Slip Stitch, go here: https://youtu.be/khed-Ni_AjM?si=X5PxoVuTXzCPkPQ3

Cylinder Body with Open Mouth and No Legs, Open Mouth with Humanlike Teeth (Upper and Lower), Thinner Eyelids for 30 mm Safety Eyes, Cute Mitten Limbs, Cute Footed Limbs, Teensy Round Ears, Ridged Spiral Horns with Accent Color, Circle Belly

**9.** Continue with the Mouth Color Yarn. You will work into the BLO loop left over from Row 7 underneath each "tooth," and you will work around the Sl St in Row 8 and into the Row 7 stitch to create a gap between "teeth." BLO stitches will be in [brackets]. Stitches worked around the Sl St in Row 8 and into the Row 7 stitch will be <u>underlined</u>. You are working a pattern of (SC 3, Inc, SC 3) x 6, for a stitch count of [48], as follows:

([SC], <u>SC</u>, [SC], <u>Inc</u>, [SC], <u>SC</u>, [SC], <u>SC</u>, [SC], <u>SC</u>, [Inc], <u>SC</u>, [SC], <u>SC</u>, [SC], <u>SC</u>, [SC], <u>Inc</u>, [SC], <u>SC 2</u>) x 2, Sl St to beginning stitch. Fasten off with a short yarn tail. [48]

# OPEN MOUTH WITH POINTY TEETH (MAKE 1)

*Approximately 4 in/10 cm wide*

*Mouth Color Yarn: Approximately 15 yd/13.75 m worsted/medium weight yarn*

*Tooth Color Yarn: Approximately 5 yd/4.5 m lighter/sport weight yarn (White recommended)*

1. Starting with Mouth Color Yarn, SC 6 in Magic Circle, Sl St to beginning stitch, Ch 1 [6]

2. Inc x 6, Sl St to beginning stitch, Ch 1 [12]

3. (SC, Inc) x 6, Sl St to beginning stitch, Ch 1 [18]

4. (SC, Inc, SC) x 6, Sl St to beginning stitch, Ch 1 [24]

5. (SC 3, Inc) x 6, Sl St to beginning stitch, Ch 1 [30]

6. (SC 2, Inc, SC 2) x 6, Sl St to beginning stitch, Ch 1 [36]

7. (SC 5, Inc) x 6, Sl St to beginning stitch, Ch 1 [42]

8. Leave the Mouth Color Yarn attached and remove your hook at the end of Row 7. Attach the Tooth Color Yarn to the FLO of the first stitch of Row 7 with a Sl St, FLO [Sl St], (Ch 3, starting in the second Ch from hook, Sl St, SC, Skip 1 stitch on Row 7, FLO [Sl St 2]) x6, FLO [Sl St 4], (Ch 3, starting in the second Ch from hook, Sl St, SC, Skip 1 stitch on Row 7, FLO [Sl St 2]) x6 , Sl St to beginning stitch. Fasten off the Tooth Color Yarn with a short yarn tail (for a total of 12 teeth)

For a video demonstration of how to work around a Slip Stitch, go here: https://youtu.be/khed-Ni_AjM?si=X5PxoVuTXzCPkPQ3

9. Continue with the Mouth Color Yarn. You will work into the BLO loop left over from Row 7 underneath each "tooth," and you will work around the Sl St in Row 8 and into the Row 7 stitch to create a gap between "teeth." BLO stitches will be in [brackets]. Stitches worked around the Sl St in Row 8 and into the Row 7 stitch will be underlined. You are working a pattern of (SC 3, Inc, SC 3) x 6, for a stitch count of [48], as follows:

SC 2, [SC], Inc, SC, [SC], SC 2, [SC], SC, Inc, [SC], SC 2, [SC], SC 2, [Inc], SC 6, [Inc], SC 2, [SC], SC 2, [SC], Inc, SC, [SC], SC 2, [SC], SC, Inc, [SC], SC 2, Sl St to beginning stitch. Fasten off with a short yarn tail.

**Sphere Body with Open Mouth, Open Mouth with Pointy Teeth (Upper and Lower), Cute Mitten Limbs, Cute Footed Limbs, Skinny Curved Horns**

# OPEN MOUTH WITH SHORT ROW OF SMALL TEETH (MAKE 1)

*Approximately 4 in/10 cm wide*

*Mouth Color Yarn: 25 yd/22.75 m worsted/medium weight yarn*

*Tooth Color Yarn: 5 yd/4.5 m lighter/sport weight yarn (White recommended)*

1. Starting with Mouth Color Yarn, SC 6 in Magic Circle, Sl St to beginning stitch, Ch 1 [6]

2. Inc x 6, Sl St to beginning stitch, Ch 1 [12]

3. (SC, Inc) x 6, Sl St to beginning stitch, Ch 1 [18]

4. (SC, Inc, SC) x 6, Sl St to beginning stitch, Ch 1 [24]

5. (SC 3, Inc) x 6, Sl St to beginning stitch, Ch 1 [30]

6. (SC 2, Inc, SC 2) x 6, Sl St to beginning stitch, Ch 1 [36]

7. (SC 5, Inc) x 6, Sl St to beginning stitch, Ch 1 [42]

> You can create both or either one of the rows of teeth for these Monsters.

8. Mark the 8th stitch of Row 7 for an upper row of teeth and the 29th stitch of Row 7 for the bottom row of teeth. Leave the Mouth Color Yarn attached, and remove your hook at the end of Row 7

## Row 8 continued to Create a Short Row of Upper Teeth

Attach Tooth Color Yarn to the FLO 8th stitch of Row 7 with a "Sl St, Ch 1," working in the FLO [SC in the same stitch you attached the yarn to, Ch 1, Sl St in the same stitch, Sl St 2, Ch 2, HDC in the same stitch as the last Sl St, Ch 2, Sl St in the same stitch, Sl St 2, Ch 2, HDC in the same stitch as the last Sl St, Ch 2, Sl St in the same stitch, Sl St 2, Ch 1, SC in the same stitch as the last Sl St, Ch 1, Sl St in the same stitch]. Fasten off the Tooth Color Yarn with a short yarn tail (for a total of 4 teeth).

Blob Body with Open Mouth, Open Mouth with Short Row of Small Teeth (Upper), Bugle Ears, Small Double-pointed Tongue

### Row 8 continued to Create a Short Row of Lower Teeth

Attach Tooth Color Yarn to the FLO 29th stitch of Row 7 with a "Sl St, Ch 1," working in the FLO [SC in the same stitch you attached the yarn to, Ch 1, Sl St in the same stitch, Sl St 2, Ch 2, HDC in the same stitch as the last Sl St, Ch 2, Sl St in the same stitch, Sl St 2, Ch 2, HDC in the same stitch as the last Sl St, Ch 2, Sl St in the same stitch, Sl St 2, Ch 1, SC in the same stitch as the last Sl St, Ch 1, Sl St in the same stitch]. Fasten off the Tooth Color Yarn with a short yarn tail (for a total of 4 teeth).

For a video demonstration of how to work around a Slip Stitch, go here: https://youtu.be/khed-Ni_AjM?si=X5PxoVuTXzCPkPQ3

**9.** Continue with the Mouth Color Yarn. You will work into the BLO loop left over from Row 7 underneath each "tooth," and you will work around the Sl St in Row 8 and into the Row 7 stitch to create a gap between "teeth." BLO stitches will be in [brackets]. Stitches worked around the Sl St in Row 8 and into the Row 7 stitch will be underlined. You are working a pattern of (SC 3, Inc, SC 3) x 6, for a stitch count of [48], as follows:

*Instructions for Top Teeth Only:* SC 3, Inc, SC 3, [SC], <u>SC</u>, [SC], <u>Inc</u>, [SC], <u>SC</u>, [SC], (SC 3, Inc, SC 3) x 4, Sl St to beginning stitch; fasten off with a short yarn tail

*Instructions for Bottom Teeth Only:* (SC 3, Inc, SC 3) x 4, [SC], <u>SC</u>, [SC], <u>Inc</u>, [SC], <u>SC</u>, [SC], SC 3, Inc, SC 3, Sl St to beginning stitch; fasten off with a short yarn tail

*Instructions for Top and Bottom Teeth:* SC 3, Inc, SC 3, [SC], <u>SC</u>, [SC], <u>Inc</u>, [SC], <u>SC</u>, [SC], SC 3, Inc, SC 6, Inc, SC 3, [SC], <u>SC</u>, [SC], <u>Inc</u>, [SC], <u>SC</u>, [SC], SC 3, Inc, SC 3, Sl St to beginning stitch; fasten off with a short yarn tail

# OPEN MOUTH WITH BUCK TEETH (MAKE 1)

*Approximately 4 in/10 cm wide*

*Mouth Color Yarn: 25 yd/22.75 m worsted/medium weight yarn*

*Tooth Color Yarn: 5 yd/4.5 m lighter/sport weight yarn (White recommended) per row of Teeth*

1. Starting with Mouth Color Yarn, SC 6 in Magic Circle, Sl St to beginning stitch, Ch 1 [6]
2. Inc x 6, Sl St to beginning stitch, Ch 1 [12]
3. (SC, Inc) x 6, Sl St to beginning stitch, Ch 1 [18]
4. (SC, Inc, SC) x 6, Sl St to beginning stitch, Ch 1 [24]
5. (SC 3, Inc) x 6, Sl St to beginning stitch, Ch 1 [30]
6. (SC 2, Inc, SC 2) x 6, Sl St to beginning stitch, Ch 1 [36]
7. (SC 5, Inc) x 6, Sl St to beginning stitch, Ch 1 [42]

> You can create both or either one of the rows of teeth for these Monsters.

8. Mark the 9th stitch of Row 7 for an upper row of teeth and the 30th stitch of Row 7 for the bottom row of teeth. Leave the Mouth Color Yarn attached, and remove your hook at the end of Row 7

### Row 8 continued to Create 2 Upper Buck Teeth

Attach Tooth Color Yarn to the FLO 9th stitch of Row 7 (the first marked stitch) with a Sl St, Ch 3, working in the FLO [Half Trip in the same stitch you attached the yarn to, Half Trip, Ch 3, Sl St in the same stitch as your last Half Trip, Sl St 2, Ch 3, Half Trip in the same stitch as the last Sl St, Half Trip, Ch 3, Sl St in the same stitch as your last Half Trip]. Fasten off the Tooth Color Yarn with a short yarn tail (for a total of 2 teeth).

### Row 8 continued to Create 2 Lower Buck Teeth

Attach Tooth Color Yarn to the FLO 30th stitch of Row 7 (the second marked stitch) with a Sl St, Ch 3, working in the FLO [Half Trip in the same stitch you attached the yarn to, Half Trip, Ch 3, Sl St in the same stitch as your last Half Trip, Sl St 2, Ch 3, Half Trip in the same stitch as the last Sl St, Half Trip, Ch 3, Sl St in the same stitch as your last Half Trip]. Fasten off Tooth Color Yarn with a short yarn tail (for a total of 2 teeth).

For a video demonstration of how to work around a Slip Stitch, go here:
https://youtu.be/khed-Ni_AjM?si=X5PxoVuTXzCPkPQ3

**9.** Continue with the Mouth Color Yarn. You will work into the BLO loop left over from Row 7 underneath each "tooth," and you will work around the Sl St in Row 8 and into the Row 7 stitch to create a gap between "teeth." BLO stitches will be in [brackets]. Stitches worked around the Sl St in Row 8 and into the Row 7 stitch will be underlined. Work one of the following options: Top Teeth, Bottom Teeth, or Top and Bottom Teeth. You are working a pattern of (SC 3, Inc, SC 3) x 6, for a stitch count of [48], as follows:

*Instructions for Top Teeth Only:* SC 3, Inc, SC 4, [SC 2], Inc, [SC 2], SC, (SC 3, Inc, SC 3) x 4, Sl St to beginning stitch [48]; fasten off with a short yarn tail

*Instructions for Bottom Teeth Only:* (SC 3, Inc, SC 3) x 4, SC, [SC 2], Inc, [SC 2], SC 4, Inc, SC 3, Sl St to beginning stitch [48]; fasten off with a short yarn tail

*Instructions for Both Top and Bottom Teeth:* SC 3, Inc, SC 4, [SC 2], Inc, [SC 2], SC 4, Inc, SC 6, Inc, SC 4, [SC 2], Inc, [SC 2], SC 4, Inc, SC 3, Sl St to beginning stitch [48]; fasten off with a short yarn tail

Cylinder Body with Open Mouth and No Legs, Open Mouth with Buck Teeth (Upper), Short Rounded Limbs, Large Footed Bent Limbs, Medium Curved Horns

Cylinder with Open Mouth and No Legs, Open Mouth with Four Pointed Teeth (Upper and Lower), Large Nubbins Limbs, Nubbin Footed Limbs, Medium Curved Horns

# OPEN MOUTH WITH FOUR POINTED TEETH (MAKE 1)

*Approximately 4 in/10 cm wide*

*Mouth Color Yarn: 25 yd/22.75 m worsted/medium weight yarn*

*Tooth Color Yarn: 10 yd/9.25 m lighter/sport weight yarn (White recommended)*

1. Starting with Mouth Color Yarn, SC 6 in Magic Circle, Sl St to beginning stitch, Ch 1 [6]

2. Inc x 6, Sl St to beginning stitch, Ch 1 [12]

3. (SC, Inc) x 6, Sl St to beginning stitch, Ch 1 [18]

4. (SC, Inc, SC) x 6, Sl St to beginning stitch, Ch 1 [24]

5. (SC 3, Inc) x 6, Sl St to beginning stitch, Ch 1 [30]

6. (SC 2, Inc, SC 2) x 6, Sl St to beginning stitch, Ch 1 [36]

7. (SC 5, Inc) x 6, Sl St to beginning stitch, Ch 1 [42]

> You can create both or either one of the rows of teeth for these Monsters.

8. Mark the 6th stitch of Row 7 for an upper row of teeth and the 27th stitch of Row 7 for the bottom row of teeth. Leave the Mouth Color Yarn attached, and remove your hook at the end of Row 7

## Row 8 continued to Create 4 Upper Pointed Teeth

Attach Tooth Color Yarn to the FLO 6th stitch of Row 7 with a Sl St, Ch 4, starting in the second Ch from hook, Sl St, SC, HDC, Skip 1 stitch, Sl St in the next 2 FLO stitches on Row 7, Ch 3, starting in the second Ch from hook, Sl St, SC, Sl St in the next 3 FLO stitches on Row 7, Ch 3, starting in the second Ch from hook, Sl St, SC, Sl St in the next 2 FLO stitches on Row 7, Ch 4, starting in the second Ch from hook, Sl St, SC, HDC, Skip 1 stitch, Sl St in the next available FLO stitch in Row 7. Fasten off the Tooth Color Yarn with a short yarn tail (for a total of 4 teeth).

## Row 8 continued to Create 4 Lower Pointed Teeth

Attach Tooth Color Yarn to the FLO 27th stitch of Row 7 with a Sl St, Ch 4, starting in the second Ch from hook, Sl St, SC, HDC, Skip 1 stitch, Sl St in the next 2 FLO stitches on Row 7, Ch 3, starting in the second Ch from hook, Sl St, SC, Sl St in the next 3 FLO stitches on Row 7, Ch 3, starting in the second Ch from hook, Sl St, SC, Sl St in the next 2 FLO stitches on Row 7, Ch 4, starting in the second Ch from hook, Sl St, SC, HDC, Skip 1 stitch, Sl St in the next available FLO stitch on Row 7. Fasten off the Tooth Color Yarn with a short yarn tail (for a total of 4 teeth).

For a video demonstration of how to work around a Slip Stitch, go here:
https://youtu.be/khed-Ni_AjM?si=X5PxoVuTXzCPkPQ3

**9.** Continue with the Mouth Color Yarn. You will work into the BLO loop left over from Row 7 underneath each "tooth," and you will work around the Sl St in Row 8 and into the Row 7 stitch to create a gap between "teeth." BLO stitches will be in [brackets]. Stitches worked around the Sl St in Row 8 and into the Row 7 stitch will be underlined. Work one of the following options: Top Teeth, Bottom Teeth, or Top and Bottom Teeth. You are working a pattern of (SC 3, Inc, SC 3) x 6, for a stitch count of [48], as follows:

*Instructions for Top Teeth Only:* SC 3, Inc, SC 2, [SC 2], <u>SC</u>, [SC], <u>Inc</u>, <u>SC</u>, [SC], <u>SC</u>, [SC 2], SC, Inc, SC 3, (SC 3, Inc, SC 3) x 3, Sl St to beginning stitch; fasten off with a short yarn tail

*Instructions for Bottom Teeth Only:* (SC 3, Inc, SC 3) x 3, SC 3, Inc, SC 2, [SC 2], <u>SC</u>, [SC], <u>Inc</u>, <u>SC</u>, [SC], <u>SC</u>, [SC 2], SC, Inc, SC 3, Sl St to beginning stitch; fasten off with a short yarn tail

*Instructions for Both Top and Bottom Teeth:* SC 3, Inc, SC 2, [SC 2], <u>SC</u>, [SC], <u>Inc</u>, <u>SC</u>, [SC], <u>SC</u>, [SC 2], SC, Inc, SC 6, Inc, SC 2, [SC 2], <u>SC</u>, [SC], <u>Inc</u>, <u>SC</u>, [SC], <u>SC</u>, [SC 2], SC, Inc, SC 3, Sl St to beginning stitch; fasten off with a short yarn tail

Blob Body with
Underbite,
Hair Puff

# Blob Style Bodies

## BLOB BODY WITH UNDERBITE (MAKE 1)

*Approximately 4.5 in/11.5 cm wide at the body, 7.5 in/19 cm tall, 6.5 in/16.5 cm wide at the base*

*Body Color Yarn: Approximately 150 yd/137.25 m worsted/medium weight yarn*

> The Blob Body is worked in a continuous spiral. *Do not* join at the end of each round unless explicitly told to do so. This Monster Body is worked from the bottom of the body to the top.

**1.** SC 6 in Magic Circle [6]

**2.** Inc x 6 [12]

**3.** (SC, Inc) x 6 [18]

**4.** (SC, Inc, SC) x 6 [24]

**5.** (SC 3, Inc) x 6 [30]

**6.** (SC 3, Ch 5, starting in the second Ch from hook, SC 4, SC in the same stitch as your last SC before the chain stitches, SC 5, Ch 8, starting in the second Ch from hook, SC 7, SC in the same stitch as your last SC before the chain stitches, SC 2) x 3 [69]

> The first 12 rows of all Blob Monster Bodies are the same. See page 33, Blob Body with Overbite section, for photos of these rows.

**7.** (SC 3, continuing up the side of the Ch stitches from Row 6 and then back down the other side, SC 3, Inc x 2, SC 5, Inc, SC 3, continuing up the side of the Ch stitches from Row 6 and then back down the other side, SC 6, Inc x 2, SC 8, Inc) x 3 [120]

**8.** (SC 2, Dec, SC 3, Inc x 2, SC 3, Dec, SC 5, Dec, SC 6, Inc x 2, SC 6, Dec, SC 3) x 3 [120]

**9.** (SC 2, Dec, SC 8, Dec, SC 5, Dec, SC 14, Dec, SC 3) x 3 [108]

**10.** SC 108 [108]

**11.** (SC 3, Dec x 4, SC 10, Dec x 4, SC 7) x 3 [84]

**12.** (SC 3, HDC Dec x 2, SC 10, HDC Dec x 2, SC 7) x 3 [72]

**13.** SC 72 [72]

**14.** (SC 5, Dec, SC 5) x 6 [66]

**15.** SC 66 [66]

**16.** (SC 9, Dec) x 6 [60]

**17–18.** (2 rows of) SC 60 [60]

**19.** (SC 4, Dec, SC 4) x 6 [54]

**20–22.** (3 rows of) SC 54 [54]

**23.** (SC 7, Dec) x 6 [48]

**24–25.** (2 rows of) SC 48 [48]

**26.** FLO [SC 12, HDC 24, SC 12] [48]

**27.** SC 12, HDC 24, SC 12 [48]

**28.** Ch 2, starting in the first BLO stitch from Row 25 and continuing working into the leftover BLO of the stitches from Row 25, BLO [SC 48] [48]

**29.** SC 48 [48]

**30.** Starting in the first available stitch of each row through both Row 29 and Row 27 at the same time SC 12, SC 24 in Row 29 only, Skip 24 stitches on Row 27, SC 12 through Row 29 and Row 27 at the same time [48]

**31–36.** (6 Rows of) SC 48 [48]

**37.** (SC 3, Dec, SC 3) x 6 [42]

**38.** (SC 5, Dec) x 6 [36]

After you've completed Row 38, insert safety eyes. Safety eye size and placement are up to your discretion; the following are guidelines only.

If using two 30 mm safety eyes, insert them between Row 33 and Row 34 with approximately 7 stitch spaces between the posts. (1)

If using three safety eyes (two 30 mm and one 40 mm recommended), insert the two 30 mm eyes between Row 34 and Row 35 on either side of the single 40 mm safety eye with approximately 5 stitch spaces between each post. (2)

If using two 40 mm safety eyes, insert between Row 34 and Row 35 with approximately 7 stitch spaces between the posts. (3)

If using one 40 mm safety eye, insert between Row 34 and Row 35. (4)

You could also skip inserting a safety eye and follow the crocheted eye instruction options, including a 2D Medium or Large Eye, an Eye Bump, or an Eye Stalk.

It is optional to put some sort of weight in the bottom of the Body. You can use glass gems, clean stones, or plastic pellets in a nylon stocking. This will make the Monster very stable when placed on a shelf, but the small pieces will make the item unsafe for babies/toddlers. Stuff the Body with fiberfill and continue to stuff as you go.

**39.** (SC 2, Dec, SC 2) x 6 [30]
**40.** (SC 3, Dec) x 6 [24]
**41.** (SC 2, Dec) x 6 [18]
**42.** (SC, Dec) x 6 [12]
**43.** Dec x 6 [6]

Fasten off with a 12 in/30.5 cm yarn tail.

## Assembly

**1.** Finish stuffing with fiberfill.
**2.** Use the yarn tail to sew the hole in the top of the head shut; weave in ends.
**3.** Add any extra details—ears, limbs, horns, etc.—you want to the body!

# BLOB BODY WITH DEEP POCKET UNDERBITE (MAKE 1)

*Approximately 4.5 in/11.5 cm wide at the body, 7.5 in/19 cm tall, 6.5 in/16.5 cm wide at the base*

*Body Color Yarn: Approximately 160 yd/146.25 m worsted/medium weight yarn*

The Blob Body is worked in a continuous spiral. *Do not* join at the end of each round unless explicitly told to do so. This Monster Body is worked from the bottom of the body to the top.

**1.** SC 6 in Magic Circle [6]

**2.** Inc x 6 [12]

**3.** (SC, Inc) x 6 [18]

**4.** (SC, Inc, SC) x 6 [24]

**5.** (SC 3, Inc) x 6 [30]

**6.** (SC 3, Ch 5, starting in the second Ch from hook, SC 4, SC in the same stitch as your last SC before the chain stitches, SC 5, Ch 8, starting in the second Ch from hook, SC 7, SC in the same stitch as your last SC before the chain stitches, SC 2) x 3 [69]

The first 12 rows of all Blob Monster Bodies are the same. See page 33, Blob Body with Overbite section, for photos of these rows.

**7.** (SC 3, continuing up the side of the Ch stitches from Row 6 and then back down the other side, SC 3, Inc x 2, SC 5, Inc, SC 3, continuing up the side of the Ch stitches from Row 6 and then back down the other side, SC 6, Inc x 2, SC 8, Inc) x 3 [120]

**8.** (SC 2, Dec, SC 3, Inc x 2, SC 3, Dec, SC 5, Dec, SC 6, Inc x 2, SC 6, Dec, SC 3) x 3 [120]

**9.** (SC 2, Dec, SC 8, Dec, SC 5, Dec, SC 14, Dec, SC 3) x 3 [108]

**10.** SC 108 [108]

**11.** (SC 3, Dec x 4, SC 10, Dec x 4, SC 7) x 3 [84]

**12.** (SC 3, HDC Dec x 2, SC 10, HDC Dec x 2, SC 7) x 3 [72]

**13.** FLO [SC 72] [72]

Insert a stitch marker into the first unused BLO from Row 12 for reference on where to start Row 28.

**14.** (SC 5, Dec, SC 5) x 6 [66]

**15.** SC 66 [66]

**16.** (SC 9, Dec) x 6 [60]

**17–18.** (2 rows of) SC 60 [60]

**19.** (SC 4, Dec, SC 4) x 6 [54]

**20–22.** (3 rows of) SC 54 [54]

**23.** (SC 7, Dec) x 6 [48]

**24–25.** (2 rows of) SC 48 [48]

**26.** SC 12, HDC 24, SC 12 [48]

**27.** SC 12, HDC 24, SC 12 [48]

Insert a stitch marker in the first stitch of Row 27 for reference when starting Row 43.

**28.** Ch 15, starting in the first BLO stitch from Row 12 and continuing working into the leftover BLO of the stitches from Row 12, BLO [SC 72] [72]

It can help to fold the outer edge down over the work (like pulling down a sock) so that you have easier access to the leftover BLO stitches from Row 12.

**29.** (SC 5, Dec, SC 5) x 6 [66]

**30.** SC 66 [66]

**31.** (SC 9, Dec) x 6 [60]

**32–33.** (2 rows of) SC 60 [60]

**34.** (SC 4, Dec, SC 4) x 6 [54]

**35–37.** (3 rows of) SC 54 [54]

**38.** (SC 7, Dec) x 6 [48]

**39–42.** (4 rows of) SC 48 [48]

**44–49.** (6 rows of) SC 48 [48]

**50.** (SC 3, Dec, SC 3) x 6 [42]

**51.** (SC 5, Dec) x 6 [36]

**52.** (SC 2, Dec, SC 2) x 6 [30]

**53.** (SC 3, Dec) x 6 [24]

**54.** (SC 2, Dec) x 6 [18]

**55.** (SC, Dec) x 6 [12]

**56.** Dec x 6 [6]

Fasten off with a 12 in/30.5 cm yarn tail.

**43.** Starting in the first available stitch of each row through both Row 42 and (the marked stitch from) Row 27 at the same time SC 12, SC 24 in Row 42 only, skip 24 stitches on Row 27, SC 12 through Row 42 and Row 27 at the same time [48]

After you've completed Row 51, insert safety eyes. Safety eye size and placement are up to your discretion; the following are guidelines only. Generalized photos of what these options look like can be found on page 28.

For two 30 mm eyes, insert between Row 46 and Row 47 with approximately 7 stitch spaces between the posts.

For three eyes (two 30 mm and one 40 mm), insert between Row 47 and Row 48, with the 40 mm eye in the center and approximately 5 stitch spaces between each post.

For one or two 40 mm eyes, insert between Row 47 and Row 48 with approximately 7 stitch spaces between the posts.

You could also skip inserting a safety eye and follow the crocheted eye instruction options, including a 2D Medium or Large Eye, an Eye Bump, or an Eye Stalk.

Glass gems are optional (for more information, see page 28). Stuff the Body with fiberfill and continue to stuff as you go.

## Assembly

**1.** Finish stuffing with fiberfill.

**2.** Use the yarn tail to sew the hole in the top of the head shut; weave in ends.

**3.** Add any extra details—ears, horns, limbs, etc.—you want to the body!

**4.** Careful with feeding this type of Monster—they tend to enjoy munching on crochet hooks.

Blob
Body with
Deep Pocket
Underbite,
Rounded
Segmented
Horns

# BLOB BODY WITH OVERBITE (MAKE 1)

*Approximately 4.5 in/11.5 cm wide at the body, 7.5 in/19 cm tall, 6.5 in/16.5 cm wide at the base*

*Body Color Yarn: Approximately 140 yd/128 m worsted/medium weight yarn*

> The Blob Body is worked in a continuous spiral. *Do not* join at the end of each round unless explicitly told to do so. This Monster Body is worked from the bottom to the top.

**1.** SC 6 in Magic Circle [6]

**2.** Inc x 6 [12]

**3.** (SC, Inc) x 6 [18]

**4.** (SC, Inc, SC) x 6 [24]

**5.** (SC 3, Inc) x 6 [30]

**6.** (SC 3, Ch 5, starting in the second Ch from hook, SC 4, SC in the same stitch as your last SC before the chain stitches, SC 5, Ch 8, starting in the second Ch from hook, SC 7, SC in the same stitch as your last SC before the chain stitches, SC 2) x 3 [69]

**7.** (SC 3, continuing up the side of the Ch stitches from Row 6 and then back down the other side, SC 3, Inc x 2, SC 5, Inc, SC 3, continuing up the side of the Ch stitches from Row 6 and then back down the other side, SC 6, Inc x 2, SC 8, Inc) x 3 [120]

**8.** (SC 2, Dec, SC 3, Inc x 2, SC 3, Dec, SC 5, Dec, SC 6, Inc x 2, SC 6, Dec, SC 3) x 3 [120]

**9.** (SC 2, Dec, SC 8, Dec, SC 5, Dec, SC 14, Dec, SC 3) x 3 [108]

**10.** SC 108 [108]

**11.** (SC 3, Dec x 4, SC 10, Dec x 4, SC 7) x 3 [84]

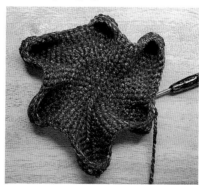

**12.** (SC 3, HDC Dec x 2, SC 10, HDC Dec x 2, SC 7) x 3 [72]

**13.** SC 72 [72]

**14.** (SC 5, Dec, SC 5) x 6 [66]

**15.** SC 66 [66]

**16.** (SC 9, Dec) x 6 [60]

**17–18.** (2 rows of) SC 60 [60]

**19.** (SC 4, Dec, SC 4) x 6 [54]

**20–22.** (3 rows of) SC 54 [54]

**23.** (SC 7, Dec) x 6 [48]

**24–25.** (2 rows of) SC 48 [48]

**26.** FLO [SC 12], Ch 24, Skip 24 stitches, FLO [SC 12] [48]

**27.** SC 12, HDC 24 into the Chain Stitches from Row 26, SC 12 [48]

**28.** SC 12, HDC 24, SC 12 [48]

**29.** Ch 2, starting in the first BLO stitch from Row 25 and continuing working into the leftover BLO of the stitches from Row 25, BLO [SC 12], SC 24, BLO [SC 12] [48]

**30.** SC 48 [48]

**31.** SC 48 [48]

**32.** SC 48 through both Row 31 and Row 28 at the same time [48]

**33–38.** (6 rows of) SC 48 [48]

**39.** (SC 3, Dec, SC 3) x 6 [42]

**40.** (SC 5, Dec) x 6 [36]

After you've completed Row 40, insert safety eyes. Safety eye size and placement are up to your discretion; the following are guidelines only. Generalized photos of what these options look like can be found on page 28.

For two 30 mm eyes, insert between Row 35 and Row 36 with approximately 7 stitch spaces between the posts.

For three eyes (two 30 mm and one 40 mm), insert between Row 36 and Row 37, with the 40 mm eye in the center and approximately 5 stitch spaces between each post.

For one or two 40 mm eyes, insert between Row 36 and Row 37 with approximately 7 stitch spaces between the posts.

You could also skip inserting a safety eye and follow the crocheted eye instruction options, including a 2D Medium or Large Eye, an Eye Bump, or an Eye Stalk.

Glass gems are optional (for more information, see page 28). Stuff the Body with fiberfill and continue to stuff as you go.

**41.** (SC 2, Dec, SC 2) x 6 [30]

**42.** (SC 3, Dec) x 6 [24]

**43.** (SC, Dec, SC) x 6 [18]

**44.** (SC, Dec) x 6 [12]

**45.** Dec x 6 [6]

Fasten off with a 12 in/30.5 cm yarn tail.

## Assembly

**1.** Finish stuffing with fiberfill.

**2.** Use the yarn tail to sew the final holes shut; weave in ends.

**3.** Add any extra details—ears, horns, limbs, etc.—you want to the body!

# BLOB BODY WITH OPEN MOUTH (MAKE 1)

*Approximately 4.5 in/11.5 cm wide at the body, 7.5 in/19 cm tall, 6.5 in/16.5 cm wide at the base*

*Body Color Yarn: Approximately 150 yd/137.25 m worsted/medium weight yarn*

> You will need to crochet one of the Open Mouth pieces (pages 15–25) prior to making this Body to attach as you go.

> The Blob Body is worked in a continuous spiral. *Do not* join at the end of each round unless explicitly told to do so. This Monster Body is worked from the bottom to the top.

1. SC 6 in Magic Circle [6]
2. Inc x 6 [12]
3. (SC, Inc) x 6 [18]
4. (SC, Inc, SC) x 6 [24]
5. (SC 3, Inc) x 6 [30]
6. (SC 3, Ch 5, starting in the second Ch from hook, SC 4, SC in the same stitch as your last SC before the chain stitches, SC 5, Ch 8, starting in the second Ch from hook, SC 7, SC in the same stitch as your last SC before the chain stitches, SC 2) x 3 [69]

> The first 12 rows of all Blob Monster Bodies are the same. See page 33, Blob Body with Overbite section, for photos of these rows.

7. (SC 3, continuing up the side of the Ch stitches from Row 6 and then back down the other side, SC 3, Inc x 2, SC 5, Inc, SC 3, continuing up the side of the Ch stitches from Row 6 and then back down the other side, SC 6, Inc x 2, SC 8, Inc) x 3 [120]

8. (SC 2, Dec, SC 3, Inc x 2, SC 3, Dec, SC 5, Dec, SC 6, Inc x 2, SC 6, Dec, SC 3) x 3 [120]
9. (SC 2, Dec, SC 8, Dec, SC 5, Dec, SC 14, Dec, SC 3) x 3 [108]
10. SC 108 [108]
11. (SC 3, Dec x 4, SC 10, Dec x 4, SC 7) x 3 [84]
12. (SC 3, HDC Dec x 2, SC 10, HDC Dec x 2, SC 7) x 3 [72]

13. SC 72 [72]
14. (SC 5, Dec, SC 5) x 6 [66]
15. SC 66 [66]
16. (SC 9, Dec) x 6 [60]
17–18. (2 rows of) SC 60 [60]
19. (SC 4, Dec, SC 4) x 6 [54]
20–22. (3 rows of) SC 54 [54]
23. (SC 7, Dec) x 6 [48]
24–27. (4 rows of) SC 48 [48]

28. Working into the Mouth and the Body at the same time, SC 24; working into the Body only, SC 24 [48]

> In Row 28, insert your hook into the right side/outside of the Body first and then into the wrong side of the last stitch of the last row of the Mouth (OR the marked stitch on the Mouth). To create these stitches, you will be working along the bottom front of the Mouth.

> In Row 29, when you work into the Mouth, you are working along the top front of the Mouth only; you do not work into the stitches you made in Row 28 in the bottom half of the mouth at all.

29. Starting in the first available stitch of the top front of the mouth, FLO [SC 24], SC 24 in the Body [48]

Blob Body with Open Mouth, Open Mouth with Buck Teeth (Upper and Lower), Thin Arms with Two Fingers, Spiral-shaped Horns

**30.** Continuing in the back loops of the Mouth left after Row 29, BLO [SC 24], SC 24 in the Body stitches from Row 29 [48]

**31–36.** (6 rows of) SC 48 [48]
**37.** (SC 3, Dec, SC 3) x 6 [42]
**38.** (SC 5, Dec) x 6 [36]
**39.** (SC 2, Dec, SC 2) x 6 [30]
**40.** (SC 3, Dec) x 6 [24]

After you've completed Row 40, insert safety eyes. Safety eye size and placement are up to your discretion; the following are guidelines only. Generalized photos of what these options look like can be found on page 28.

For two 30 mm eyes, insert between Row 31 and Row 32 with approximately 7 stitch spaces between the posts.

For three eyes (two 30 mm and one 40 mm), insert between Row 31 and Row 32, with the 40 mm eye in the center and approximately 5 stitch spaces between each post.

For one or two 40 mm eyes, insert between Row 31 and Row 32 with approximately 7 stitch spaces between the posts.

You could also skip inserting a safety eye and follow the crocheted eye instruction options, including a 2D Medium or Large Eye, an Eye Bump, or an Eye Stalk.

Glass gems are optional (for more information, see page 28). Stuff the Body with fiberfill and continue to stuff as you go. Do not overstuff; make sure the Mouth is folded over itself when you stuff (like a hard taco shell) so that the Blob Monster Mouth can be closed when you finish.

**41.** (SC, Dec, SC) x 6 [18]
**42.** (SC, Dec) x 6 [12]
**43.** Dec x 6 [6]

Fasten off with a 12 in/30.5 cm yarn tail.

### Assembly

**1.** Finish stuffing with fiberfill.
**2.** Use the yarn tail to sew the final holes shut; weave in ends.
**3.** Add any extra details—ears, horns, limbs, etc.—you want to the body!

# BLOB BODY WITH NO MOUTH (MAKE 1)

*Approximately 4.5 in/11.5 cm wide at the body, 7.5 in/19 cm tall, 6.5 in/16.5 cm wide at the base*

*Body Color Yarn: Approximately 140 yd/128 m worsted/medium weight yarn*

> The Blob Body is worked in a continuous spiral. *Do not* join at the end of each round unless explicitly told to do so. This Monster Body is worked from the bottom to the top.

**1.** SC 6 in Magic Circle [6]

**2.** Inc x 6 [12]

**3.** (SC, Inc) x 6 [18]

**4.** (SC, Inc, SC) x 6 [24]

**5.** (SC 3, Inc) x 6 [30]

**6.** (SC 3, Ch 5, starting in the second Ch from hook, SC 4, SC in the same stitch as your last SC before the chain stitches, SC 5, Ch 8, starting in the second Ch from hook, SC 7, SC in the same stitch as your last SC before the chain stitches, SC 2) x 3 [69]

> The first 12 rows of all Blob Monster Bodies are the same. See page 33, Blob Body with Overbite section, for photos of these rows.

**7.** (SC 3, continuing up the side of the Ch stitches from Row 6 and then back down the other side, SC 3, Inc x 2, SC 5, Inc, SC 3, continuing up the side of the Ch stitches from Row 6 and then back down the other side, SC 6, Inc x 2, SC 8, Inc) x 3 [120]

**8.** (SC 2, Dec, SC 3, Inc x 2, SC 3, Dec, SC 5, Dec, SC 6, Inc x 2, SC 6, Dec, SC 3) x 3 [120]

**9.** (SC 2, Dec, SC 8, Dec, SC 5, Dec, SC 14, Dec, SC 3) x 3 [108]

**10.** SC 108 [108]

**11.** (SC 3, Dec x 4, SC 10, Dec x 4, SC 7) x 3 [84]

**12.** (SC 3, HDC Dec x 2, SC 10, HDC Dec x 2, SC 7) x 3 [72]

**13.** SC 72 [72]

**14.** (SC 5, Dec, SC 5) x 6 [66]

**15.** SC 66 [66]

**16.** (SC 9, Dec) x 6 [60]

**17–18.** (2 rows of) SC 60 [60]

**19.** (SC 4, Dec, SC 4) x 6 [54]

**20–22.** (3 rows of) SC 54 [54]

**23.** (SC 7, Dec) x 6 [48]

**24–35.** (12 rows of) SC 48 [48]

**36.** (SC 3, Dec, SC 3) x 6 [42]

**37.** (SC 5, Dec) x 6 [36]

> After you've completed Row 37, insert safety eyes. Safety eye size and placement are up to your discretion; the following are guidelines only. Generalized photos of what these options look like can be found on page 28.
>
> For two 30 mm eyes, insert between Row 31 and Row 32 with approximately 7 stitch spaces between the posts.
>
> For three eyes (two 30 mm and one 40 mm), insert between Row 31 and Row 32, with the 40 mm eye in the center and approximately 5 stitch spaces between each post.
>
> For one or two 40 mm eyes, insert between Row 31 and Row 32 with approximately 7 stitch spaces between the posts.
>
> You could also skip inserting a safety eye and follow the crocheted eye instruction options, including a 2D Medium or Large Eye, an Eye Bump, or an Eye Stalk.

> Glass gems are optional (for more information, see page 28). Stuff the Body with fiberfill and continue to stuff as you go.

**38.** (SC 2, Dec, SC 2) x 6 [30]

**39.** (SC 3, Dec) x 6 [24]

**40.** (SC 2, Dec) x 6 [18]

**41.** (SC, Dec) x 6 [12]

**42.** Dec x 6 [6]

Fasten off with a 12 in/30.5 cm yarn tail.

## Assembly

1. Finish stuffing with fiberfill.

2. Use the yarn tail to sew the hole in the top of the head shut; weave in ends.

3. Add any extra details—ears, horns, limbs, etc.—you want to the body!

**Blob Body with No Mouth, Eye Bumps, 2D Open Mouth in Round Shape with Fangs, Medium Tongue, Row of Spikes**

Cylinder with Underbite and No Legs, Wide Flat-ended Short Limbs, Larger Cone Limbs, Tail with Hair Puff, Ridged Horns, Pointy Teeth, Embroidered Claws

# Cylinder Bodies

## CYLINDER WITH UNDERBITE AND NO LEGS (MAKE 1)

***Approximately 7.5 in/19 cm tall, 4.5 in/11.5 cm wide at the body***

***Body Color Yarn: Approximately 100 yd/91.5 m worsted/medium weight yarn***

This Monster Body is worked from the bottom to the top.

**1.** SC 6 in Magic Circle, Sl St to beginning stitch, Ch 1 [6]

**2.** Inc x 6, Sl St to beginning stitch, Ch 1 [12]

**3.** (SC, Inc) x 6, Sl St to beginning stitch, Ch 1 [18]

**4.** (SC, Inc, SC) x 6, Sl St to beginning stitch, Ch 1 [24]

**5.** (SC 3, Inc) x 6, Sl St to beginning stitch, Ch 1 [30]

**6.** (SC 2, Inc, SC 2) x 6, Sl St to beginning stitch, Ch 1 [36]

**7.** (SC 5, Inc) x 6, Sl St to beginning stitch, Ch 1 [42]

**8.** (SC 3, Inc, SC 3) x 6, Sl St to beginning stitch, Ch 1 [48]

**9–21.** (13 rows of) SC 48, Sl St to beginning stitch, Ch 1 [48]

**22.** FLO [SC 12, HDC 24, SC 12], Sl St to beginning stitch, Ch 1 [48]

**23.** SC 12, HDC 24, SC 12, Sl St to beginning stitch, Ch 1 [48]

**24.** Ch 2, starting in the first BLO stitch from Row 21 and continuing working into the leftover BLO of the stitches from Row 21, BLO [SC 48], Sl St to beginning stitch, Ch 1 [48]

**25.** SC 48, Sl St to beginning stitch, Ch 1 [48]

**26.** Starting in the first available stitch of each row through both Row 25 and Row 23 at the same time SC 12, SC 24 in Row 25 only, Skip 24 stitches on Row 23, SC 12 through Row 25 and Row 23 at the same time, Sl St to beginning stitch, Ch 1 [48]

**27–33.** (7 rows of) SC 48, Sl St to beginning stitch, Ch 1 [48]

**34.** (SC 3, Dec, SC 3) x 6, Sl St to beginning stitch, Ch 1 [42]

**35.** (SC 5, Dec) x 6, Sl St to beginning stitch, Ch 1 [36]

After you've completed Row 35, insert safety eyes. Safety eye size and placement are up to your discretion; the following are guidelines only. Generalized photos of what these options look like can be found on page 28.

For two 30 mm eyes, insert between Row 30 and Row 31 with approximately 7 stitch spaces between the posts.

For three eyes (two 30 mm and one 40 mm), insert between Row 31 and Row 32, with the 40 mm eye in the center and approximately 5 stitch spaces between each post.

For one or two 40 mm eyes, insert between Row 31 and Row 32 with approximately 7 stitch spaces between the posts.

You could also skip inserting a safety eye and follow the crocheted eye instruction options, including a 2D Medium or Large Eye, an Eye Bump, or an Eye Stalk.

Glass gems are optional (for more information, see page 28). Stuff the Body with fiberfill and continue to stuff as you go.

**36.** (SC 2, Dec, SC 2) x 6, Sl St to beginning stitch, Ch 1 [30]

**37.** (SC 3, Dec) x 6, Sl St to beginning stitch, Ch 1 [24]

**38.** (SC, Dec, SC) x 6, Sl St to beginning stitch, Ch 1 [18]

**39.** (SC, Dec) x 6, Sl St to beginning stitch, Ch 1 [12]

**40.** Dec x 6, Sl St to beginning stitch [6]

Fasten off with a 12 in/30.5 cm yarn tail.

### Assembly

**1.** Finish stuffing with fiberfill.

**2.** Use the yarn tail to sew the hole in the top of the head shut; weave in ends.

**3.** Add any extra details—ears, horns, limbs, etc.—you want to the body!

Cylinder with Underbite and Legs, Small Cone Limbs, Medium Pointy Antlers, Two Close Together Rounded Teeth

# CYLINDER WITH UNDERBITE AND LEGS (MAKE 1)

*Approximately 8.5 in/21.5 cm tall, 4.5 in/11.5 cm wide at the body*

*Body Color Yarn: Approximately 110 yd/100.5 m worsted/medium weight yarn*

This Monster Body is worked from the bottom of the feet to the top.

**1.** SC 6 in Magic Circle, Sl St to beginning stitch, Ch 1 [6]

**2.** Inc x 6, Sl St to beginning stitch, Ch 1 [12]

**3.** (SC, Inc) x 6, Sl St to beginning stitch, Ch 1 [18]

**4.** (SC, Inc, SC) x 6, Sl St to beginning stitch, Ch 1 [24]

**5.** BLO [SC 24], Sl St to beginning stitch, Ch 1 [24]

**6–8.** (3 rows of) SC 24, Sl St to beginning stitch, Ch 1 [24]

**9.** SC 8, Dec x 4, SC 8, Sl St to beginning stitch, Ch 1 [20]

**10–12.** (3 rows of) SC 20, Sl St to beginning stitch, Ch 1 [20]

**13.** (SC 4, Inc) x 4, Sl St to beginning stitch, Ch 1 [24]

**14.** SC 24, Sl St to beginning stitch, Ch 1 [24]

**15.** SC 24, Sl St to beginning stitch [24]

Fasten off the first leg with a short yarn tail.

Mark the 19th stitch of the final row of the first leg for reference in Row 16.

Repeat instructions for Rows 1 through 15 for the second leg, do not fasten off, and continue to Row 16.

It is optional to add flat reinforcement to the bottom of the inside of the foot. See page 49 for details.

**16.** Ch 1, SC 6, working into the first leg, starting in the marked stitch, SC 24, continuing into the next available stitch on the current leg, SC 18, Sl St to beginning stitch, Ch 1 [48]

**17–27.** (11 rows of) SC 48, Sl St to beginning stitch, Ch 1 [48]

**28.** FLO [SC 19, HDC 24, SC 5], Sl St to beginning stitch, Ch 1 [48]

**29.** SC 19, HDC 24, SC 5, Sl St to beginning stitch, Ch 1 [48]

**30.** Ch 2, starting in the first BLO stitch from Row 27 and continuing working into the leftover BLO of the stitches from Row 27, BLO [SC 48], Sl St to beginning stitch, Ch 1 [48]

**31.** SC 48, Sl St to beginning stitch, Ch 1 [48]

**32.** Starting in the first available stitch of each row through both Row 29 and Row 31 at the same time SC 19, SC 24 in Row 31 only, Skip 24 stitches on Row 29, SC 12 through Row 29 and Row 31 at the same time, Sl St to beginning stitch, Ch 1 [48]

**33–39.** (7 rows of) SC 48, Sl St to beginning stitch, Ch 1 [48]

**40.** (SC 3, Dec, SC 3) x 6, Sl St to beginning stitch, Ch 1 [42]

**41.** (SC 5, Dec) x 6, Sl St to beginning stitch, Ch 1 [36]

After you've completed Row 41, insert safety eyes. Safety eye size and placement are up to your discretion; the following are guidelines only. Generalized photos of what these options look like can be found on page 28.

For two 30 mm eyes, insert between Row 36 and Row 37 with approximately 7 stitch spaces between the posts.

For three eyes (two 30 mm and one 40 mm), insert between Row 37 and Row 38, with the 40 mm eye in the center and approximately 5 stitch spaces between each post.

For one or two 40 mm eyes, insert between Row 37 and Row 38 with approximately 7 stitch spaces between the posts.

You could also skip inserting a safety eye and follow the crocheted eye instruction options, including a 2D Medium or Large Eye, an Eye Bump, or an Eye Stalk.

Glass gems are optional (for more information, see page 28). Stuff the Body with fiberfill and continue to stuff as you go.

**42.** (SC 2, Dec, SC 2) x 6, Sl St to beginning stitch, Ch 1 [30]

**43.** (SC 3, Dec) x 6, Sl St to beginning stitch, Ch 1 [24]

**44.** (SC, Dec, SC) x 6, Sl St to beginning stitch, Ch 1 [18]

**45.** (SC, Dec) x 6, Sl St to beginning stitch, Ch 1 [12]

**46.** Dec x 6, Sl St to beginning stitch [6]

Fasten off with a 12 in/30.5 cm yarn tail.

## Assembly

**1.** Finish stuffing with fiberfill.

**2.** Use the yarn tails to sew the hole in the top of the head shut and between the legs (if necessary); weave in ends.

**3.** Add any extra details—ears, horns, limbs, etc.—you want to the body!

# CYLINDER WITH DEEP POCKET UNDERBITE AND NO LEGS (MAKE 1)

*Approximately 7.5 in/19 cm tall, 4.5 in/11.5 cm wide at the body*

*Body Color Yarn: Approximately 110 yd/100.5 m worsted/medium weight yarn*

This Monster Body is worked from the bottom to the top.

**1.** SC 6 in Magic Circle, Sl St to beginning stitch, Ch 1 [6]

**2.** Inc x 6, Sl St to beginning stitch, Ch 1 [12]

**3.** (SC, Inc) x 6, Sl St to beginning stitch, Ch 1 [18]

**4.** (SC, Inc, SC) x 6, Sl St to beginning stitch, Ch 1 [24]

**5.** (SC 3, Inc) x 6, Sl St to beginning stitch, Ch 1 [30]

**6.** (SC 2, Inc, SC 2) x 6, Sl St to beginning stitch, Ch 1 [36]

**7.** (SC 5, Inc) x 6, Sl St to beginning stitch, Ch 1 [42]

**8.** (SC 3, Inc, SC 3) x 6, Sl St to beginning stitch, Ch 1 [48]

**9.** SC 48, Sl St to beginning stitch, Ch 1 [48]

**10.** FLO [SC 48], Sl St to beginning stitch, Ch 1 [48]

Insert a stitch marker into the first unused BLO from Row 9 for reference on where to start Row 24.

**11–21.** (11 rows of) SC 48, Sl St to beginning stitch, Ch 1 [48]

**22–23.** (2 rows of) SC 12, HDC 24, SC 12, Sl St to beginning stitch, Ch 1 [48]

**24.** Ch 13, starting in the first BLO stitch from Row 9 and continuing working into the leftover BLO of the stitches from Row 9, BLO [SC 48], Sl St to beginning stitch, Ch 1 [48]

It can help to fold the outer edge down over the work (like pulling down a sock) so that you have easier access to the leftover BLO stitches from Row 9.

**25–37.** (13 rows of) SC 48, Sl St to beginning stitch, Ch 1 [48]

**38.** Starting in the first available stitch of each row through both Row 23 and Row 37 at the same time SC 12, SC 24 in Row 37 only, Skip 24 stitches on Row 23, SC 12 through Row 23 and Row 37 at the same time, Sl St to beginning stitch, Ch 1 [48]

**39–45.** (7 rows of) SC 48, Sl St to beginning stitch, Ch 1 [48]

**46.** (SC 3, Dec, SC 3) x 6, Sl St to beginning stitch, Ch 1 [42]

**47.** (SC 5, Dec) x 6, Sl St to beginning stitch, Ch 1 [36]

After you've completed Row 47, insert safety eyes. Safety eye size and placement are up to your discretion; the following are guidelines only. Generalized photos of what these options look like can be found on page 28.

For two 30 mm eyes, insert between Row 42 and Row 43 with approximately 7 stitch spaces between the posts.

For three eyes (two 30 mm and one 40 mm), insert between Row 43 and Row 44, with the 40 mm eye in the center and approximately 5 stitch spaces between each post.

For one or two 40 mm eyes, insert between Row 43 and Row 44 with approximately 7 stitch spaces between the posts.

You could also skip inserting a safety eye and follow the crocheted eye instruction options, including a 2D Medium or Large Eye, an Eye Bump, or an Eye Stalk.

Glass gems are optional (for more information, see page 28). Stuff the Body with fiberfill and continue to stuff as you go.

**48.** (SC 2, Dec, SC 2) x 6, Sl St to beginning stitch, Ch 1 [30]

**49.** (SC 3, Dec) x 6, Sl St to beginning stitch, Ch 1 [24]

**50.** (SC, Dec, SC) x 6, Sl St to beginning stitch, Ch 1 [18]

**51.** (SC, Dec) x 6, Sl St to beginning stitch, Ch 1 [12]

**52.** Dec x 6, Sl St to beginning stitch [6]

Fasten off with a 12 in/30.5 cm yarn tail.

## Assembly

**1.** Finish stuffing with fiberfill.

**2.** Use the yarn tail to sew the hole in the top of the head shut; weave in ends.

**3.** Add any extra details—ears, horns, limbs, etc.—you want to the body!

Cylinder with Deep Pocket Underbite and No Legs, Three-fingered Wide Limbs, Small Feet with Tiny Nubbin Toes, Thin Curved Antennae

Cylinder with Deep Pocket Underbite and Legs, Large Bulb Antennae, Large Cone Limbs, Big Double-layer Round Ears

# CYLINDER WITH DEEP POCKET UNDERBITE AND LEGS (MAKE 1)

***Approximately 8.5 in/21.5 cm tall, 4.5 in/11.5 cm wide at the body***

***Body Color Yarn: Approximately 140 yd/128 m worsted/medium weight yarn***

This Monster Body is worked from the bottom of the Feet to the top of the Body.

1. SC 6 in Magic Circle, Sl St to beginning stitch, Ch 1 [6]
2. Inc x 6, Sl St to beginning stitch, Ch 1 [12]
3. (SC, Inc) x 6, Sl St to beginning stitch, Ch 1 [18]
4. (SC, Inc, SC) x 6, Sl St to beginning stitch, Ch 1 [24]
5. BLO [SC 24], Sl St to beginning stitch, Ch 1 [24]
6–8. (3 rows of) SC 24, Sl St to beginning stitch, Ch 1 [24]
9. SC 8, Dec x 4, SC 8, Sl St to beginning stitch, Ch 1 [20]
10–12. (3 rows of) SC 20, Sl St to beginning stitch, Ch 1 [20]
13. (SC 4, Inc) x 4, Sl St to beginning stitch, Ch 1 [24]
14. SC 24, Sl St to beginning stitch, Ch 1 [24]

It is optional to use a piece of plastic canvas cut to size, a bottle cap, furniture felt pad, and so on to reinforce the bottom of the inside of the feet of your monster. At this point, insert this flat object into the bottom of the inside of the feet to help keep the feet flat and make it easier for your monster to stand securely. If you are also adding optional weight like glass gems, they should go on top of the plastic canvas.

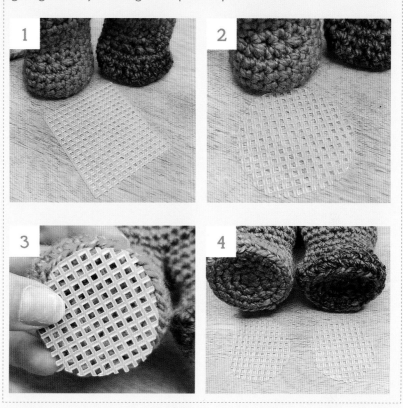

15. SC 24, Sl St to beginning stitch [24]

Fasten off the first leg with a short yarn tail.

Mark the 19th stitch of the final row of the first leg for reference in Row 16.

Repeat instructions for Rows 1 through 15 for the second leg, do not fasten off, and continue to Row 16.

**16.** Ch 1, SC 6, working into the first leg, starting in the marked stitch, SC 24, continuing into the next available stitch on the current or second leg, SC 18, Sl St to beginning stitch, Ch 1 [48]

**17.** FLO [SC 48], Sl St to beginning stitch, Ch 1 [48]

Insert a stitch marker into the first unused BLO from Row 16 for reference on where to start Row 30.

**18–27.** (10 rows of) SC 48, Sl St to beginning stitch, Ch 1 [48]

**28–29.** (2 rows of) SC 20, HDC 24, SC 4, Sl St to beginning stitch, Ch 1 [48]

**30.** Ch 13, starting in the first BLO stitch from Row 16 and continuing working into the leftover BLO of the stitches from Row 16, BLO [SC 48], Sl St to beginning stitch, Ch 1 [48]

It can help to fold the outer edge down over the work (like pulling down a sock) so that you have easier access to the leftover BLO stitches from Row 16.

**31–42.** (12 rows of) SC 48, Sl St to beginning stitch, Ch 1 [48]

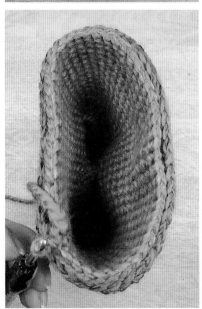

**43.** Starting in the first available stitch of each row through both Row 29 and Row 42 at the same time SC 20, SC 24 in Row 42 only, Skip 24 stitches on Row 29, SC 4 through Row 29 and Row 42 at the same time, Sl St to beginning stitch, Ch 1 [48]

**44–50.** (7 rows of) SC 48, Sl St to beginning stitch, Ch 1 [48]

**51.** (SC 3, Dec, SC 3) x 6, Sl St to beginning stitch, Ch 1 [42]

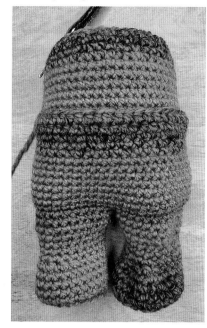

After you've completed Row 51, insert safety eyes. Safety eye size and placement are up to your discretion; the following are guidelines only. Generalized photos of what these options look like can be found on page 28.

For two 30 mm eyes, insert between Row 46 and Row 47 with approximately 7 stitch spaces between the posts.

For three eyes (two 30 mm and one 40 mm), insert between Row 47 and Row 48, with the 40 mm eye in the center and approximately 5 stitch spaces between each post.

For one or two 40 mm eyes, insert between Row 47 and Row 48 with approximately 7 stitch spaces between the posts.

You could also skip inserting a safety eye and follow the crocheted eye instruction options, including a 2D Medium or Large Eye, an Eye Bump, or an Eye Stalk.

Glass gems are optional (for more information, see page 28). Stuff the Body with fiberfill and continue to stuff as you go.

**52.** (SC 5, Dec) x 6, Sl St to beginning stitch, Ch 1 [36]

**53.** (SC 2, Dec, SC 2) x 6, Sl St to beginning stitch, Ch 1 [30]

**54.** (SC 3, Dec) x 6, Sl St to beginning stitch, Ch 1 [24]

**55.** (SC, Dec, SC) x 6, Sl St to beginning stitch, Ch 1 [18]

**56.** (SC, Dec) x 6, Sl St to beginning stitch, Ch 1 [12]

**57.** Dec x 6, Sl St to beginning stitch [6]

Fasten off with a 12 in/30.5 cm yarn tail.

## Assembly

**1.** Finish stuffing with fiberfill.

**2.** Use the yarn tails to sew shut the hole in the top of the head and between the legs (if necessary); weave in ends.

**3.** Add any extra details—ears, horns, limbs, etc.—you want to the body!

# CYLINDER WITH OVERBITE AND NO LEGS (MAKE 1)

*Approximately 7.5 in/19 cm tall, 4.5 in/11.5 cm wide at the body*

*Body Color Yarn: Approximately 120 yd/109.75 m worsted/medium weight yarn*

> This Monster Body is worked from the top of the head down to the bottom of the Body.

1. SC 6 in Magic Circle, Sl St to beginning stitch, Ch 1 [6]

2. Inc x 6, Sl St to beginning stitch, Ch 1 [12]

3. (SC, Inc) x 6, Sl St to beginning stitch, Ch 1 [18]

4. (SC, Inc, SC) x 6, Sl St to beginning stitch, Ch 1 [24]

5. (SC 3, Inc) x 6, Sl St to beginning stitch, Ch 1 [30]

6. (SC 2, Inc, SC 2) x 6, Sl St to beginning stitch, Ch 1 [36]

7. (SC 5, Inc) x 6, Sl St to beginning stitch, Ch 1 [42]

8. (SC 3, Inc, SC 3) x 6, Sl St to beginning stitch, Ch 1 [48]

9–14. (6 rows of) SC 48, Sl St to beginning stitch, Ch 1 [48]

15. FLO [SC 12, HDC 24, SC 12], Sl St to beginning stitch, Ch 1 [48]

16. SC 12, HDC 24, SC 12, Sl St to beginning stitch, do not Ch 1 [48]

17. Ch 2, starting in the first BLO stitch from Row 14 and continuing working into the leftover BLO of the stitches from Row 14, BLO [SC 48], Sl St to beginning stitch, Ch 1 [48]

18. SC 48, Sl St to beginning stitch, Ch 1 [48]

19. Starting in the first available stitch of each row through both Row 16 and Row 18 at the same time SC 12, SC 24 in Row 18 only, Skip 24 stitches on Row 16, SC 12 through Row 16 and Row 18 at the same time, Sl St to beginning stitch, Ch 1 [48]

20–32. (13 rows of) SC 48, Sl St to beginning stitch, Ch 1 [48]

33. (SC 3, Dec, SC 3) x 6, Sl St to beginning stitch, Ch 1 [42]

After you've completed Row 33, insert safety eyes. Safety eye size and placement are up to your discretion; the following are guidelines only. Generalized photos of what these options look like can be found on page 28.

For two 30 mm eyes, insert between Row 27 and Row 28 with approximately 7 stitch spaces between the posts.

For three eyes (two 30 mm and one 40 mm), insert between Row 28 and Row 29, with the 40 mm eye in the center and approximately 5 stitch spaces between each post.

For one or two 40 mm eyes, insert between Row 28 and Row 29 with approximately 7 stitch spaces between the posts.

You could also skip inserting a safety eye and follow the crocheted eye instruction options, including a 2D Medium or Large Eye, an Eye Bump, or an Eye Stalk.

Glass gems are optional (for more information, see page 28). Stuff the Body with fiberfill and continue to stuff as you go.

**34.** (SC 5, Dec) x 6, Sl St to beginning stitch, Ch 1 [36]

**35.** (SC 2, Dec, SC 2) x 6, Sl St to beginning stitch, Ch 1 [30]

**36.** (SC 3, Dec) x 6, Sl St to beginning stitch, Ch 1 [24]

**37.** (SC, Dec, SC) x 6, Sl St to beginning stitch, Ch 1 [18]

**38.** (SC, Dec) x 6, Sl St to beginning stitch, Ch 1 [12]

**39.** Dec x 6, Sl St to beginning stitch [6]

Fasten off with a 12 in/30.5 cm yarn tail.

## Assembly

**1.** Finish stuffing with fiberfill.

**2.** Use the yarn tail to sew shut the hole in the top of the head; weave in ends.

**3.** Add any extra details—ears, horns, limbs, etc.—you want to the body!

**Cylinder with Overbite and No Legs, Short Rounded Limbs, Long Rounded Limbs, Triangular Spikes of Varying Size, Pointed Folded Ears, Squared Teeth**

Cylinder with
Overbite and
Legs, Thick Curved
Antennae, Three-
fingered Wide Limbs,
Two Pointed Teeth
Two Flat Teeth

# CYLINDER WITH OVERBITE AND LEGS (MAKE 1)

*Approximately 8.5 in/21.5 cm tall, 4.5 in/11.5 cm wide at the body*

*Body Color Yarn: Approximately 150 yd/137.25 m worsted/medium weight yarn*

> This Monster Body is worked from the top of the head down to the bottom of the Body.

1. SC 6 in Magic Circle, Sl St to beginning stitch, Ch 1 [6]

2. Inc x 6, Sl St to beginning stitch, Ch 1 [12]

3. (SC, Inc) x 6, Sl St to beginning stitch, Ch 1 [18]

4. (SC, Inc, SC) x 6, Sl St to beginning stitch, Ch 1 [24]

5. (SC 3, Inc) x 6, Sl St to beginning stitch, Ch 1 [30]

6. (SC 2, Inc, SC 2) x 6, Sl St to beginning stitch, Ch 1 [36]

7. (SC 5, Inc) x 6, Sl St to beginning stitch, Ch 1 [42]

8. (SC 3, Inc, SC 3) x 6, Sl St to beginning stitch, Ch 1 [48]

9-14. (6 rows of) SC 48, Sl St to beginning stitch, Ch 1 [48]

15. FLO [SC 12, HDC 24, SC 12], Sl St to beginning stitch, Ch 1 [48]

16. SC 12, HDC 24, SC 12, Sl St to beginning stitch, Ch 1 [48]

17. Ch 2, starting in the first BLO stitch from Row 14 and continuing working into the leftover BLO of the stitches from Row 14, BLO [SC 48], Sl St to beginning stitch, Ch 1 [48]

18. SC 48, Sl St to beginning stitch, Ch 1 [48]

19. Starting in the first available stitch of each row through both Row 16 and Row 18 at the same time SC 12, SC 24 in Row 18 only, Skip 24 stitches on Row 16, SC 12 through Row 16 and Row 18 at the same time, Sl St to beginning stitch, Ch 1 [48]

After you've completed Row 19, insert safety eyes. Safety eye size and placement are up to your discretion; the following are guidelines only. Generalized photos of what these options look like can be found on page 28.

For two 30 mm eyes, insert between Row 11 and Row 12 with approximately 7 stitch spaces between the posts.

For three eyes (two 30 mm and one 40 mm), insert between Row 10 and Row 11, with the 40 mm eye in the center and approximately 5 stitch spaces between each post.

For one or two 40 mm eyes, insert between Row 10 and Row 11 with approximately 7 stitch spaces between the posts.

You could also skip inserting a safety eye and follow the crocheted eye instruction options, including a 2D Medium or Large Eye, an Eye Bump, or an Eye Stalk.

20-32. (13 rows of) SC 48, Sl St to beginning stitch, Ch 1 [48]

**33.** SC 2, Skip 24 stitches, SC 22, Sl St to beginning stitch, Ch 1 [24]

**34.** SC 24, Sl St to beginning stitch, Ch 1 [24]

> Stuff the Body of the Monster medium-firm; continue to stuff each leg as you crochet it.

**35.** (SC 4, Dec) x 4, Sl St to beginning stitch, Ch 1 [20]

**36–38.** (3 rows of) SC 20, Sl St to beginning stitch, Ch 1 [20]

**39.** SC 5, Inc x 4, SC 11, Sl St to beginning stitch, Ch 1 [24]

**40–42.** (3 rows of) SC 24, Sl St to beginning stitch, Ch 1 [24]

**43.** BLO [(SC 2, Dec) x 6], Sl St to beginning stitch, Ch 1 [18]

**44.** (SC, Dec) x 6, Sl St to beginning stitch, Ch 1 [12]

**45.** Dec x 6, Sl St to beginning stitch [6]

Fasten off with a 12 in/30.5 cm yarn tail.

For the second leg, attach the yarn to the third stitch on Row 32.

**46.** Working into all available remaining stitches on Row 32, SC 24, Sl St to beginning stitch, Ch 1 [24]

**47.** SC 24, Sl St to beginning stitch, Ch 1 [24]

> It is optional to add flat reinforcement to the bottom of the inside of the foot; see page 49 for details. Place reinforcement into the bottom of the first leg before continuing to stuff. Reinforcement for the bottom of the second leg will need to be placed after Row 55, after the piece has been stuffed.
>
> Glass gems are optional for use at the bottom of each foot—after you've made the first leg, and then at the end of the instructions for the second leg (for more information, see page 28). Stuff the Body with fiberfill and continue to stuff as you go.

**48.** (SC 4, Dec) x 4, Sl St to beginning stitch, Ch 1 [20]

**49–51.** (3 rows of) SC 20, Sl St to beginning stitch, Ch 1 [20]

**52.** SC 14, Inc x 4, SC 2, Sl St to beginning stitch, Ch 1 [24]

**53–55.** (3 rows of) SC 24, Sl St to beginning stitch, Ch 1 [24]

**56.** BLO [(SC, Dec, SC) x 6], Sl St to beginning stitch, Ch 1 [18]

**57.** (SC, Dec) x 6, Sl St to beginning stitch, Ch 1 [12]

**58.** Dec x 6, Sl St to beginning stitch [6]

Fasten off with a 12 in/30.5 cm yarn tail.

### Assembly

**1.** Finish stuffing with fiberfill.

**2.** Use the yarn tails to sew shut the final holes, including between the legs (if necessary); weave in ends.

**3.** Add any extra details—ears, horns, limbs, etc.—you want to the body!

Cylinder with Open Mouth and No Legs, Open Mouth with Buck Teeth (Upper), Short Rounded Limbs, Large Footed Bent Limbs, Medium Curved Horns

# CYLINDER WITH OPEN MOUTH AND NO LEGS (MAKE 1)

*Approximately 7.5 in/19 cm tall, 4.5 in/11.5 cm wide at the body*

*Body Color Yarn: Approximately 95 yd/86.75 m worsted/medium weight yarn*

You will need to crochet one of the Open Mouth pieces (pages 15–25) prior to making this Body to attach as you go.

This Monster Body is worked from the bottom to the top.

1. SC 6 in Magic Circle, Sl St to beginning stitch, Ch 1 [6]

2. Inc x 6, Sl St to beginning stitch, Ch 1 [12]

3. (SC, Inc) x 6, Sl St to beginning stitch, Ch 1 [18]

4. (SC, Inc, SC) x 6, Sl St to beginning stitch, Ch 1 [24]

5. (SC 3, Inc) x 6, Sl St to beginning stitch, Ch 1 [30]

6. (SC 2, Inc, SC 2) x 6, Sl St to beginning stitch, Ch 1 [36]

7. (SC 5, Inc) x 6, Sl St to beginning stitch, Ch 1 [42]

8. (SC 3, Inc, SC 3) x 6, Sl St to beginning stitch, Ch 1 [48]

9–21. (13 rows of) SC 48, Sl St to beginning stitch, Ch 1 [48]

In Row 22, insert your hook into the right side/outside of the Body first and then into the wrong side/inside of the last stitch of the last row of the Mouth (OR the marked stitch on the Mouth) to create these stitches. You are working along the bottom front of the Mouth.

22. SC 12, working into the Mouth and the Body at the same time, SC 24, working into the Body only, SC 12, Sl St to beginning stitch, Ch 1 [48]

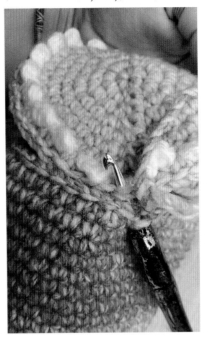

In Row 23, when you work into the Mouth, you are working along the top front of the Mouth only; you do not work into the stitches you made in Row 22 in the bottom half of the Mouth at all.

23. SC 12, working into the Mouth only, FLO [SC 24], SC 12 in the Body, Sl St to beginning stitch, Ch 1 [48]

**24.** SC 12, continuing in the back loops of the Mouth left after Row 23, BLO [SC 24], SC 12 in Row 23, Sl St to beginning stitch, Ch 1 [48]

After you've completed Row 33, insert safety eyes. Safety eye size and placement are up to your discretion; the following are guidelines only. Generalized photos of what these options look like can be found on page 28.

For two 30 mm eyes, insert between Row 27 and Row 28 with approximately 7 stitch spaces between the posts.

For three eyes (two 30 mm and one 40 mm), insert between Row 28 and Row 29, with the 40 mm eye in the center and approximately 5 stitch spaces between each post.

For one or two 40 mm eyes, insert between Row 28 and Row 29 with approximately 7 stitch spaces between the posts.

You could also skip inserting a safety eye and follow the crocheted eye instruction options, including a 2D Medium or Large Eye, an Eye Bump, or an Eye Stalk.

Glass gems are optional (for more information, see page 28). Stuff the Body with fiberfill and continue to stuff as you go. Do not overstuff; make sure the Mouth is folded over itself when you stuff (like a hard taco shell) so that the Monster Mouth can be closed when you finish.

**34.** (SC 2, Dec, SC 2) x 6, Sl St to beginning stitch, Ch 1 [30]

**35.** (SC 3, Dec) x 6, Sl St to beginning stitch, Ch 1 [24]

**36.** (SC, Dec, SC) x 6, Sl St to beginning stitch, Ch 1 [18]

**37.** (SC, Dec) x 6, Sl St to beginning stitch, Ch 1 [12]

**38.** Dec x 6, Sl St to beginning stitch [6]

Fasten off with a 12 in/30.5 cm yarn tail.

### Assembly

**1.** Finish stuffing with fiberfill.

**2.** Use the yarn tail to sew shut the hole in the top of the head; weave in ends.

**3.** Add any extra details—ears, horns, limbs, etc.—you want to the body!

**25–31.** (7 rows of) SC 48, Sl St to beginning stitch, Ch 1 [48]

**32.** (SC 3, Dec, SC 3) x 6, Sl St to beginning stitch, Ch 1 [42]

**33.** (SC 5, Dec) x 6, Sl St to beginning stitch, Ch 1 [36]

# CYLINDER WITH OPEN MOUTH AND LEGS (MAKE 1)

*Approximately 8.5 in/21.5 cm tall, 4.5 in/11.5 cm wide at the body*

*Body Color Yarn: 80 yd/73.25 m worsted/medium weight yarn*

You will need to crochet one of the Open Mouth pieces (pages 15–25) prior to making this Body to attach as you go.

This Monster Body is worked from the bottom of the Feet to the top of the Body.

1. SC 6 in Magic Circle, Sl St to beginning stitch, Ch 1 [6]

2. Inc x 6, Sl St to beginning stitch, Ch 1 [12]

3. (SC, Inc) x 6, Sl St to beginning stitch, Ch 1 [18]

4. (SC, Inc, SC) x 6, Sl St to beginning stitch, Ch 1 [24]

5. BLO [SC 24], Sl St to beginning stitch, Ch 1 [24]

6–8. (3 rows of) SC 24, Sl St to beginning stitch, Ch 1 [24]

9. SC 8, Dec x 4, SC 8, Sl St to beginning stitch, Ch 1 [20]

10–12. (3 rows of) SC 20, Sl St to beginning stitch, Ch 1 [20]

13. (SC 4, Inc) x 4, Sl St to beginning stitch, Ch 1 [24]

14. SC 24, Sl St to beginning stitch, Ch 1 [24]

15. SC 24, Sl St to beginning stitch [24]

Fasten off the first leg with a short yarn tail.

Mark the 19th stitch of the final row of the first leg for reference in Row 16.

Repeat instructions for Rows 1 through 15 for the second leg, do not fasten off, and continue to Row 16.

It is optional to add flat reinforcement to the bottom of the inside of the foot; see page 49 for details.

16. SC 6, working into the first leg, starting in the marked stitch, SC 24, continuing into the next available stitch on the current leg, SC 18, Sl St to beginning stitch, Ch 1 [48]

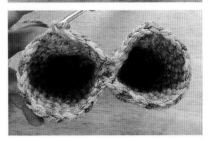

17–27. (11 rows of) SC 48, Sl St to beginning stitch, Ch 1 [48]

In Row 28, insert your hook into the right side/outside of the Body first and then into the wrong side/inside of the last stitch of the last row of the Mouth (OR the marked stitch on the Mouth) to create these stitches. You are working along the bottom front of the Mouth.

**28.** SC 21, working into the Mouth and the Body at the same time, SC 24, working into the Body only, SC 3, Sl St to beginning stitch, Ch 1 [48]

In Row 29, when you work into the Mouth, you are working along the top front of the Mouth only; you do not work into the stitches you made in Row 28 in the bottom half of the Mouth at all.

**29.** SC 21, working into the Mouth only, FLO [SC 24], SC 3 in the Body, Sl St to beginning stitch, Ch 1 [48]

**30.** SC 21, continuing in the back loops of the Mouth left after Row 29, BLO [SC 24], SC 3 in Row 29, Sl St to beginning stitch, Ch 1 [48]

**31–37.** (7 rows of) SC 48, Sl St to beginning stitch, Ch 1 [48]

**38.** (SC 3, Dec, SC 3) x 6, Sl St to beginning stitch, Ch 1 [42]

**39.** (SC 5, Dec) x 6, Sl St to beginning stitch, Ch 1 [36]

After you've completed Row 39, insert safety eyes. Safety eye size and placement are up to your discretion; the following are guidelines only. Generalized photos of what these options look like can be found on page 28.

For two 30 mm eyes, insert between Row 33 and Row 34 with approximately 7 stitch spaces between the posts.

For three eyes (two 30 mm and one 40 mm), insert between Row 34 and Row 35, with the 40 mm eye in the center and approximately 5 stitch spaces between each post.

For one or two 40 mm eyes, insert between Row 34 and Row 35 with approximately 7 stitch spaces between the posts.

You could also skip inserting a safety eye and follow the crocheted eye instruction options, including a 2D Medium or Large Eye, an Eye Bump, or an Eye Stalk.

Glass gems are optional (for more information, see page 28). Stuff the Body with fiberfill and continue to stuff as you go. Do not overstuff; make sure the Mouth is folded over itself when you stuff (like a hard taco shell) so that the Monster Mouth can be closed when you finish.

**40.** (SC 2, Dec, SC 2) x 6, Sl St to beginning stitch, Ch 1 [30]

**41.** (SC 3, Dec) x 6, Sl St to beginning stitch, Ch 1 [24]

**42.** (SC, Dec, SC) x 6, Sl St to beginning stitch, Ch 1 [18]

**43.** (SC, Dec) x 6, Sl St to beginning stitch, Ch 1 [12]

**44.** Dec x 6, Sl St to beginning stitch [6]

Fasten off with a 12 in/30.5 cm yarn tail.

## Assembly

**1.** Finish stuffing with fiberfill.

**2.** Use the yarn tails to sew shut the final holes, including between the legs (if necessary); weave in ends.

**3.** Add any extra details—ears, horns, limbs, etc.—you want to the body!

**Cylinder with Open Mouth and Legs, Open Mouth Four Pointed Teeth (Lower), Thin Arms with Two Fingers, Skinny Spikes, Long Reptile Tail, Long Slightly Curved Horns**

Cylinder
with No Mouth
and No Legs, 2D Open
Mouth in Lima Bean Shape
with Straight Teeth and
Tongue, Eye Stalks,
Three-fingered Hand with
Elbow and Arm,
Two- toed Feet with
Knees and Legs

If you want to add
metal spikes to
any part of your
Monster, go to
page 172 for tips
on how to do that.

# CYLINDER WITH NO MOUTH AND NO LEGS (MAKE 1)

*Approximately 7.5 in/19 cm tall, 4.5 in/11.5 cm wide at the body*

*Body Color Yarn: Approximately 85 yd/77.75 m worsted/medium weight yarn*

This Monster Body is worked from the bottom to the top.

**1.** SC 6 in Magic Circle, Sl St to beginning stitch, Ch 1 [6]

**2.** Inc x 6, Sl St to beginning stitch, Ch 1 [12]

**3.** (SC, Inc) x 6, Sl St to beginning stitch, Ch 1 [18]

**4.** (SC, Inc, SC) x 6, Sl St to beginning stitch, Ch 1 [24]

**5.** (SC 3, Inc) x 6, Sl St to beginning stitch, Ch 1 [30]

**6.** (SC 2, Inc, SC 2) x 6, Sl St to beginning stitch, Ch 1 [36]

**7.** (SC 5, Inc) x 6, Sl St to beginning stitch, Ch 1 [42]

**8.** (SC 3, Inc, SC 3) x 6, Sl St to beginning stitch, Ch 1 [48]

**9–29.** (21 rows of) SC 48, Sl St to beginning stitch, Ch 1 [48]

**30.** (SC 3, Dec, SC 3) x 6, Sl St to beginning stitch, Ch 1 [42]

After you've completed Row 30, insert safety eyes. Safety eye size and placement are up to your discretion; the following are guidelines only. Generalized photos of what these options look like can be found on page 28.

For two 30 mm eyes, insert between Row 25 and Row 26 with approximately 7 stitch spaces between the posts.

For three eyes (two 30 mm and one 40 mm), insert between Row 26 and Row 27, with the 40 mm eye in the center and approximately 5 stitch spaces between each post.

For one or two 40 mm eyes, insert between Row 26 and Row 27 with approximately 7 stitch spaces between the posts.

You could also skip inserting a safety eye and follow the crocheted eye instruction options, including a 2D Medium or Large Eye, an Eye Bump, or an Eye Stalk.

Glass gems are optional (for more information, see page 28). Stuff the Body with fiberfill and continue to stuff as you go.

**31.** (SC 5, Dec) x 6, Sl St to beginning stitch, Ch 1 [36]

**32.** (SC 2, Dec, SC 2) x 6, Sl St to beginning stitch, Ch 1 [30]

**33.** (SC 3, Dec) x 6, Sl St to beginning stitch, Ch 1 [24]

**34.** (SC, Dec, SC) x 6, Sl St to beginning stitch, Ch 1 [18]

**35.** (SC, Dec) x 6, Sl St to beginning stitch, Ch 1 [12]

**36.** Dec x 6, Sl St to beginning stitch [6]

Fasten off with a 12 in/30.5 cm yarn tail.

## Assembly

**1.** Finish stuffing with fiberfill.

**2.** Use the yarn tail to sew shut the final holes; weave in ends.

**3.** Add any extra details—ears, horns, limbs, etc.—you want to the body!

Cylinder with No Mouth and Legs, 2D Open Mouth in Rectangular Shape with Humanlike Teeth, Eye Stalks, Bulb-ended Short Limbs

# CYLINDER WITH NO MOUTH AND LEGS (MAKE 1)

*Approximately 8.5 in/21.5 cm tall, 4.5 in/11.5 cm wide at the body*

*Body Color Yarn: Approximately 120 yd/109.75 m worsted/medium weight yarn*

> This Monster Body is worked from the bottom of the Feet to the top of the Body.

1. SC 6 in Magic Circle, Sl St to beginning stitch, Ch 1 [6]

2. Inc x 6, Sl St to beginning stitch, Ch 1 [12]

3. (SC, Inc) x 6, Sl St to beginning stitch, Ch 1 [18]

4. (SC, Inc, SC) x 6, Sl St to beginning stitch, Ch 1 [24]

5. BLO [SC 24], Sl St to beginning stitch, Ch 1 [24]

6-8. (3 rows of) SC 24, Sl St to beginning stitch, Ch 1 [24]

9. SC 8, Dec x 4, SC 8, Sl St to beginning stitch, Ch 1 [20]

10-12. (3 rows of) SC 20, Sl St to beginning stitch, Ch 1 [20]

13. (SC 4, Inc) x 4, Sl St to beginning stitch, Ch 1 [24]

14. SC 24, Sl St to beginning stitch, Ch 1 [24]

15. SC 24, Sl St to beginning stitch [24]

Fasten off the first leg with a short yarn tail.

Mark the 19th stitch of the final row of the first leg for reference in Row 16.

Repeat instructions for Rows 1 through 15 for the second leg, do not fasten off, and continue to Row 16.

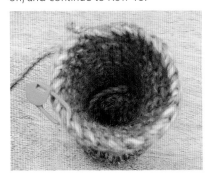

> It is optional to add flat reinforcement to the bottom of the inside of the foot; see page 49 for details.

16. Ch 1, SC 6, working into the marked stitch on the first leg, SC 24, continuing into the next available stitch on the second leg, SC 18, Sl St to beginning stitch, Ch 1 [48]

17-37. (21 rows of) SC 48, Sl St to beginning stitch, Ch 1 [48]

38. (SC 3, Dec, SC 3) x 6, Sl St to beginning stitch, Ch 1 [42]

> After you've completed Row 38, insert safety eyes. Safety eye size and placement are up to your discretion; the following are guidelines only. Generalized photos of what these options look like can be found on page 28.
>
> For two 30 mm eyes, insert between Row 33 and Row 34 with approximately 7 stitch spaces between the posts.
>
> For three eyes (two 30 mm and one 40 mm), insert between Row 34 and Row 35, with the 40 mm eye in the center and approximately 5 stitch spaces between each post.
>
> For one or two 40 mm eyes, insert between Row 34 and Row 35 with approximately 7 stitch spaces between the posts.
>
> You could also skip inserting a safety eye and follow the crocheted eye instruction options, including a 2D Medium or Large Eye, an Eye Bump, or an Eye Stalk.

Glass gems are optional (for more information, see page 28). Stuff the Body with fiberfill and continue to stuff as you go.

**39.** (SC 5, Dec) x 6, Sl St to beginning stitch, Ch 1 [36]

**40.** (SC 2, Dec, SC 2) x 6, Sl St to beginning stitch, Ch 1 [30]

**41.** (SC 3, Dec) x 6, Sl St to beginning stitch, Ch 1 [24]

**42.** (SC, Dec, SC) x 6, Sl St to beginning stitch, Ch 1 [18]

**43.** (SC, Dec) x 6, Sl St to beginning stitch, Ch 1 [12]

**44.** Dec x 6, Sl St to beginning stitch [6]

Fasten off with a 12 in/30.5 cm yarn tail.

## Assembly

**1.** Finish stuffing with fiberfill.

**2.** Use the yarn tails to sew shut the final holes, including between the legs (if necessary); weave in ends.

**3.** Add any extra details—ears, horns, limbs, etc.—you want to the body!

# Egg-shaped Bodies

## EGG SHAPE WITH UNDERBITE AND NO LEGS (MAKE 1)

*Approximately 8 in/20.5 cm tall, 6 in/15 cm wide at the body*

*Body Color Yarn: Approximately 140 yd/128 m worsted/medium weight yarn*

This Monster Body is worked from the bottom to the top.

**1.** SC 6 in Magic Circle, Sl St to beginning stitch, Ch 1 [6]

**2.** Inc x 6, Sl St to beginning stitch, Ch 1 [12]

**3.** (SC, Inc) x 6, Sl St to beginning stitch, Ch 1 [18]

**4.** (SC, Inc, SC) x 6, Sl St to beginning stitch, Ch 1 [24]

**5.** (SC 3, Inc) x 6, Sl St to beginning stitch, Ch 1 [30]

**6.** (SC 2, Inc, SC 2) x 6, Sl St to beginning stitch, Ch 1 [36]

**7.** (SC 5, Inc) x 6, Sl St to beginning stitch, Ch 1 [42]

**8.** (SC 3, Inc, SC 3) x 6, Sl St to beginning stitch, Ch 1 [48]

**9.** (SC 7, Inc) x 6, Sl St to beginning stitch, Ch 1 [54]

**10.** (SC 4, Inc, SC 4) x 6, Sl St to beginning stitch, Ch 1 [60]

**11.** (SC 9, Inc) x 6, Sl St to beginning stitch, Ch 1 [66]

**12.** SC 66, Sl St to beginning stitch, Ch 1 [66]

**13.** (SC 21, Inc) x 3, Sl St to beginning stitch, Ch 1 [69]

**14–20.** (7 rows of) SC 69, Sl St to beginning stitch, Ch 1 [69]

**21.** (SC 21, Dec) x 3, Sl St to beginning stitch, Ch 1 [66]

**22–24.** (3 rows of) SC 66, Sl St to beginning stitch, Ch 1 [66]

**25.** (SC 9, Dec) x 6, Sl St to beginning stitch, Ch 1 [60]

**26–27.** (2 rows of) SC 60, Sl St to beginning stitch, Ch 1 [60]

**28.** SC 21, (Dec, SC) x 3, (SC, Dec) x 3, SC 21, Sl St to beginning stitch, Ch 1 [54]

**29.** FLO [SC 54], Sl St to beginning stitch, Ch 1 [54]

**30.** SC 22, HDC 10, SC 22, Sl St to beginning stitch, Ch 2 [54]

**31.** Starting in the first BLO stitch from Row 28 and continuing working into the leftover BLO of the stitches from Row 28, BLO [SC 54], Sl St to beginning stitch, Ch 1 [54]

**32.** SC 54, Sl St to beginning stitch, Ch 1 [54]

**33.** Starting in the first available stitch of each row through both Row 30 and Row 32 at the same time SC 8, Dec, SC 12, then working in Row 32 only, SC 4, Dec, SC 4, Skip 10 stitches on Row 30, then working through Row 30 and Row 32 at the same time, SC 12, Dec, SC 8, Sl St to beginning stitch, Ch 1 [51]

**34.** SC 51, Sl St to beginning stitch, Ch 1 [51]

**35.** (SC 15, Dec) x 3, Sl St to beginning stitch, Ch 1 [48]

**36.** SC 48, Sl St to beginning stitch, Ch 1 [48]

**37.** (SC 7, Dec, SC 7) x 3, Sl St to beginning stitch, Ch 1 [45]

**38.** (SC 13, Dec) x 3, Sl St to beginning stitch, Ch 1 [42]

**39.** (SC 6, Dec, SC 6) x 3, Sl St to beginning stitch, Ch 1 [39]

**40.** (SC 11, Dec) x 3, Sl St to beginning stitch, Ch 1 [36]

**41.** (SC 2, Dec, SC 2) x 6, Sl St to beginning stitch, Ch 1 [30]

**42.** (SC 3, Dec) x 6, Sl St to beginning stitch, Ch 1 [24]

After you've completed Row 42, insert safety eyes. Safety eye size and placement are up to your discretion; the following are guidelines only. Generalized photos of what these options look like can be found on page 28.

For two 30 mm eyes, insert between Row 37 and Row 38 with approximately 7 stitch spaces between the posts.

For three eyes (two 30 mm and one 40 mm), insert between Row 37 and Row 38, with the 40 mm eye in the center and approximately 5 stitch spaces between each post.

For one or two 40 mm eyes, insert between Row 37 and Row 38 with approximately 7 stitch spaces between the posts.

You could also skip inserting a safety eye and follow the crocheted eye instruction options, including a 2D Medium or Large Eye, an Eye Bump, or an Eye Stalk.

Glass gems are optional (for more information, see page 28). Stuff the Body with fiberfill and continue to stuff as you go.

**43.** (SC, Dec, SC) x 6, Sl St to beginning stitch, Ch 1 [18]

**44.** (SC, Dec) x 6, Sl St to beginning stitch, Ch 1 [12]

**45.** Dec x 6, Sl St to beginning stitch [6]

Fasten off with a 12 in/30.5 cm yarn tail.

## Assembly

**1.** Finish stuffing with fiberfill.

**2.** Use the yarn tail to sew shut the final holes; weave in ends.

**3.** Add any extra details—ears, horns, limbs, etc.—you want to the body!

# EGG SHAPE WITH UNDERBITE AND LEGS (MAKE 1)

*Approximately 9.5 in/24 cm tall, 6 in/15 cm wide at the body*

*Body Color Yarn: Approximately 160 yd/146.25 m worsted/medium weight yarn*

> This Monster Body is worked from the bottom of the Feet to the top of the Body.

**1.** SC 6 in Magic Circle, Sl St to beginning stitch, Ch 1 [6]

**2.** Inc x 6, Sl St to beginning stitch, Ch 1 [12]

**3.** (SC, Inc) x 6, Sl St to beginning stitch, Ch 1 [18]

**4.** (SC, Inc, SC) x 6, Sl St to beginning stitch, Ch 1 [24]

**5.** (SC 3, Inc) x 6, Sl St to beginning stitch, Ch 1 [30]

**6.** BLO [SC 30], Sl St to beginning stitch, Ch 1 [30]

**7–9.** (3 rows of) SC 30, Sl St to beginning stitch, Ch 1 [30]

**10.** SC 11, Dec x 4, SC 11, Sl St to beginning stitch, Ch 1 [26]

**11.** SC 10, Dec, SC 2, Dec, SC 10, Sl St to beginning stitch, Ch 1 [24]

**12–13.** (2 rows of) SC 24, Sl St to beginning stitch, Ch 1 [24]

**14.** (SC 3, Inc) x 6, Sl St to beginning stitch, Ch 1 [30]

**15.** SC 30, Sl St to beginning stitch, Ch 1 [30]

**16.** (SC 9, Inc) x 3, Sl St to beginning stitch [33]

Fasten off the first leg with a short yarn tail.

Mark the 27th stitch of the final row of the first leg for reference in Row 17.

Repeat instructions for Rows 1 through 16 for the second leg, do not fasten off, and continue to Row 17.

> It is optional to add flat reinforcement to the bottom of the inside of the foot; see page 49 for details.

**17.** Ch 1, SC 9, working into the first leg, starting in the marked stitch, SC 33, continuing into the next available stitch on the second leg, SC 24, Sl St to beginning stitch, Ch 1 [66]

**18.** (SC 21, Inc) x 3, Sl St to beginning stitch, Ch 1 [69]

**19–25.** (7 rows of) SC 69, Sl St to beginning stitch, Ch 1 [69]

**26.** (SC 21, Dec) x 3, Sl St to beginning stitch, Ch 1 [66]

**27–29.** (3 rows of) SC 66, Sl St to beginning stitch, Ch 1 [66]

**30.** (SC 9, Dec) x 6, Sl St to beginning stitch, Ch 1 [60]

**31–32.** (2 rows of) SC 60, Sl St to beginning stitch, Ch 1 [60]

**33.** SC 32, (Dec, SC) x 3, (SC, Dec) x 3, SC 10, Sl St to beginning stitch, Ch 1 [54]

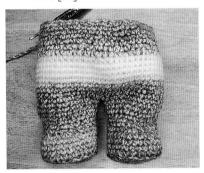

**34.** FLO [SC 54], Sl St to beginning stitch, Ch 1 [54]

**35.** SC 34, HDC 10, SC 10, Sl St to beginning stitch, Ch 2 [54]

**36.** Starting in the first BLO stitch from Row 33 and continuing working into the leftover BLO of the stitches from Row 33, BLO [SC 54], Sl St to beginning stitch, Ch 1 [54]

**37.** SC 54, Sl St to beginning stitch, Ch 1 [54]

**38.** Starting in the first available stitch of each row through both Row 35 and Row 37 at the same time SC 8, Dec, SC 16, Dec, SC 6, then working in Row 37 only, SC 10, Skip 10 stitches on Row 35, then working through Row 35 and Row 37 at the same time, Dec, SC 8, Sl St to beginning stitch, Ch 1 [51]

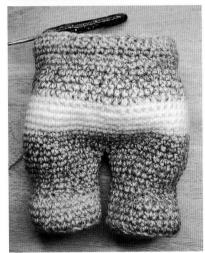

**39.** SC 51, Sl St to beginning stitch, Ch 1 [51]

**40.** (SC 15, Dec) x 3, Sl St to beginning stitch, Ch 1 [48]

**41.** SC 48, Sl St to beginning stitch, Ch 1 [48]

**42.** (SC 7, Dec, SC 7) x 3, Sl St to beginning stitch, Ch 1 [45]

**43.** (SC 13, Dec) x 3, Sl St to beginning stitch, Ch 1 [42]

**44.** (SC 6, Dec, SC 6) x 3, Sl St to beginning stitch, Ch 1 [39]

**45.** (SC 11, Dec) x 3, Sl St to beginning stitch, Ch 1 [36]

**46.** (SC 2, Dec, SC 2) x 6, Sl St to beginning stitch, Ch 1 [30]

**47.** (SC 3, Dec) x 6, Sl St to beginning stitch, Ch 1 [24]

After you've completed Row 47, insert safety eyes at this point between Row 42 and Row 43. Safety eye size and placement are up to your discretion; the following are guidelines only. Generalized photos of what these options look like can be found on page 28.

For two 30 mm eyes, insert with approximately 7 stitch spaces between the posts.

For three eyes (two 30 mm and one 40 mm), insert with approximately 5 stitch spaces between each post.

For one or two 40 mm eyes, insert with approximately 7 stitch spaces between the posts.

You could also skip inserting a safety eye and follow the crocheted eye instruction options, including a 2D Medium or Large Eye, an Eye Bump, or an Eye Stalk.

Glass gems are optional (for more information, see page 28). Stuff the Body with fiberfill and continue to stuff as you go.

**48.** (SC, Dec, SC) x 6, Sl St to beginning stitch, Ch 1 [18]

**49.** (SC, Dec) x 6, Sl St to beginning stitch, Ch 1 [12]

**50.** Dec x 6, Sl St to beginning stitch [6]

Fasten off with a 12 in/30.5 cm yarn tail.

## Assembly

**1.** Finish stuffing with fiberfill.

**2.** Use the yarn tails to sew shut the final holes, including between the legs (if necessary); weave in ends.

**3.** Add any extra details—ears, horns, limbs, etc.—you want to the body!

Egg Shape with Underbite and No Legs, Small Short Limbs, Feet with Big Toes, Big Round Horns, Two Small Fangs

Egg Shape with Underbite and Legs, Small Cone Limbs, Medium Curved Horns, Six Sharp Teeth

Egg Shape with Overbite and No Legs, Small Short Limbs, Rounded Feet, Small Half Circle Ears, Mohawk, Small Tongue

# EGG SHAPE WITH OVERBITE AND NO LEGS (MAKE 1)

***Approximately 8 in/20.5 cm tall, 6 in/15 cm wide at the body***

***Body Color Yarn: Approximately 150 yd/137.25 m worsted/medium weight yarn***

This Monster Body is worked from the top of the head down to the bottom of the body.

1. SC 6 in Magic Circle, Sl St to beginning stitch, Ch 1 [6]
2. Inc x 6, Sl St to beginning stitch, Ch 1 [12]
3. (SC, Inc) x 6, Sl St to beginning stitch, Ch 1 [18]
4. (SC, Inc, SC) x 6, Sl St to beginning stitch, Ch 1 [24]
5. (SC 3, Inc) x 6, Sl St to beginning stitch, Ch 1 [30]
6. (SC 2, Inc, SC 2) x 6, Sl St to beginning stitch, Ch 1 [36]
7. (SC 11, Inc) x 3, Sl St to beginning stitch, Ch 1 [39]
8. (SC 6, Inc, SC 6) x 3, Sl St to beginning stitch, Ch 1 [42]
9. (SC 13, Inc) x 3, Sl St to beginning stitch, Ch 1 [45]
10. (SC 7, Inc, SC 7) x 3, Sl St to beginning stitch, Ch 1 [48]
11. SC 48, Sl St to beginning stitch, Ch 1 [48]
12. (SC 15, Inc) x 3, Sl St to beginning stitch, Ch 1 [51]
13. SC 51, Sl St to beginning stitch, Ch 1 [51]
14. FLO [(SC 8, Inc, SC 8) x 3], Sl St to beginning stitch, Ch 1 [54]

15. SC 23, HDC 10, SC 21, Sl St to beginning stitch [54]

16. Ch 3, starting in the first BLO stitch from Row 13 and continuing working into the leftover BLO of the stitches from Row 13, BLO [(SC 8, Inc, SC 8) x 3], Sl St to beginning stitch, Ch 1 [54]
17. SC 54, Sl St to beginning stitch, Ch 1 [54]

18. Starting in the first available stitch of each row through both Row 15 and Row 17 at the same time SC 23, then working in Row 17 only, SC 10, , Skip 10 stitches on Row 15, then working through Row 15 and Row 17 at the same time, SC 21, Sl St to beginning stitch, Ch 1 [54]

After you've completed Row 18, insert safety eyes between Row 10 and Row 11. Safety eye size and placement are up to your discretion; the following are guidelines only. Generalized photos of what these options look like can be found on page 28.

For two 30 mm eyes, insert with approximately 7 stitch spaces between the posts.

For three eyes (two 30 mm and one 40 mm), insert with approximately 5 stitch spaces between each post.

For one or two 40 mm eyes, insert with approximately 7 stitch spaces between the posts.

You could also skip inserting a safety eye and follow the crocheted eye instruction options, including a 2D Medium or Large Eye, an Eye Bump, or an Eye Stalk.

19. SC 22, (Inc, SC) x 3, (SC, Inc) x 3, SC 20, Sl St to beginning stitch, Ch 1 [60]
20–21. (2 rows of) SC 60, Sl St to beginning stitch, Ch 1 [60]
22. (SC 9, Inc) x 6, Sl St to beginning stitch, Ch 1 [66]
23–25. (3 rows of) SC 66, Sl St to beginning stitch, Ch 1 [66]

**26.** (SC 21, Inc) x 3, Sl St to beginning stitch, Ch 1 [69]

**27–33.** (7 rows of) SC 69, Sl St to beginning stitch, Ch 1 [69]

**34.** (SC 21, Dec) x 3, Sl St to beginning stitch, Ch 1 [66]

**35.** SC 66, Sl St to beginning stitch, Ch 1 [66]

**36.** (SC 9, Dec) x 6, Sl St to beginning stitch, Ch 1 [60]

**37.** (SC 4, Dec, SC 4) x 6, Sl St to beginning stitch, Ch 1 [54]

**38.** (SC 7, Dec) x 6, Sl St to beginning stitch, Ch 1 [48]

**39.** (SC 3, Dec, SC 3) x 6, Sl St to beginning stitch, Ch 1 [42]

**40.** (SC 5, Dec) x 6, Sl St to beginning stitch, Ch 1 [36]

**41.** (SC 2, Dec, SC 2) x 6, Sl St to beginning stitch, Ch 1 [30]

**42.** (SC 3, Dec) x 6, Sl St to beginning stitch, Ch 1 [24]

> Glass gems are optional (for more information, see page 28). Stuff the Body with fiberfill and continue to stuff as you go.

**43.** (SC, Dec, SC) x 6, Sl St to beginning stitch, Ch 1 [18]

**44.** (SC, Dec) x 6, Sl St to beginning stitch, Ch 1 [12]

**45.** Dec x 6, Sl St to beginning stitch [6]

Fasten off with a 12 in/30.5 cm yarn tail.

## Assembly

**1.** Finish stuffing with fiberfill.

**2.** Use the yarn tail to sew shut the final holes; weave in ends.

**3.** Add any extra details—ears, horns, limbs, etc.—you want to the body!

# EGG SHAPE WITH OVERBITE AND LEGS (MAKE 1)

*Approximately 9.5 in/24 cm tall, 6 in/15 cm wide at the body*

*Body Color Yarn: Approximately 160 yd/146.25 m worsted/medium weight yarn*

> This Monster Body is worked from the top of the head down to the bottom of the feet.

**1.** SC 6 in Magic Circle, Sl St to beginning stitch, Ch 1 [6]

**2.** Inc x 6, Sl St to beginning stitch, Ch 1 [12]

**3.** (SC, Inc) x 6, Sl St to beginning stitch, Ch 1 [18]

**4.** (SC, Inc, SC) x 6, Sl St to beginning stitch, Ch 1 [24]

**5.** (SC 3, Inc) x 6, Sl St to beginning stitch, Ch 1 [30]

**6.** (SC 2, Inc, SC 2) x 6, Sl St to beginning stitch, Ch 1 [36]

**7.** (SC 11, Inc) x 3, Sl St to beginning stitch, Ch 1 [39]

**8.** (SC 6, Inc, SC 6) x 3, Sl St to beginning stitch, Ch 1 [42]

**9.** (SC 13, Inc) x 3, Sl St to beginning stitch, Ch 1 [45]

**10.** (SC 7, Inc, SC 7) x 3, Sl St to beginning stitch, Ch 1 [48]

**11.** SC 48, Sl St to beginning stitch, Ch 1 [48]

**12.** (SC 15, Inc) x 3, Sl St to beginning stitch, Ch 1 [51]

**13.** SC 51, Sl St to beginning stitch, Ch 1 [51]

**14.** FLO [(SC 8, Inc, SC 8) x 3], Sl St to beginning stitch, Ch 1 [54]

**15.** SC 23, HDC 10, SC 21, Sl St to beginning stitch, Ch 1 [54]

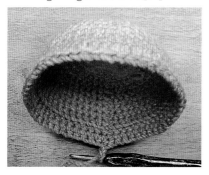

**16.** Ch 2, starting in the first BLO stitch from Row 13 and continuing working into the leftover BLO of the stitches from Row 13, BLO [(SC 8, Inc, SC 8) x 3], Sl St to beginning stitch, Ch 1 [54]

**17.** SC 54, Sl St to beginning stitch, Ch 1 [54]

**18.** Starting in the first available stitch of each row through both Row 15 and Row 17 at the same time SC 23, then working in Row 17 only, SC 10, Skip 10 stitches on Row 15, then working through Row 15 and Row 17 at the same time, SC 21, Sl St to beginning stitch, Ch 1 [54]

After you've completed Row 18, insert safety eyes between Row 10 and Row 11. Safety eye size and placement are up to your discretion; the following are guidelines only. Generalized photos of what these options look like can be found on page 28.

For two 30 mm eyes, insert with approximately 7 stitch spaces between the posts.

For three eyes (two 30 mm and one 40 mm), insert with approximately 5 stitch spaces between each post.

For one or two 40 mm eyes, insert with approximately 7 stitch spaces between the posts.

You could also skip inserting a safety eye and follow the crocheted eye instruction options, including a 2D Medium or Large Eye, an Eye Bump, or an Eye Stalk.

**19.** SC 22, (Inc, SC) x 3, (SC, Inc) x 3, SC 20, Sl St to beginning stitch, Ch 1 [60]

**20–21.** (2 rows of) SC 60, Sl St to beginning stitch, Ch 1 [60]

**22.** (SC 9, Inc) x 6, Sl St to beginning stitch, Ch 1 [66]

**23–25.** (3 rows of) SC 66, Sl St to beginning stitch, Ch 1 [66]

**26.** (SC 21, Inc) x 3, Sl St to beginning stitch, Ch 1 [69]

**27–33.** (7 rows of) SC 69, Sl St to beginning stitch, Ch 1 [69]

**34.** (SC 21, Dec) x 3, Sl St to beginning stitch, Ch 1 [66]

Insert a stitch marker into the 12th stitch on Row 34 for reference on where to attach the yarn for the second leg.

**35.** SC 4, Skip 33 stitches, SC 29, Sl St to beginning stitch, Ch 1 [33]

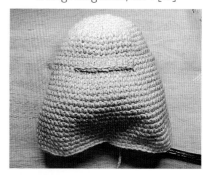

**36.** (SC 9, Dec) x 3, Sl St to beginning stitch, Ch 1 [30]

Ignore the Skipped stitches from Row 35.

**37.** SC 30, Sl St to beginning stitch, Ch 1 [30]

**38.** (SC 3, Dec) x 6, Sl St to beginning stitch, Ch 1 [24]

**39–40.** (2 rows of) SC 24, Sl St to beginning stitch, Ch 1 [24]

**41.** SC 8, Inc, SC 2, Inc, SC 12, Sl St to beginning stitch, Ch 1 [26]

**42.** SC 9, Inc x 4, SC 13, Sl St to beginning stitch, Ch 1 [30]

**43–46.** (4 rows of) SC 30, Sl St to beginning stitch, Ch 1 [30]

**47.** BLO [(SC 3, Dec) x 6], Sl St to beginning stitch, Ch 1 [24]

**48.** (SC, Dec, SC) x 6, Sl St to beginning stitch, Ch 1 [18]

**49.** (SC, Dec) x 6, Sl St to beginning stitch, Ch 1 [12]

**50.** Dec x 6, Sl St to beginning stitch [6]

Fasten off with a 12 in/30.5 cm yarn tail.

For the second leg, attach the yarn to the marked stitch from Row 34.

**51.** Working into all available remaining stitches on Row 34, SC 33, Sl St to beginning stitch, Ch 1 [33]

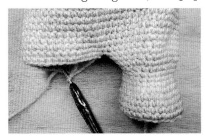

**52.** (SC 9, Dec) x 3, Sl St to beginning stitch, Ch 1 [30]

Glass gems are optional for use in the bottom of each foot—after you've made the first leg, and then at the end of the instructions for the second leg (for more information, see page 28). Stuff the Body with fiberfill and continue to stuff as you go.

**53.** SC 30, Sl St to beginning stitch, Ch 1 [30]

**54.** (SC 3, Dec) x 6, Sl St to beginning stitch, Ch 1 [24]

**55–56.** (2 rows of) SC 24, Sl St to beginning stitch, Ch 1 [24]

**57.** SC 13, Inc, SC 2, Inc, SC 7, Sl St to beginning stitch, Ch 1 [26]

**58.** SC 14, Inc x 4, SC 8, Sl St to beginning stitch, Ch 1 [30]

**59–62.** (4 rows of) SC 30, Sl St to beginning stitch, Ch 1 [30]

It is optional to add flat reinforcement to the bottom of the inside of the foot; see page 49 for details.

**63.** BLO [(SC 3, Dec) x 6], Sl St to beginning stitch, Ch 1 [24]

**64.** (SC, Dec, SC) x 6, Sl St to beginning stitch, Ch 1 [18]

**65.** (SC, Dec) x 6, Sl St to beginning stitch, Ch 1 [12]

**66.** Dec x 6, Sl St to beginning stitch [6]

Fasten off with a 12 in/30.5 cm yarn tail.

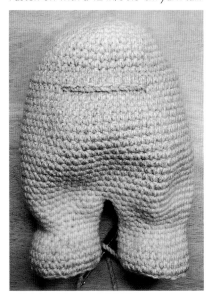

## Assembly

**1.** Finish stuffing with fiberfill.

**2.** Use the yarn tails to sew shut the final holes, including between the legs (if necessary); weave in ends.

**3.** Add any extra details—ears, horns, limbs, etc.—you want to the body!

## EGG SHAPE WITH OPEN MOUTH AND NO LEGS (MAKE 1)

*Approximately 8 in/20.5 cm tall, 6 in/15 cm wide at the body*

*Body Color Yarn: Approximately 155 yd/141.75 m worsted/medium weight yarn*

You will need to crochet one of the Open Mouth pieces (pages 15–25) prior to making this Body to attach as you go.

This Monster Body is worked from the bottom to the top.

**1.** SC 6 in Magic Circle, Sl St to beginning stitch, Ch 1 [6]

**2.** Inc x 6, Sl St to beginning stitch, Ch 1 [12]

**3.** (SC, Inc) x 6, Sl St to beginning stitch, Ch 1 [18]

**4.** (SC, Inc, SC) x 6, Sl St to beginning stitch, Ch 1 [24]

**5.** (SC 3, Inc) x 6, Sl St to beginning stitch, Ch 1 [30]

**6.** (SC 2, Inc, SC 2) x 6, Sl St to beginning stitch, Ch 1 [36]

**7.** (SC 5, Inc) x 6, Sl St to beginning stitch, Ch 1 [42]

**8.** (SC 3, Inc, SC 3) x 6, Sl St to beginning stitch, Ch 1 [48]

**9.** (SC 7, Inc) x 6, Sl St to beginning stitch, Ch 1 [54]

**10.** (SC 4, Inc, SC 4) x 6, Sl St to beginning stitch, Ch 1 [60]

**11.** (SC 9, Inc) x 6, Sl St to beginning stitch, Ch 1 [66]

**12.** SC 66, Sl St to beginning stitch, Ch 1 [66]

**13.** (SC 21, Inc) x 3, Sl St to beginning stitch, Ch 1 [69]

**14–20.** (7 rows of) SC 69, Sl St to beginning stitch, Ch 1 [69]

**21.** (SC 21, Dec) x 3, Sl St to beginning stitch, Ch 1 [66]

**22–24.** (3 rows of) SC 66, Sl St to beginning stitch, Ch 1 [66]

**25.** (SC 9, Dec) x 6, Sl St to beginning stitch, Ch 1 [60]

**26–27.** (2 rows of) SC 60, Sl St to beginning stitch, Ch 1 [60]

Egg Shape with Open Mouth and No Legs, Open Mouth with Buck Teeth (Lower), Small Short Rounded Limbs, Large Rounded Feet, Triangular Scales, Curved Dragon/Dinosaur Tail, Fin Ears, Large Ridged Belly

**28.** SC 21, (Dec, SC) x 3, (SC, Dec) x 3, SC 21, Sl St to beginning stitch, Ch 1 [54]

In Row 29, insert your hook into the right side/outside of the Body first and then into the wrong side/inside of the last stitch of the last row of the Mouth (OR the marked stitch on the Mouth) to create these stitches. You are working along the bottom front of the Mouth.

**29.** SC 15, working into the Mouth and the Body at the same time, SC 24, working into the Body only, SC 15, Sl St to beginning stitch, Ch 1 [54]

In Row 30, when you work into the Mouth, you are working along the top front of the Mouth only; you do not work into the stitches you made in Row 29 in the bottom half of the Mouth at all.

**30.** SC 15, working into the Mouth only, FLO [SC 24], SC 15 in the Body, Sl St to beginning stitch, Ch 1 [54]

**31.** SC 8, Dec, SC 5, continuing in the back loops of the Mouth left after Row 30, BLO [SC 11, Dec, SC 11], SC 5, Dec, SC 8 in Row 30, Sl St to beginning stitch, Ch 1 [51]

**32.** SC 51, Sl St to beginning stitch, Ch 1 [51]

**33.** (SC 15, Dec) x 3, Sl St to beginning stitch, Ch 1 [48]

**34.** SC 48, Sl St to beginning stitch, Ch 1 [48]

**35.** (SC 7, Dec, SC 7) x 3, Sl St to beginning stitch, Ch 1 [45]

**36.** (SC 13, Dec) x 3, Sl St to beginning stitch, Ch 1 [42]

**37.** (SC 6, Dec, SC 6) x 3, Sl St to beginning stitch, Ch 1 [39]

**38.** (SC 11, Dec) x 3, Sl St to beginning stitch, Ch 1 [36]

**39.** (SC 2, Dec, SC 2) x 6, Sl St to beginning stitch, Ch 1 [30]

**40.** (SC 3, Dec) x 6, Sl St to beginning stitch, Ch 1 [24]

After you've completed Row 40, insert safety eyes between Row 34 and Row 35. Safety eye size and placement are up to your discretion; the following are guidelines only. Generalized photos of what these options look like can be found on page 28.

For two 30 mm eyes, insert with approximately 7 stitch spaces between the posts.

For three eyes (two 30 mm and one 40 mm), insert with approximately 5 stitch spaces between each post.

For one or two 40 mm eyes, insert with approximately 7 stitch spaces between the posts.

You could also skip inserting a safety eye and follow the crocheted eye instruction options, including a 2D Medium or Large Eye, an Eye Bump, or an Eye Stalk.

Glass gems are optional (for more information, see page 28). Stuff the Body with fiberfill and continue to stuff as you go. Do not overstuff; make sure the Mouth is folded over itself when you stuff (like a hard taco shell) so that the Monster Mouth can be closed when you finish.

**41.** (SC, Dec, SC) x 6, Sl St to beginning stitch, Ch 1 [18]

**42.** (SC, Dec) x 6, Sl St to beginning stitch, Ch 1 [12]

**43.** Dec x 6, Sl St to beginning stitch [6]

Fasten off with a 12 in/30.5 cm yarn tail.

## Assembly

**1.** Finish stuffing with fiberfill.

**2.** Use the yarn tail to sew shut the final holes; weave in ends.

**3.** Add any extra details—ears, horns, limbs, etc.—you want to the body!

# EGG SHAPE WITH OPEN MOUTH AND LEGS (MAKE 1)

*Approximately 9.5 in/24 cm tall, 6 in/15 cm wide at the body*

*Body Color Yarn: Approximately 170 yd/155.5 m worsted/medium weight yarn*

> You will need to crochet one of the Open Mouth pieces (pages 15–25) prior to making this Body to attach as you go.

> This Monster Body is worked from the bottom of the Feet to the top of the Body.

**1.** SC 6 in Magic Circle, Sl St to beginning stitch, Ch 1 [6]

**2.** Inc x 6, Sl St to beginning stitch, Ch 1 [12]

**3.** (SC, Inc) x 6, Sl St to beginning stitch, Ch 1 [18]

**4.** (SC, Inc, SC) x 6, Sl St to beginning stitch, Ch 1 [24]

**5.** (SC 3, Inc) x 6, Sl St to beginning stitch, Ch 1 [30]

**6.** BLO [SC 30], Sl St to beginning stitch, Ch 1 [30]

**7–9.** (3 rows of) SC 30, Sl St to beginning stitch, Ch 1 [30]

**10.** SC 11, Dec x 4, SC 11, Sl St to beginning stitch, Ch 1 [26]

**11.** SC 10, Dec, SC 2, Dec, SC 10, Sl St to beginning stitch, Ch 1 [24]

**12–13.** (2 rows of) SC 24, Sl St to beginning stitch, Ch 1 [24]

**14.** (SC 3, Inc) x 6, Sl St to beginning stitch, Ch 1 [30]

**15.** SC 30, Sl St to beginning stitch, Ch 1 [30]

**16.** (SC 9, Inc) x 3, Sl St to beginning stitch [33]

Fasten off the first leg with a short yarn tail.

Mark the 27th stitch of the final row of the first leg for reference in Row 17.

Repeat instructions for Rows 1 through 16 for the second leg, do not fasten off, and continue to Row 17.

> It is optional to add flat reinforcement to the bottom of the inside of the foot; see page 49 for details.

**17.** Ch 1, SC 9, working into the first leg, starting in the marked stitch, SC 33, continuing into the next available stitch on the second leg, SC 24, Sl St to beginning stitch, Ch 1 [66]

**18.** (SC 21, Inc) x 3, Sl St to beginning stitch, Ch 1 [69]

**19–25.** (7 rows of) SC 69, Sl St to beginning stitch, Ch 1 [69]

**26.** (SC 21, Dec) x 3, Sl St to beginning stitch, Ch 1 [66]

**27–29.** (3 rows of) SC 66, Sl St to beginning stitch, Ch 1 [66]

**30.** (SC 9, Dec) x 6, Sl St to beginning stitch, Ch 1 [60]

**31–32.** (2 rows of) SC 60, Sl St to beginning stitch, Ch 1 [60]

**33.** SC 32, (Dec, SC) x 3, (SC, Dec) x 3, SC 10, Sl St to beginning stitch, Ch 1 [54]

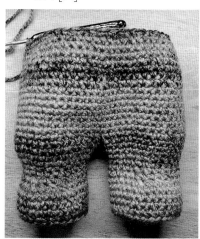

In Row 34, insert your hook into the right side/outside of the Body first and then into the wrong side/inside of the last stitch of the last row of the Mouth (OR the marked stitch on the Mouth) to create these stitches. You are working along the bottom front of the Mouth.

**34.** SC 26, working into the Mouth and the Body at the same time, SC 24, working into the Body only, SC 4, Sl St to beginning stitch, Ch 1 [54]

In Row 35, when you work into the Mouth, you are working along the top front of the Mouth only; you do not work into the stitches you made in Row 34 in the bottom half of the Mouth at all.

**35.** SC 26, working into the Mouth only, FLO [SC 24], SC 4 in the Body, Sl St to beginning stitch, Ch 1 [54]

**36.** SC 8, Dec, SC 16, continuing in the back loops of the Mouth left after Row 35, BLO [Dec, SC 16, Dec, SC 4], SC 4 in Row 35, Sl St to beginning stitch, Ch 1 [51]

**37.** SC 51, Sl St to beginning stitch, Ch 1 [51]

**38.** (SC 15, Dec) x 3, Sl St to beginning stitch, Ch 1 [48]

**39.** SC 48, Sl St to beginning stitch, Ch 1 [48]

**40.** (SC 7, Dec, SC 7) x 3, Sl St to beginning stitch, Ch 1 [45]

**41.** (SC 13, Dec) x 3, Sl St to beginning stitch, Ch 1 [42]

**42.** (SC 6, Dec, SC 6) x 3, Sl St to beginning stitch, Ch 1 [39]

**43.** (SC 11, Dec) x 3, Sl St to beginning stitch, Ch 1 [36]

**44.** (SC 2, Dec, SC 2) x 6, Sl St to beginning stitch, Ch 1 [30]

**45.** (SC 3, Dec) x 6, Sl St to beginning stitch, Ch 1 [24]

After you've completed Row 45, insert safety eyes between Row 40 and Row 41. Safety eye size and placement are up to your discretion; the following are guidelines only. Generalized photos of what these options look like can be found on page 28.

For two 30 mm eyes, insert with approximately 7 stitch spaces between the posts.

For three eyes (two 30 mm and one 40 mm), insert with approximately 5 stitch spaces between each post.

For one or two 40 mm eyes, insert with approximately 7 stitch spaces between the posts.

You could also skip inserting a safety eye and follow the crocheted eye instruction options, including a 2D Medium or Large Eye, an Eye Bump, or an Eye Stalk.

Glass gems are optional (for more information, see page 28). Stuff the Body with fiberfill and continue to stuff as you go. Do not overstuff; make sure the Mouth is folded over itself when you stuff (like a hard taco shell) so that the Monster Mouth can be closed when you finish.

**46.** (SC, Dec, SC) x 6, Sl St to beginning stitch, Ch 1 [18]

**47.** (SC, Dec) x 6, Sl St to beginning stitch, Ch 1 [12]

**48.** Dec x 6, Sl St to beginning stitch [6]

Fasten off with a 12 in/30.5 cm yarn tail.

## Assembly

**1.** Finish stuffing with fiberfill.

**2.** Use the yarn tails to sew shut the final holes, including between the legs (if necessary); weave in ends.

**3.** Add any extra details—ears, horns, limbs, etc.—you want to the body!

Egg Shape with
Open Mouth and
Legs, Open Mouth
with Four Pointed Teeth
(Upper), Thick Short Arms,
S-shaped Horns, Pointed
Tongue, Embroidered
Sutures

Egg Shape with No Mouth and No Legs, 2D Mouth in Round Shape with Fang Teeth and Tongue, Eye Stalks, Four-toed Crouching Frog Rear Leg

If you want to add metal spikes to any part of your Monster, go to page 172 for tips on how to do that.

# EGG SHAPE WITH NO MOUTH AND NO LEGS (MAKE 1)

***Approximately 8 in/20.5 cm tall, 6 in/15 cm wide at the body***

***Body Color Yarn: Approximately 130 yd/119 m worsted/medium weight yarn***

> This Monster Body is worked from the bottom to the top.

1. SC 6 in Magic Circle, Sl St to beginning stitch, Ch 1 [6]
2. Inc x 6, Sl St to beginning stitch, Ch 1 [12]
3. (SC, Inc) x 6, Sl St to beginning stitch, Ch 1 [18]
4. (SC, Inc, SC) x 6, Sl St to beginning stitch, Ch 1 [24]
5. (SC 3, Inc) x 6, Sl St to beginning stitch, Ch 1 [30]
6. (SC 2, Inc, SC 2) x 6, Sl St to beginning stitch, Ch 1 [36]
7. (SC 5, Inc) x 6, Sl St to beginning stitch, Ch 1 [42]
8. (SC 3, Inc, SC 3) x 6, Sl St to beginning stitch, Ch 1 [48]
9. (SC 7, Inc) x 6, Sl St to beginning stitch, Ch 1 [54]
10. (SC 4, Inc, SC 4) x 6, Sl St to beginning stitch, Ch 1 [60]
11. (SC 9, Inc) x 6, Sl St to beginning stitch, Ch 1 [66]
12. SC 66, Sl St to beginning stitch, Ch 1 [66]
13. (SC 21, Inc) x 3, Sl St to beginning stitch, Ch 1 [69]
14–20. (7 rows of) SC 69, Sl St to beginning stitch, Ch 1 [69]
21. (SC 21, Dec) x 3, Sl St to beginning stitch, Ch 1 [66]
22–24. (3 rows of) SC 66, Sl St to beginning stitch, Ch 1 [66]
25. (SC 9, Dec) x 6, Sl St to beginning stitch, Ch 1 [60]
26–27. (2 rows of) SC 60, Sl St to beginning stitch, Ch 1 [60]
28. SC 22, (Dec, SC) x 3, (SC, Dec) x 3, SC 20, Sl St to beginning stitch, Ch 1 [54]
29–30. (2 rows of) SC 54, Sl St to beginning stitch, Ch 1 [54]
31. (SC 8, Dec, SC 8) x 3, Sl St to beginning stitch, Ch 1 [51]
32. SC 51, Sl St to beginning stitch, Ch 1 [51]
33. (SC 15, Dec) x 3, Sl St to beginning stitch, Ch 1 [48]
34. SC 48, Sl St to beginning stitch, Ch 1 [48]
35. (SC 7, Dec, SC 7) x 3, Sl St to beginning stitch, Ch 1 [45]
36. (SC 13, Dec) x 3, Sl St to beginning stitch, Ch 1 [42]
37. (SC 6, Dec, SC 6) x 3, Sl St to beginning stitch, Ch 1 [39]
38. (SC 11, Dec) x 3, Sl St to beginning stitch, Ch 1 [36]
39. (SC 2, Dec, SC 2) x 6, Sl St to beginning stitch, Ch 1 [30]
40. (SC 3, Dec) x 6, Sl St to beginning stitch, Ch 1 [24]

> After you've completed Row 40, insert safety eyes between Row 35 and Row 36. Safety eye size and placement are up to your discretion; the following are guidelines only. Generalized photos of what these options look like can be found on page 28.
>
> For two 30 mm eyes, insert with approximately 7 stitch spaces between the posts.
>
> For three eyes (two 30 mm and one 40 mm), insert with approximately 5 stitch spaces between each post.
>
> For one or two 40 mm eyes, insert with approximately 7 stitch spaces between the posts.
>
> You could also skip inserting a safety eye and follow the crocheted eye instruction options, including a 2D Medium or Large Eye, an Eye Bump, or an Eye Stalk.

> Glass gems are optional (for more information, see page 28). Stuff the Body with fiberfill and continue to stuff as you go.

41. (SC, Dec, SC) x 6, Sl St to beginning stitch, Ch 1 [18]
42. (SC, Dec) x 6, Sl St to beginning stitch, Ch 1 [12]
43. Dec x 6, Sl St to beginning stitch [6]

Fasten off with a 12 in/30.5 cm yarn tail.

## Assembly

1. Finish stuffing with fiberfill.
2. Use the yarn tail to sew shut the final holes; weave in ends.
3. Add any extra details—ears, horns, limbs, etc.—you want to the body!

**Egg
Shape with
No Mouth and
Legs, Small Rounded
Overbite, Small Short
Limbs, Medium to the
Side Curved Horns, Hair
Puff, Two Small Fangs,
Nose with Wide
Nostrils**

If you want to add metal spikes to any part of your Monster, go to page 172 for tips on how to do that.

# EGG SHAPE WITH NO MOUTH AND LEGS (MAKE 1)

***Approximately 9.5 in/24 cm tall, 6 in/15 cm wide at the body***

***Body Color Yarn: Approximately 145 yd/132.5 m worsted/medium weight yarn***

> This Monster Body is worked from the bottom of the Feet to the top of the Body.

**1.** SC 6 in Magic Circle, Sl St to beginning stitch, Ch 1 [6]

**2.** Inc x 6, Sl St to beginning stitch, Ch 1 [12]

**3.** (SC, Inc) x 6, Sl St to beginning stitch, Ch 1 [18]

**4.** (SC, Inc, SC) x 6, Sl St to beginning stitch, Ch 1 [24]

**5.** (SC 3, Inc) x 6, Sl St to beginning stitch, Ch 1 [30]

**6.** BLO [SC 30], Sl St to beginning stitch, Ch 1 [30]

**7–9.** (3 rows of) SC 30, Sl St to beginning stitch, Ch 1 [30]

**10.** SC 11, Dec x 4, SC 11, Sl St to beginning stitch, Ch 1 [26]

**11.** SC 10, Dec, SC 2, Dec, SC 10, Sl St to beginning stitch, Ch 1 [24]

**12–13.** (2 rows of) SC 24, Sl St to beginning stitch, Ch 1 [24]

**14.** (SC 3, Inc) x 6, Sl St to beginning stitch, Ch 1 [30]

**15.** SC 30, Sl St to beginning stitch, Ch 1 [30]

**16.** (SC 9, Inc) x 3, Sl St to beginning stitch [33]

Fasten off the first leg with a short yarn tail.

Mark the 27th stitch of the final row of the first leg for reference in Row 17.

Repeat instructions for Rows 1 through 16 for the second leg, do not fasten off, and continue to Row 17.

> It is optional to add flat reinforcement to the bottom of the inside of the foot; see page 49 for details.

**17.** Ch 1, SC 9, working into the first leg, starting in the marked stitch, SC 33, continuing into the next available stitch on the second leg, SC 24, Sl St to beginning stitch, Ch 1 [66]

**18.** (SC 21, Inc) x 3, Sl St to beginning stitch, Ch 1 [69]

**19–25.** (7 rows of) SC 69, Sl St to beginning stitch, Ch 1 [69]

**26.** (SC 21, Dec) x 3, Sl St to beginning stitch, Ch 1 [66]

**27–29.** (3 rows of) SC 66, Sl St to beginning stitch, Ch 1 [66]

**30.** (SC 9, Dec) x 6, Sl St to beginning stitch, Ch 1 [60]

**31–32.** (2 rows of) SC 60, Sl St to beginning stitch, Ch 1 [60]

**33.** SC 32, (Dec, SC) x 3, (SC, Dec) x 3, SC 10, Sl St to beginning stitch, Ch 1 [54]

**34–35.** (2 rows of) SC 54, Sl St to beginning stitch, Ch 1 [54]

**36.** (SC 8, Dec, SC 8) x 3, Sl St to beginning stitch, Ch 1 [51]

**37.** SC 51, Sl St to beginning stitch, Ch 1 [51]

**38.** (SC 15, Dec) x 3, Sl St to beginning stitch, Ch 1 [48]

**39.** SC 48, Sl St to beginning stitch, Ch 1 [48]

**40.** (SC 7, Dec, SC 7) x 3, Sl St to beginning stitch, Ch 1 [45]

**41.** (SC 13, Dec) x 3, Sl St to beginning stitch, Ch 1 [42]

**42.** (SC 6, Dec, SC 6) x 3, Sl St to beginning stitch, Ch 1 [39]

**43.** (SC 11, Dec) x 3, Sl St to beginning stitch, Ch 1 [36]

**44.** (SC 2, Dec, SC 2) x 6, Sl St to beginning stitch, Ch 1 [30]

**45.** (SC 3, Dec) x 6, Sl St to beginning stitch, Ch 1 [24]

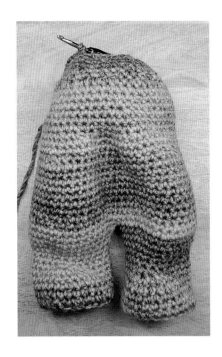

**46.** (SC, Dec, SC) x 6, Sl St to beginning stitch, Ch 1 [18]

**47.** (SC, Dec) x 6, Sl St to beginning stitch, Ch 1 [12]

**48.** Dec x 6, Sl St to beginning stitch [6]

Fasten off with a 12 in/30.5 cm yarn tail.

## Assembly

**1.** Finish stuffing with fiberfill.

**2.** Use the yarn tails to sew shut the final holes, including between the legs (if necessary); weave in ends.

**3.** Add any extra details—ears, horns, limbs, etc.—you want to the body!

After you've completed Row 45, insert safety eyes between Row 40 and Row 41. Safety eye size and placement are up to your discretion; the following are guidelines only. Generalized photos of what these options look like can be found on page 28.

For two 30 mm eyes, insert with approximately 7 stitch spaces between the posts.

For three eyes (two 30 mm and one 40 mm), insert with approximately 5 stitch spaces between each post.

For one or two 40 mm eyes, insert with approximately 7 stitch spaces between the posts.

You could also skip inserting a safety eye and follow the crocheted eye instruction options, including a 2D Medium or Large Eye, an Eye Bump, or an Eye Stalk.

Glass gems are optional (for more information, see page 28). Stuff the Body with fiberfill and continue to stuff as you go.

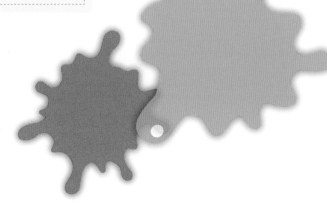

Sphere with Underbite, Thinner Eyelids/Eyebrows for 30 mm Safety Eyes, Bulb-ended Short Limbs, Bulb-ended Long Limbs, Thin L-shaped Horns, Squared Teeth

# Sphere Bodies

## SPHERE WITH UNDERBITE (MAKE 1)

*Approximately 4 in/10 cm in diameter*

*Body Color Yarn: Approximately 75 yd/68.5 m worsted/medium weight yarn*

This Monster Body is worked from the bottom to the top.

1. SC 6 in Magic Circle, Sl St to beginning stitch, Ch 1 [6]

2. Inc x 6, Sl St to beginning stitch, Ch 1 [12]

3. (SC, Inc) x 6, Sl St to beginning stitch, Ch 1 [18]

4. (SC, Inc, SC) x 6, Sl St to beginning stitch, Ch 1 [24]

5. (SC 3, Inc) x 6, Sl St to beginning stitch, Ch 1 [30]

6. (SC 2, Inc, SC 2) x 6, Sl St to beginning stitch, Ch 1 [36]

7. (SC 5, Inc) x 6, Sl St to beginning stitch, Ch 1 [42]

8. (SC 3, Inc, SC 3) x 6, Sl St to beginning stitch, Ch 1 [48]

9-12. (4 rows of) SC 48, Sl St to beginning stitch, Ch 1 [48]

13. FLO [SC 18, HDC 12, SC 18], Sl St to beginning stitch, Ch 1 [48]

14. SC 18, HDC 12, SC 18, Sl St to beginning stitch, Ch 1 [48]

15. Ch 2, starting in the first BLO stitch from Row 12 and continuing working into the leftover BLO of the stitches from Row 12, BLO [SC 48], Sl St to beginning stitch, Ch 1 [48]

16. SC 48, Sl St to beginning stitch, Ch 1 [48]

17. Starting in the first available stitch of each row through both Row 16 and Row 14 at the same time SC 18, then working in Row 16 only, SC 12, Skip 12 stitches on Row 14, then working through Row 16 and Row 14 at the same time, SC 18, Sl St to beginning stitch, Ch 1 [48]

18-23. (6 rows of) SC 48, Sl St to beginning stitch, Ch 1 [48]

24. (SC 3, Dec, SC 3) x 6, Sl St to beginning stitch, Ch 1 [42]

25. (SC 5, Dec) x 6, Sl St to beginning stitch, Ch 1 [36]

26. (SC 2, Dec, SC 2) x 6, Sl St to beginning stitch, Ch 1 [30]

27. (SC 3, Dec) x 6, Sl St to beginning stitch, Ch 1 [24]

28. (SC 2, Dec) x 6, Sl St to beginning stitch, Ch 1 [18]

After you've completed Row 28, insert safety eyes between Row 21 and Row 22. Safety eye size and placement are up to your discretion; the following are guidelines only. Generalized photos of what these options look like can be found on page 28.

For two 30 mm eyes, insert with approximately 6-7 stitch spaces between the posts.

For three eyes (two 30 mm and one 40 mm), insert with approximately 5 stitch spaces between each post.

For one or two 40 mm eyes, insert with approximately 7 stitch spaces between the posts.

You could also skip inserting a safety eye and follow the crocheted eye instruction options, including a 2D Medium or Large Eye, an Eye Bump, or an Eye Stalk.

Stuff the body with fiberfill and continue to stuff as you go.

29. (SC, Dec) x 6, Sl St to beginning stitch, Ch 1 [12]
30. Dec x 6, Sl St to beginning stitch [6]

Fasten off with a 12 in/30.5 cm yarn tail.

## Assembly

1. Finish stuffing with fiberfill.
2. Use the yarn tail to sew shut the final holes; weave in ends.
3. Add any extra details—ears, horns, limbs, etc.—you want to the body!

If you want to add metal spikes to any part of your Monster, go to page 172 for tips on how to do that.

Sphere with Overbite, Small Short Limbs, Feet with Pointy Toes, Medium Curved Horns, Two Small Uneven Pointy Fangs

# SPHERE WITH OVERBITE (MAKE 1)

*Approximately 4 in/10 cm in diameter*

*Body Color Yarn: Approximately 75 yd/68.5 m worsted/medium weight yarn*

> This Monster Body is worked from the top to the bottom.

1. SC 6 in Magic Circle, Sl St to beginning stitch, Ch 1 [6]
2. Inc x 6, Sl St to beginning stitch, Ch 1 [12]
3. (SC, Inc) x 6, Sl St to beginning stitch, Ch 1 [18]
4. (SC, Inc, SC) x 6, Sl St to beginning stitch, Ch 1 [24]
5. (SC 3, Inc) x 6, Sl St to beginning stitch, Ch 1 [30]
6. (SC 2, Inc, SC 2) x 6, Sl St to beginning stitch, Ch 1 [36]
7. (SC 5, Inc) x 6, Sl St to beginning stitch, Ch 1 [42]
8. (SC 3, Inc, SC 3) x 6, Sl St to beginning stitch, Ch 1 [48]
9–14. (6 rows of) SC 48, Sl St to beginning stitch, Ch 1 [48]

15. FLO [SC 18, HDC 12, SC 18], Sl St to beginning stitch, Ch 1 [48]
16. SC 18, HDC 12, SC 18, Sl St to beginning stitch, Ch 1 [48]

17. Ch 2, starting in the first BLO stitch from Row 14 and continuing working into the leftover BLO of the stitches from Row 14, BLO [SC 48], Sl St to beginning stitch, Ch 1 [48]
18. SC 48, Sl St to beginning stitch, Ch 1 [48]

19. Starting in the first available stitch of each row through both Row 18 and Row 16 at the same time SC 18, then working in Row 18 only, SC 12 , Skip 12 stitches on Row 16, then working through Row 18 and Row 16 at the same time, SC 18, Sl St to beginning stitch, Ch 1 [48]

20–23. (4 rows of) SC 48, Sl St to beginning stitch, Ch 1 [48]
24. (SC 3, Dec, SC 3) x 6, Sl St to beginning stitch, Ch 1 [42]
25. (SC 5, Dec) x 6, Sl St to beginning stitch, Ch 1 [36]

26. (SC 2, Dec, SC 2) x 6, Sl St to beginning stitch, Ch 1 [30]

> After you've completed Row 26, insert safety eyes between Row 11 and Row 12. Safety eye size and placement are up to your discretion; the following are guidelines only. Generalized photos of what these options look like can be found on page 28.
>
> For two 30 mm eyes, insert with approximately 7 stitch spaces between the posts.
>
> For three eyes (two 30 mm and one 40 mm), insert with approximately 5 stitch spaces between each post.
>
> For one or two 40 mm eyes, insert with approximately 7 stitch spaces between the posts.
>
> You could also skip inserting a safety eye and follow the crocheted eye instruction options, including a 2D Medium or Large Eye, an Eye Bump, or an Eye Stalk.

**27.** (SC 3, Dec) x 6, Sl St to beginning stitch, Ch 1 [24]

**28.** (SC 2, Dec) x 6, Sl St to beginning stitch, Ch 1 [18]

**29.** (SC, Dec) x 6, Sl St to beginning stitch, Ch 1 [12]

**30.** Dec x 6, Sl St to beginning stitch [6]

Fasten off with a 12 in/30.5 cm yarn tail.

## Assembly

**1.** Finish stuffing with fiberfill.

**2.** Use the yarn tail to sew shut the final holes; weave in ends.

**3.** Add any extra details—ears, horns, limbs, etc.—you want to the body!

# SPHERE WITH OPEN MOUTH (MAKE 1)

*Approximately 4 in/10 cm in diameter*

*Body Color Yarn: Approximately 50 yd/45.75 m worsted/medium weight yarn*

You will need to crochet one of the Open Mouth pieces (pages 15–25) prior to making this Body to attach as you go.

This Monster Body is worked from the bottom to the top.

**1.** SC 6 in Magic Circle, Sl St to beginning stitch, Ch 1 [6]

**2.** Inc x 6, Sl St to beginning stitch, Ch 1 [12]

**3.** (SC, Inc) x 6, Sl St to beginning stitch, Ch 1 [18]

**4.** (SC, Inc, SC) x 6, Sl St to beginning stitch, Ch 1 [24]

**5.** (SC 3, Inc) x 6, Sl St to beginning stitch, Ch 1 [30]

**6.** (SC 2, Inc, SC 2) x 6, Sl St to beginning stitch, Ch 1 [36]

**7.** (SC 5, Inc) x 6, Sl St to beginning stitch, Ch 1 [42]

**8.** (SC 3, Inc, SC 3) x 6, Sl St to beginning stitch, Ch 1 [48]

**9–12.** (4 rows of) SC 48, Sl St to beginning stitch, Ch 1 [48]

In Row 13, when working into the Mouth, insert your hook into the right side/outside of the Body first and then into the wrong side/inside of the last stitch of the last row of the Mouth (OR the marked stitch on the Mouth) to create these stitches. You are working along the bottom front of the Mouth.

**13.** SC 12, working into the Mouth and the Body at the same time, SC 24, working into the Body only, SC 12, Sl St to beginning stitch, Ch 1 [48]

In Row 14, when you work into the Mouth, you are working along the top front of the Mouth only; you do not work into the stitches you made in Row 13 in the bottom half of the Mouth at all.

**14.** SC 12, working into the Mouth only, FLO [SC 24], SC 12 in the Body, Sl St to beginning stitch, Ch 1 [48]

**15.** SC 12, continuing in the back loops of the Mouth left after Row 14, BLO [SC 24], SC 12 in Row 14 [48]

**16–19.** (4 rows of) SC 48, Sl St to beginning stitch, Ch 1 [48]

**20.** (SC 3, Dec, SC 3) x 6, Sl St to beginning stitch, Ch 1 [42]

**21.** (SC 5, Dec) x 6, Sl St to beginning stitch, Ch 1 [36]

After you've completed Row 21, insert safety eyes between Row 17 and Row 18. Safety eye size and placement are up to your discretion; the following are guidelines only. Generalized photos of what these options look like can be found on page 28.

For two 30 mm eyes, insert with approximately 7 stitch spaces between the posts.

For three eyes (two 30 mm and one 40 mm), insert with approximately 5 stitch spaces between each post.

For one or two 40 mm eyes, insert with approximately 7 stitch spaces between the posts.

You could also skip inserting a safety eye and follow the crocheted eye instruction options, including a 2D Medium or Large Eye, an Eye Bump, or an Eye Stalk.

Stuff the body with fiberfill and continue to stuff as you go.

**22.** (SC 2, Dec, SC 2) x 6, Sl St to beginning stitch, Ch 1 [30]

**23.** (SC 3, Dec) x 6, Sl St to beginning stitch, Ch 1 [24]

**24.** (SC 2, Dec) x 6, Sl St to beginning stitch, Ch 1 [18]

**25.** (SC, Dec) x 6, Sl St to beginning stitch, Ch 1 [12]

**26.** Dec x 6, Sl St to beginning stitch [6]

Fasten off with a 12 in/30.5 cm yarn tail.

## Assembly

**1.** Finish stuffing with fiberfill.

**2.** Use the yarn tail to sew shut the final holes; weave in ends.

**3.** Add any extra details—ears, horns, limbs, etc.—you want to the body!

Sphere with Open Mouth, Open Mouth with Pointy Teeth, Cute Mitten Limbs, Cute Footed Limbs, Skinny Curved Horns

# SPHERE WITH NO MOUTH (MAKE 1)

*Approximately 4 in/10 cm in diameter*

*Body Color Yarn: Approximately 60 yd/54.75 m worsted/medium weight yarn*

This Monster Body is worked from the bottom to the top.

1. SC 6 in Magic Circle, Sl St to beginning stitch, Ch 1 [6]
2. Inc x 6, Sl St to beginning stitch, Ch 1 [12]
3. (SC, Inc) x 6, Sl St to beginning stitch, Ch 1 [18]
4. (SC, Inc, SC) x 6, Sl St to beginning stitch, Ch 1 [24]
5. (SC 3, Inc) x 6, Sl St to beginning stitch, Ch 1 [30]
6. (SC 2, Inc, SC 2) x 6, Sl St to beginning stitch, Ch 1 [36]
7. (SC 5, Inc) x 6, Sl St to beginning stitch, Ch 1 [42]
8. (SC 3, Inc, SC 3) x 6, Sl St to beginning stitch, Ch 1 [48]
9–20. (12 rows of) SC 48, Sl St to beginning stitch, Ch 1 [48]
21. (SC 3, Dec, SC 3) x 6, Sl St to beginning stitch, Ch 1 [42]
22. (SC 5, Dec) x 6, Sl St to beginning stitch, Ch 1 [36]

After you've completed Row 22, insert safety eyes between Row 17 and Row 18. Safety eye size and placement are up to your discretion; the following are guidelines only. Generalized photos of what these options look like can be found on page 28.

For two 30 mm eyes, insert with approximately 7 stitch spaces between the posts.

For three eyes (two 30 mm and one 40 mm), insert with approximately 5 stitch spaces between each post.

For one or two 40 mm eyes, insert with approximately 7 stitch spaces between the posts.

You could also skip inserting a safety eye and follow the crocheted eye instruction options, including a 2D Medium or Large Eye, an Eye Bump, or an Eye Stalk.

Stuff the body with fiberfill and continue to stuff as you go.

23. (SC 2, Dec, SC 2) x 6, Sl St to beginning stitch, Ch 1 [30]
24. (SC 3, Dec) x 6, Sl St to beginning stitch, Ch 1 [24]
25. (SC 2, Dec) x 6, Sl St to beginning stitch, Ch 1 [18]
26. (SC, Dec) x 6, Sl St to beginning stitch, Ch 1 [12]
27. Dec x 6, Sl St to beginning stitch [6]

Fasten off with a 12 in/30.5 cm yarn tail.

## Assembly

1. Finish stuffing with fiberfill.
2. Use the yarn tail to sew shut the final holes; weave in ends.
3. Add any extra details—ears, horns, limbs, etc.—you want to the body!

Sphere with No Mouth, Medium Rounded Underbite, Short Arms with Two Fingers, Tiny Little Footed Legs, Medium Curved Horns, Individual Small Short Fangs, Long Thin Tongue

## Square Bodies

### SQUARE WITH UNDERBITE AND NO LEGS (MAKE 1)

*Approximately 6.5 in/16.5 cm tall, 5.5 in/14 cm wide, 3 in/7.5 cm deep*

*Body Color Yarn: Approximately 150 yd/137.25 m worsted/medium weight yarn*

> This Monster Body is worked from the bottom to the top.

1. Ch 11, starting in the second Ch from hook, SC 9, Inc, continue to crochet around to the other side of the starting chain stitches, SC 8, SC in the same Ch stitch as the first SC in this row, Sl St to beginning stitch, Ch 1 [20]

2. (Inc, SC 8, Inc) x 2, Sl St to beginning stitch, Ch 1 [24]

3. (SC & HDC, HDC & SC, SC 8, SC & HDC, HDC & SC) x 2, Sl St to beginning stitch, Ch 1 [32]

4. (SC, SC & HDC, HDC & SC, SC 10, SC & HDC, HDC & SC, SC) x 2, Sl St to beginning stitch, Ch 1 [40]

**5.** (SC 2, SC & HDC, HDC & SC, SC 12, SC & HDC, HDC & SC, SC 2) x 2, Sl St to beginning stitch, Ch 1 [48]

**6.** (SC 3, SC & HDC, HDC & SC, SC 14, SC & HDC, HDC & SC, SC 3) x 2, Sl St to beginning stitch, Ch 1 [56]

**7.** (SC 5, <Dec>, SC 18, <Dec>, SC 5) x 2, Sl St to beginning stitch, Ch 1 [60]

"<Dec>" is a stitch that is defined in the Glossary.

**8–13.** (6 rows of) SC 60, Sl St to beginning stitch, Ch 1 [60]

This row (14) and all rows like it (Rows 21 and 30) are optional but recommended. They create scaffolding inside the Monster Body to reinforce the square shaping. These rows will not be visible when the Body is complete. If you skip these rows, when the piece is stuffed, it will have a much rounder shape. None of the Slip Stitches in these rows are worked into any of the chain stitches.

In Row 14 (and 21 and 30), you will make eight Slip Stitches and a number of chains, but there is no stitch count associated with the row, because you will not work into any of these stitches again.

**14.** Ch 6, Skip 4 stitches, BLO [Sl St], Ch 1, Skip 3 stitches, BLO [Sl St], Ch 18, Skip 14 stitches, BLO [Sl St], Ch 1, Skip 3 stitches, BLO [Sl St], Ch 10, Skip 6 stitches, BLO [Sl St], Ch 1, Skip 3 stitches, BLO [Sl St], Ch 18, Skip 14 stitches, BLO [Sl St], Ch 1, Skip 3 stitches, BLO [Sl St], Ch 6; continue working rows as normal, ignoring the chain sections and slip stitches and keeping them on the inside of your work

In Row 15, work into all stitches in Row 13 as normal, ignoring all the stitches from Row 14.

**15–20.** (6 rows of) SC 60, Sl St to beginning stitch, Ch 1 [60]

**21.** Ch 7, Skip 5 stitches, BLO [Sl St], Ch 1, Skip 3 stitches, BLO [Sl St], Ch 18, Skip 14 stitches, BLO [Sl St], Ch 1, Skip 3 stitches, BLO [Sl St], Ch 10, Skip 6 stitches, BLO [Sl St], Ch 1, Skip 3 stitches, BLO [Sl St], Ch 18, Skip 14 stitches, BLO [Sl St], Ch 1, Skip 2 stitches, BLO [Sl St], Ch 3, Skip the last 2 stitches; continue working rows as normal, ignoring the chain sections and slip stitches and keeping them on the inside of your work

In Row 22, work into all stitches in Row 20 as normal, ignoring all the stitches from Row 21.

**22.** SC 60, Sl St to beginning stitch, Ch 1 [60]

**23.** FLO [SC 13, HDC 10, SC 37], Sl St to beginning stitch, Ch 1 [60]

**24.** SC 13, HDC 10, SC 37, Sl St to beginning stitch, Ch 1 [60]

**25.** Ch 2, starting in the first BLO stitch from Row 22 and continuing working into the leftover BLO of the stitches from Row 24, BLO [SC 60], Sl St to beginning stitch, Ch 1 [60]

**26.** SC 60, Sl St to beginning stitch, Ch 1 [60]

**27.** Starting in the first available stitch of each row through both Row 26 and Row 24 at the same time SC 13, then working in Row 26 only, SC 10 , Skip 10 stitches on Row 24, then working through Row 26 and Row 24 at the same time, SC 37, Sl St to beginning stitch, Ch 1 [60]

**28–29.** (2 rows of) SC 60, Sl St to beginning stitch, Ch 1 [60]

**30.** Ch 8, Skip 6 stitches, BLO [Sl St], Ch 1, Skip 3 stitches, BLO [Sl St], Ch 18, Skip 14 stitches, BLO [Sl St], Ch 1, Skip 3 stitches, BLO [Sl St], Ch 10, Skip 6 stitches, BLO [Sl St], Ch 1, Skip 3 stitches, BLO [Sl St], Ch 18, Skip 14 stitches, BLO [Sl St], Ch 1, Skip 2 stitches, BLO [Sl St], Ch 3, Skip the last stitch; continue working rows as normal, ignoring the chain sections and slip stitches and keeping them on the inside of your work

In Row 31, work into all stitches in Row 29 as normal, ignoring all the stitches from Row 30.

**31–36.** (6 rows of) SC 60, Sl St to beginning stitch, Ch 1 [60]

**37.** SC 8, Triple SC Dec, SC 16, Triple SC Dec, SC 8, Triple SC Dec, SC 16, Triple SC Dec, continue in spiral [52]

> To work a Triple SC Dec, work a decrease stitch across 3 stitches.

**38.** SC 7, Triple SC Dec, SC 14, Triple SC Dec, SC 6, Triple SC Dec, SC 14, Triple SC Dec [44]

> Row 38 overlaps itself by 1 stitch. This and all stitch counts reflect the number of stitches available to work into the next row.

**39.** SC 5, Triple SC Dec, SC 12, Triple SC Dec, SC 4, Triple SC Dec, SC 12, Triple SC Dec [36]

> Row 39 overlaps itself by 1 stitch.

After you've completed Row 39, insert safety eyes between Row 32 and Row 33. Safety eye size and placement are up to your discretion; the following are guidelines only. Generalized photos of what these options look like can be found on page 28.

For two 30 mm eyes, insert with approximately 7 stitch spaces between the posts.

For three eyes (two 30 mm and one 40 mm), insert with approximately 5 stitch spaces between each post.

For one or two 40 mm eyes, insert with approximately 7 stitch spaces between the posts.

You could also skip inserting a safety eye and follow the crocheted eye instruction options, including a 2D Medium or Large Eye, an Eye Bump, or an Eye Stalk.

It is optional to insert a panel of plastic canvas cut to size against the inside of any of the walls of the Square Monster Body. Doing so will help to keep the walls from bowing or curving once the Body is stuffed with fiberfill. Cut the plastic canvas slightly smaller than the side you want to stabilize. The Monster Body pictured has two pieces of plastic canvas inside of it lining the two largest sides. If you are attaching safety eyes, be sure to make the plastic canvas on the side with the eyes shorter/lower than where you are attaching the eyes, or the backs of the eyes will interfere with the plastic canvas lining being snug up against the inside wall of the Monster Body.

Glass gems are optional (for more information, see page 28). Stuff the Body with fiberfill and continue to stuff as you go.

**40.** SC 3, Triple SC Dec, SC 10, Triple SC Dec, SC 2, Triple SC Dec, SC 10, Triple SC Dec [28]

Row 40 overlaps itself by 1 stitch.

**41.** SC, Triple SC Dec, SC 8, Triple SC Dec x 2, SC 8, Triple SC Dec [20]

Row 41 overlaps itself by 1 stitch.

Fasten off with a 12 in/30.5 cm yarn tail.

## Assembly

**1.** Finish stuffing the body; shape the stuffing inside the body as needed to fill out the shaping of the crochet work.

**2.** Finalize the eye options—if you are attaching safety eyes, make sure you have attached them at this point.

**3.** Using the yarn tail, sew shut the top opening of the body, as shown; weave in ends.

**4.** Add any extra details—ears, horns, limbs, etc.—you want to the body!

Square with Underbite and No Legs, Squarish Short Limbs, Squarish Long Limbs, Medium Slight Curved Striped Horns, Two Separated Rounded Teeth

Square with Underbite and Legs, Short Rounded Limbs, Long Rounded Striped Tail, Thin L-shaped Horns, Hair Puff, Two Medium Uneven Pointy Fangs

## SQUARE WITH UNDERBITE AND LEGS (MAKE 1)

*Approximately 6.5 in/16.5 cm tall, 8.5 in/21.5 cm wide, 3 in/ 7.5 cm deep*

*Body Color Yarn: Approximately 175 yd/160 m worsted/medium weight yarn*

This Monster Body is worked from the bottom of the Feet to the top of the Body.

1. SC 6 in Magic Circle, Sl St to beginning stitch, Ch 1 [6]

2. Inc x 6, Sl St to beginning stitch, Ch 1 [12]

3. (SC, Inc) x 6, Sl St to beginning stitch, Ch 1 [18]

4. (SC, Inc, SC) x 6, Sl St to beginning stitch, Ch 1 [24]

5. (SC 3, Inc) x 6, Sl St to beginning stitch, Ch 1 [30]

6. BLO [SC 30], Sl St to beginning stitch, Ch 1 [30]

7–9. (3 rows of) SC 30, Sl St to beginning stitch, Ch 1 [30]

10. SC 11, Dec x 4, SC 11, Sl St to beginning stitch, Ch 1 [26]

11. SC 10, Dec, SC 2, Dec, SC 10, Sl St to beginning stitch, Ch 1 [24]

12–13. (2 rows of) SC 24, Sl St to beginning stitch, Ch 1 [24]

14. (SC 3, Inc) x 6, Sl St to beginning stitch, Ch 1 [30]

15. SC 30, Sl St to beginning stitch, Ch 1 [30]

16. SC 30, Sl St to beginning stitch [30]

Fasten off the first leg with a short yarn tail.

Mark the 25th stitch of the final row of the first leg for reference in Row 17.

Repeat instructions for Rows 1 through 16 for the second leg, do not fasten off, and continue to Row 17.

It is optional to add flat reinforcement to the bottom of the inside of the foot; see page 49 for details.

17. Ch 1, SC 8, working into the marked stitch on the first leg, SC 30, continuing into the next available stitch on the second leg, SC 22, Sl St to beginning stitch, Ch 1 [60]

This row (18) and all rows like it (Rows 25, 32, and 41) are optional but recommended. They create scaffolding inside the Monster Body to reinforce the square shaping. These rows will not be visible when the Body is complete. If you skip these rows, when the piece is stuffed, it will have a much rounder shape. None of the Slip Stitches in these rows are worked into any of the chain stitches.

If you choose to skip these rows, you will still need to follow the first two instructions of Row 18 (Ch 11, Skip 9 stitches) to shift the start of the next row.

In Row 18 (and 25, 32, and 41), you will make 8 or 9 Slip Stitches and a number of chains, but there is no stitch count associated with the row, because you will not work into any of these stitches again.

18. Ch 11, Skip 9 stitches, BLO [Sl St] (*this stitch is the new start of the next row*), Ch 7, Skip 5 stitches, BLO [Sl St], Ch 1, Skip 3 stitches, BLO [Sl St], Ch 10, Skip 6 stitches, BLO [Sl St], Ch 1, Skip 3 stitches, BLO [Sl St], Ch 18, Skip 14 stitches, BLO [Sl St], Ch 1, Skip 3 stitches, BLO [Sl St], Ch 10, Skip 6 stitches, BLO [Sl St], Ch 1, Skip 3 stitches, BLO [Sl St], Ch 11; continue working rows as normal, ignoring the chain sections and slip stitches and keeping them on the inside of your work

In Row 19, work into all stitches in Row 17 as normal (starting into the same stitch that you first Slip Stitched into in Row 18), ignoring all the stitches from Row 18.

**19–24.** (6 rows of) SC 60, Sl St to beginning stitch, Ch 1 [60]

**25.** Ch 9, Skip 7 stitches, BLO [Sl St], Ch 1, Skip 3 stitches, BLO [Sl St], Ch 10, Skip 6 stitches, BLO [Sl St], Ch 1, Skip 3 stitches, BLO [Sl St], Ch 18, Skip 14 stitches, BLO [Sl St], Ch 1, Skip 3 stitches, BLO [Sl St], Ch 10, Skip 6 stitches, BLO [Sl St], Ch 1, Skip 3 stitches, BLO [Sl St], Ch 9, Skip 7 stitches; continue working rows as normal, ignoring the chain sections and slip stitches and keeping them on the inside of your work

In Row 26, work into all stitches in Row 24 as normal, ignoring all the stitches from Row 25.

**26–31.** (6 rows of) SC 60, Sl St to beginning stitch, Ch 1 [60]

**32.** Ch 10, Skip 8 stitches, BLO [Sl St], Ch 1, Skip 3 stitches, BLO [Sl St], Ch 10, Skip 6 stitches, BLO [Sl St], Ch 1, Skip 3 stitches, BLO [Sl St], Ch 18, Skip 14 stitches, BLO [Sl St], Ch 1, Skip 3 stitches, BLO [Sl St], Ch 10, Skip 6 stitches, BLO [Sl St], Ch 1, Skip 3 Stitches, BLO [Sl St], Ch 9, Skip 6 stitches; continue working rows as normal, ignoring the chain sections and slip stitches and keeping them on the inside of your work

In Row 33, work into all the stitches from Row 31 as normal, ignoring all the stitches from Row 32.

**33.** SC 60, Sl St to beginning stitch, Ch 1 [60]

**34.** FLO [SC 26, HDC 10, SC 24], Sl St to beginning stitch, Ch 1 [60]

**35.** SC 26, HDC 10, SC 24, Sl St to beginning stitch, Ch 1 [60]

**36.** Ch 2, starting in the first BLO stitch from Row 33 and continuing working into the leftover BLO of the stitches from Row 34, BLO [SC 60], Sl St to beginning stitch, Ch 1 [60]

**37.** SC 60, Sl St to beginning stitch, Ch 1 [60]

**38.** Starting in the first available stitch of each row through both Row 35 and Row 37 at the same time SC 26, then working in Row 37 only, SC 10, Skip 10 stitches on Row 35, then working through Row 35 and Row 37 at the same time, SC 24, Sl St to beginning stitch, Ch 1 [60]

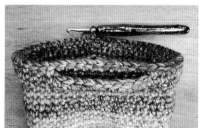

**39–40.** (2 rows of) SC 60, Sl St to beginning stitch, Ch 1 [60]

**41.** Ch 11, Skip 9 stitches, BLO [Sl St], Ch 1, Skip 3 stitches, BLO [Sl St], Ch 10, Skip 6 stitches, BLO [Sl St], Ch 1, Skip 3 stitches, BLO [Sl St], Ch 18, Skip 14 stitches, BLO [Sl St], Ch 1, Skip 3 stitches, BLO [Sl St], Ch 10, Skip 6 stitches, BLO [Sl St], Ch 1, Skip 3 stitches, BLO [Sl St], Ch 9, Skip the last 5 stitches; continue working rows as normal, ignoring the chain sections and slip stitches and keeping them on the inside of your work

In Row 42, work into all stitches in Row 40 as normal, ignoring all the stitches from Row 41.

**42–47.** (6 rows of) SC 60, Sl St to beginning stitch, Ch 1 [60]

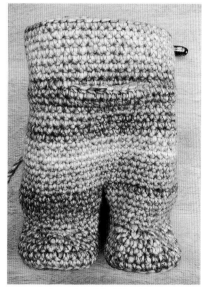

**48.** SC 10, Triple SC Dec, SC 8, Triple SC Dec, SC 16, Triple SC Dec, SC 8, Triple SC Dec, SC 6, Sl St to beginning stitch, Ch 1 [52]

> To make a Triple SC Dec, work a decrease stitch across 3 stitches.

**49.** SC 9, Triple SC Dec, SC 6, Triple SC Dec, SC 14, Triple SC Dec, SC 6, Triple SC Dec, SC 5, Sl St to beginning stitch, Ch 1 [44]

**50.** SC 8, Triple SC Dec, SC 4, Triple SC Dec, SC 12, Triple SC Dec, SC 4, Triple SC Dec, SC 4, Sl St to beginning stitch, Ch 1 [36]

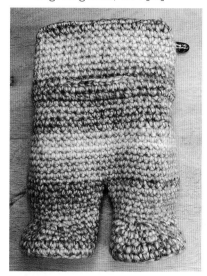

After you've completed Row 50, insert safety eyes between Row 43 and Row 44. Safety eye size and placement are up to your discretion; the following are guidelines only. Generalized photos of what these options look like can be found on page 28.

For two 30 mm eyes, insert with approximately 7 stitch spaces between the posts.

For three eyes (two 30 mm and one 40 mm), insert with approximately 5 stitch spaces between each post.

For one or two 40 mm eyes, insert with approximately 7 stitch spaces between the posts.

You could also skip inserting a safety eye and follow the crocheted eye instruction options, including a 2D Medium or Large Eye, an Eye Bump, or an Eye Stalk.

Plastic canvas as an inner body wall support is optional; for more information, see page 102.

Glass gems are optional (for more information, see page 28). Stuff the Body with fiberfill and continue to stuff as you go.

51. SC 7, Triple SC Dec, SC 2, Triple SC Dec, SC 10, Triple SC Dec, SC 2, Triple SC Dec, SC 3, Sl St to beginning stitch, Ch 1 [28]
52. SC 6, Triple SC Dec x 2, SC 8, Triple SC Dec x 2, SC 2, Sl St to beginning stitch [20]

Fasten off with a 24 in/61 cm yarn tail.

## Assembly

1. Finish stuffing the body; shape the stuffing inside the body as needed to fill out the shaping of the crochet work.
2. Finalize the eye options—if you are attaching safety eyes, make sure you have attached them at this point.
3. Using the yarn tail, sew shut the top opening of the body, as shown. Also sew the hole between the legs (if necessary); weave in ends.

4. Add any extra details—ears, horns, limbs, etc.—you want to the body!

# SQUARE WITH DEEP POCKET UNDERBITE AND NO LEGS (MAKE 1)

*Approximately 6.5 in/16.5 cm tall, 5.5 in/14 cm wide, 3 in/7.5 cm deep*

*Body Color Yarn: Approximately 160 yd/146.25 m worsted/medium weight yarn*

This Monster Body is worked from the bottom to the top.

1. Ch 11, starting in the second Ch from hook, SC 9, Inc, continue to crochet around to the other side of the starting chain stitches, SC 8, SC in the same Ch stitch as the first SC in this row, Sl St to beginning stitch, Ch 1 [20]
2. (Inc, SC 8, Inc) x 2, Sl St to beginning stitch, Ch 1 [24]

3. (SC & HDC, HDC & SC, SC 8, SC & HDC, HDC & SC) x 2, Sl St to beginning stitch, Ch 1 [32]
4. (SC, SC & HDC, HDC & SC, SC 10, SC & HDC, HDC & SC, SC) x 2, Sl St to beginning stitch, Ch 1 [40]

**5.** (SC 2, SC & HDC, HDC & SC, SC 12, SC & HDC, HDC & SC, SC 2) x 2, Sl St to beginning stitch, Ch 1 [48]

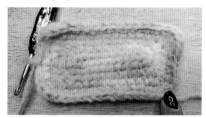

**6.** (SC 3, SC & HDC, HDC & SC, SC 14, SC & HDC, HDC & SC, SC 3) x 2, Sl St to beginning stitch, Ch 1 [56]

**7.** (SC 5, <Dec>, SC 18, <Dec>, SC 5) x 2, Sl St to beginning stitch, Ch 1 [60]

> "<Dec>" is a stitch that is defined in the Glossary.

**8.** SC 60, Sl St to beginning stitch, Ch 1 [60]

**9.** FLO [SC 60], Sl St to beginning stitch, Ch 1 [60]

> Insert a stitch marker into the first unused BLO from Row 8 for reference on where to start Row 23.

**10–20.** (11 rows of) SC 60, Sl St to beginning stitch, Ch 1 [60]

**21.** SC 13, HDC 10, SC 37, Sl St to beginning stitch, Ch 1 [60]

**22.** SC 13, HDC 10, SC 37, Sl St to beginning stitch, Ch 1 [60]

**23.** Ch 12, starting in the first BLO stitch from Row 8 and continuing working into the leftover BLO of the stitches from Row 8, BLO [SC 60], Sl St to beginning stitch, Ch 1 [60]

> It can help to fold the outer edge down over the work (like pulling down a sock) so that you have easier access to the leftover BLO stitches from Row 8.

**24–27.** (4 rows of) SC 60, Sl St to beginning stitch, Ch 1 [60]

> This row (28) and all rows like it (Rows 35 and 42) are optional but recommended. They create scaffolding inside the Monster Body to reinforce the square shaping. These rows will not be visible when the Body is complete. If you skip these rows, when the piece is stuffed, it will have a much rounder shape. None of the Slip Stitches in these rows are worked into any of the chain stitches.
>
> In Row 28 (and 35 and 42), you will make 8 Slip Stitches and a number of chains, but there is no stitch count associated with the row, because you will not work into any of these stitches again.

**28.** Ch 6, Skip 4 stitches, BLO [Sl St], Ch 1, Skip 3 stitches, BLO [Sl St], Ch 18, Skip 14 stitches, BLO [Sl St], Ch 1, Skip 3 stitches, BLO [Sl St], Ch 10, Skip 6 stitches, BLO [Sl St], Ch 1, Skip 3 stitches, BLO [Sl St], Ch 18, Skip 14 stitches, BLO [Sl St], Ch 1, Skip 3 stitches, BLO [Sl St], Ch 6, Skip the last 2 stitches; continue working rows as normal, ignoring the chain sections and slip stitches and keeping them on the inside of your work

In Row 29, work into all stitches in Row 27 as normal, ignoring all the stitches from Row 28.

**29–34.** (6 rows of) SC 60, Sl St to beginning stitch, Ch 1 [60]

**35.** Ch 7, Skip 5 stitches, BLO [Sl St], Ch 1, Skip 3 stitches, BLO [Sl St], Ch 18, Skip 14 stitches, BLO [Sl St], Ch 1, Skip 3 stitches, BLO [Sl St], Ch 10, Skip 6 stitches, BLO [Sl St], Ch 1, Skip 3 stitches, BLO [Sl St], Ch 18, Skip 14 stitches, BLO [Sl St], Ch 1, Skip 2 stitches, BLO [Sl St], Ch 5, Skip the last 2 stitches; continue working rows as normal, ignoring the chain sections and slip stitches and keeping them on the inside of your work

In Row 36, work into all stitches in Row 34 as normal, ignoring all the stitches from Row 35.

**36–38.** (3 rows of) SC 60, Sl St to beginning stitch, Ch 1 [60]

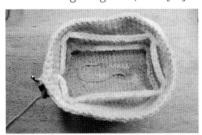

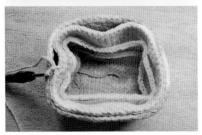

**39.** Starting in the first available stitch of each row through both Row 22 and Row 38 at the same time SC 13, then working in Row 38 only, SC 10 , Skip 10 stitches on Row 22, then working through Row 22 and Row 38 at the same time, SC 37, Sl St to beginning stitch, Ch 1 [60]

**40–41.** (2 rows of) SC 60, Sl St to beginning stitch, Ch 1 [60]

**42.** Ch 8, Skip 6 stitches, BLO [Sl St], Ch 1, Skip 3 stitches, BLO [Sl St], Ch 18, Skip 14 stitches, BLO [Sl St], Ch 1, Skip 3 stitches, BLO [Sl St], Ch 10, Skip 6 stitches, BLO [Sl St], Ch 1, Skip 3 stitches, BLO [Sl St], Ch 18, Skip 14 stitches, BLO [Sl St], Ch 1, Skip 2 stitches, BLO [Sl St], Ch 3, Skip the final stitch; continue working rows as normal, ignoring the chain sections and slip stitches and keeping them on the inside of your work

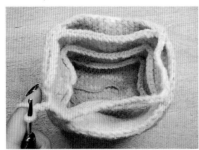

In Row 43, work into all stitches in Row 41 as normal, ignoring all the stitches from Row 42.

**43–48.** (6 rows of) SC 60, Sl St to beginning stitch, Ch 1 [60]

**49.** SC 8, Triple SC Dec, SC 16, Triple SC Dec, SC 8, Triple SC Dec, SC 16, Triple SC Dec, continue in spiral [52]

To make a Triple SC Dec, work a decrease stitch across 3 stitches.

**50.** SC 7, Triple SC Dec, SC 14, Triple SC Dec, SC 6, Triple SC Dec, SC 14, Triple SC Dec [44]

Row 50 overlaps itself by 1 stitch. This and all stitch counts reflect the number of stitches available to work into in the next row.

**51.** SC 5, Triple SC Dec, SC 12, Triple SC Dec, SC 4, Triple SC Dec, SC 12, Triple SC Dec [36]

Row 51 overlaps itself by 1 stitch.

Square with Deep Pocket Underbite and No Legs, Curved Arms, Crouching Rounded Hind Legs, Rounded Scales, Straight Dragon/Dinosaur Tail, Short Bunny Ears

After you've completed Row 51, insert safety eyes between Row 45 and Row 46. Safety eye size and placement are up to your discretion; the following are guidelines only. Generalized photos of what these options look like can be found on page 28.

For two 30 mm eyes, insert with approximately 7 stitch spaces between the posts.

For three eyes (two 30 mm and one 40 mm), insert with approximately 5 stitch spaces between each post.

For one or two 40 mm eyes, insert with approximately 7 stitch spaces between the posts.

You could also skip inserting a safety eye and follow the crocheted eye instruction options, including a 2D Medium or Large Eye, an Eye Bump, or an Eye Stalk.

Plastic canvas as an inner body wall support is optional; for more information, see page 102.

Glass gems are optional (for more information, see page 28). Stuff the Body with fiberfill and continue to stuff as you go.

**52.** SC 3, Triple SC Dec, SC 10, Triple SC Dec, SC 2, Triple SC Dec, SC 10, Triple SC Dec [28]

Row 52 overlaps itself by 1 stitch.

**53.** SC, Triple SC Dec, SC 8, Triple SC Dec x 2, SC 8, Triple SC Dec [20]

Row 53 overlaps itself by 1 stitch.

Fasten off with a 12 in/30.5 cm yarn tail.

## Assembly

**1.** Finish stuffing the body; shape the stuffing inside the body as needed to fill out the shaping of the crochet work.

**2.** Finalize the eye options—if you are attaching the safety eyes, make sure you have attached them at this point.

**3.** Using the yarn tail, sew shut the top opening of the body, as shown; weave in ends.

**4.** Add any extra details—ears, horns, limbs, etc.—you want to the body!

# SQUARE WITH DEEP POCKET UNDERBITE AND LEGS (MAKE 1)

*Approximately 8.5 in/21.5 cm tall, 5.5 in/14 cm wide, 3 in/7.5 cm deep*

*Body Color Yarn: Approximately 180 yd/164.5 m worsted/medium weight yarn*

This Monster Body is worked from the bottom of the Feet to the top of the Body.

**1.** SC 6 in Magic Circle, Sl St to beginning stitch, Ch 1 [6]

**2.** Inc x 6, Sl St to beginning stitch, Ch 1 [12]

**3.** (SC, Inc) x 6, Sl St to beginning stitch, Ch 1 [18]

**4.** (SC, Inc, SC) x 6, Sl St to beginning stitch, Ch 1 [24]

**5.** (SC 3, Inc) x 6, Sl St to beginning stitch, Ch 1 [30]

**6.** BLO [SC 30], Sl St to beginning stitch, Ch 1 [30]

**7–9.** (3 rows of) SC 30, Sl St to beginning stitch, Ch 1 [30]

**10.** SC 11, Dec x 4, SC 11, Sl St to beginning stitch, Ch 1 [26]

**11.** SC 10, Dec, SC 2, Dec, SC 10, Sl St to beginning stitch, Ch 1 [24]

**12–13.** (2 rows of) SC 24, Sl St to beginning stitch, Ch 1 [24]

**14.** (SC 3, Inc) x 6, Sl St to beginning stitch, Ch 1 [30]

**15.** SC 30, Sl St to beginning stitch, Ch 1 [30]

**16.** SC 30, Sl St to beginning stitch [30]

Fasten off the first leg with a short yarn tail.

Mark the 25th stitch of the final row of the first leg for reference in Row 17.

Repeat instructions for Rows 1 through 16 for the second leg, do not fasten off, and continue to Row 17.

It is optional to add flat reinforcement to the bottom of the inside of the foot; see page 49 for details.

**17.** Ch 1, SC 8, working into the marked stitch on the first leg, SC 30, continuing into the next available stitch on the second leg, SC 22, Sl St to beginning stitch, Ch 1 [60]

**18.** FLO [SC 60], Sl St to beginning stitch, Ch 1 [60]

Insert a stitch marker into the first unused BLO from Row 17 for reference on where to start Row 32.

**19–29.** (11 rows of) SC 60, Sl St to beginning stitch, Ch 1 [60]

**30.** SC 35, HDC 10, SC 15, Sl St to beginning stitch, Ch 1 [60]

**31.** SC 35, HDC 10, SC 15, Sl St to beginning stitch, Ch 1 [60]

**32.** Ch 12, starting in the first BLO stitch from Row 17 and continuing working into the leftover BLO of the stitches from Row 17, BLO [SC 60], Sl St to beginning stitch, Ch 1 [60]

It can help to fold the outer edge down over the work (like pulling down a sock) so that you have easier access to the leftover BLO stitches from Row 17.

**33–36.** (4 rows of) SC 60, Sl St to beginning stitch, Ch 1 [60]

Square with Deep Pocket Underbite and Legs, Small Nubbins Limbs, Double-layer Wedge Folded Ears, Tiny Curved Horns

This row (37) and all rows like it (Rows 44 and 51) are optional but recommended. They create scaffolding inside the Monster Body to reinforce the square shaping. These rows will not be visible when the Body is complete. If you skip these rows, when the piece is stuffed, it will have a much rounder shape. None of the Slip Stitches in these rows are worked into any of the chain stitches.

If you choose to skip these rows, you will still need to follow the first two instructions of Row 37 (Ch 11, Skip 9 stitches) to shift the start of the row.

Row 37 in particular overlaps itself, and the final "Skip 3 stitches, BLO [Sl St]" instruction goes beyond where the row started by 3 stitches, leaving only 6 stitches remaining until you're back at the new starting stitch of the next row.

In Row 37 (and 44 and 51), you will make 8 or 9 Slip Stitches and a number of chains, but there is no stitch count associated with the row, because you will not work into any of these stitches again.

**37.** Ch 11, Skip 9 stitches, BLO [Sl St] (*this stitch is the new start of the next row*), Ch 9, Skip 7 stitches, BLO [Sl St], Ch 1, Skip 3 stitches, BLO [Sl St], Ch 10, Skip 6 stitches, BLO [Sl St], Ch 1, Skip 3 stitches, BLO [Sl St], Ch 18, Skip 14 stitches, BLO [Sl St], Ch 1, Skip 3 stitches, BLO [Sl St], Ch 10, Skip 6 stitches, BLO [Sl St], Ch 1, Skip 3 stitches, BLO [Sl St], Ch 9, Skip the next 6 stitches; continue working rows as normal, ignoring the chain sections and slip stitches and keeping them on the inside of your work

In Row 38, work into all stitches in Row 36 as normal, ignoring all the stitches from Row 37.

**38–43.** (6 rows of) SC 60, Sl St to beginning stitch, Ch 1 [60]

**44.** Ch 10, Skip 8 stitches, BLO [Sl St], Ch 1, Skip 3 stitches, BLO [Sl St], Ch 10, Skip 6 stitches, BLO [Sl St], Ch 1, Skip 3 stitches, BLO [Sl St], Ch 18, Skip 14 stitches, BLO [Sl St], Ch 1, Skip 3 stitches, BLO [Sl St], Ch 10, Skip 6 stitches, BLO [Sl St], Ch 1, Skip 3 stitches, BLO [Sl St], Ch 9, skip the remaining 6 stitches; continue working rows as normal, ignoring the chain sections and slip stitches and keeping them on the inside of your work

In Row 45, work into all stitches in Row 43 as normal, ignoring all the stitches from Row 44.

**45–47.** (3 rows of) SC 60, Sl St to beginning stitch, Ch 1 [60]

**48.** Starting in the first available stitch of Row 47 and the 10th stitch of Row 31 at the same time SC 26, then working in Row 47 only, SC 10, Skip 10 stitches on Row 31, then working through Row 47 and Row 31 at the same time, SC 24, Sl St to beginning stitch, Ch 1 [60]

**49–50.** (2 rows of) SC 60, Sl St to beginning stitch, Ch 1 [60]

**51.** Ch 11, Skip 9 stitches, BLO [Sl St], Ch 1, Skip 3 stitches, BLO [Sl St], Ch 10, Skip 6 stitches, BLO [Sl St], Ch 1, Skip 3 stitches, BLO [Sl St], Ch 18, Skip 14 stitches, BLO [Sl St], Ch 1, Skip 3 stitches, BLO [Sl St], Ch 10, Skip 6 stitches, BLO [Sl St], Ch 1, Skip 3 stitches, BLO [Sl St], Ch 9, Skip the remaining 5 stitches; continue working rows as normal, ignoring the chain sections and slip stitches and keeping them on the inside of your work

In Row 52, work into all stitches in Row 50 as normal, ignoring all the stitches from Row 51.

**52–57.** (6 rows of) SC 60, Sl St to beginning stitch, Ch 1 [60]

**58.** SC 10, Triple SC Dec, SC 8, Triple SC Dec, SC 16, Triple SC Dec, SC 8, Triple SC Dec, SC 6, Sl St to beginning stitch, Ch 1 [52]

> To make a Triple SC Dec, work a decrease stitch across 3 stitches.

**59.** SC 9, Triple SC Dec, SC 6, Triple SC Dec, SC 14, Triple SC Dec, SC 6, Triple SC Dec, SC 5, Sl St to beginning stitch, Ch 1 [44]

**60.** SC 8, Triple SC Dec, SC 4, Triple SC Dec, SC 12, Triple SC Dec, SC 4, Triple SC Dec, SC 4, Sl St to beginning stitch, Ch 1 [36]

After you've completed Row 60, insert Safety eyes between Row 54 and Row 55. Safety eye size and placement are up to your discretion; the following are guidelines only. Generalized photos of what these options look like can be found on page 28.

For two 30 mm eyes, insert with approximately 7 stitch spaces between the posts.

For three eyes (two 30 mm and one 40 mm), insert with approximately 5 stitch spaces between each post.

For one or two 40 mm eyes, insert with approximately 7 stitch spaces between the posts.

You could also skip inserting a safety eye and follow the crocheted eye instruction options, including a 2D Medium or Large Eye, an Eye Bump, or an Eye Stalk.

Plastic canvas as an inner body wall support is optional; for more information, see page 102.

Glass gems are optional (for more information, see page 28). Stuff the Body with fiberfill and continue to stuff as you go.

**61.** SC 7, Triple SC Dec, SC 2, Triple SC Dec, SC 10, Triple SC Dec, SC 2, Triple SC Dec, SC 3, Sl St to beginning stitch, Ch 1 [28]

**62.** SC 6, Triple SC Dec x 2, SC 8, Triple SC Dec x 2, SC 2, Sl St to beginning stitch [20]

Fasten off with a 24 in/61 cm yarn tail.

## Assembly

**1.** Finish stuffing the body; shape the stuffing inside the body as needed to fill out the shaping of the crochet work.

**2.** Finalize the eye options—if you are attaching the safety eyes, make sure you have attached them at this point.

**3.** Using the yarn tail, sew shut the top opening of the body, as shown. Also sew the hole between the legs (if necessary); weave in ends.

**4.** Add any extra details—ears, horns, limbs, etc.—you want to the body!

**Square with Overbite and No Legs, Bulb-ended Short Limbs, Large-footed Bent Limbs, Double-layer Pointed Folded Ears, Small Antlers, Two Long Fangs**

If you want to add metal spikes to any part of your Monster, go to page 172 for tips on how to do that.

# SQUARE WITH OVERBITE AND NO LEGS (MAKE 1)

*Approximately 6.5 in/16.5 cm tall, 5.5 in/14 cm wide, 3 in/7.5 cm deep*

*Body Color Yarn: Approximately 135 yd/123.5 m worsted/medium weight yarn*

This Monster Body is worked from the bottom to the top.

1. Ch 11, starting in the second Ch from hook, SC 9, Inc, continue to crochet around to the other side of the starting chain stitches, SC 8, SC in the same Ch stitch as the first SC in this row, Sl St to beginning stitch, Ch 1 [20]

2. (Inc, SC 8, Inc) x 2, Sl St to beginning stitch, Ch 1 [24]

3. (SC & HDC, HDC & SC, SC 8, SC & HDC, HDC & SC) x 2, Sl St to beginning stitch, Ch 1 [32]

4. (SC, SC & HDC, HDC & SC, SC 10, SC & HDC, HDC & SC, SC) x 2, Sl St to beginning stitch, Ch 1 [40]

5. (SC 2, SC & HDC, HDC & SC, SC 12, SC & HDC, HDC & SC, SC 2) x 2, Sl St to beginning stitch, Ch 1 [48]

6. (SC 3, SC & HDC, HDC & SC, SC 14, SC & HDC, HDC & SC, SC 3) x 2, Sl St to beginning stitch, Ch 1 [56]

7. (SC 5, <Dec>, SC 18, <Dec>, SC 5) x 2, Sl St to beginning stitch, Ch 1 [60]

"<Dec>" is a stitch that is defined in the Glossary.

8-13. (6 rows of) SC 60, Sl St to beginning stitch, Ch 1 [60]

This row (14) and all rows like it (Rows 21 and 31) are optional but recommended. They create scaffolding inside the Monster Body to reinforce the square shaping. These rows will not be visible when the Body is complete. If you skip these rows, when the piece is stuffed, it will have a much rounder shape. None of the Slip Stitches in these rows are worked into any of the chain stitches.

In Row 14 (and 21 and 31), you will make 8 Slip Stitches and a number of chains, but there is no stitch count associated with the row, because you will not work into any of these stitches again.

14. Ch 6, Skip 4 stitches, BLO [Sl St], Ch 1, Skip 3 stitches, BLO [Sl St], Ch 18, Skip 14 stitches, BLO [Sl St], Ch 1, Skip 3 stitches, BLO [Sl St], Ch 10, Skip 6 stitches, BLO [Sl St], Ch 1, Skip 3 stitches, BLO [Sl St], Ch 18, Skip 14 stitches, BLO [Sl St], Ch 1, Skip 3 stitches, BLO [Sl St], Ch 6, Skip 2 stitches; continue working rows as normal, ignoring the chain sections and slip stitches and keeping them on the inside of your work

In Row 15, work into all stitches in Row 13 as normal, ignoring all the stitches from Row 14.

15-20. (6 rows of) SC 60, Sl St to beginning stitch, Ch 1 [60]

21. Ch 7, Skip 5 stitches, BLO [Sl St], Ch 1, Skip 3 stitches, BLO [Sl St], Ch 18, Skip 14 stitches, BLO [Sl St], Ch 1, Skip 3 stitches, BLO [Sl St], Ch 10, Skip 6 stitches, BLO [Sl St], Ch 1, Skip 3 stitches, BLO [Sl St], Ch 18, Skip 14 stitches, BLO [Sl St], Ch 1, Skip 2 stitches, BLO [Sl St], Ch 3, Skip the last two remaining stitches; continue working rows as normal, ignoring the chain sections and slip stitches and keeping them on the inside of your work

In Row 22, work into all stitches in Row 20 as normal, ignoring all the stitches from Row 21.

22. SC 60, Sl St to beginning stitch, Ch 1 [60]

**23.** FLO [SC 13, Ch 10, Skip 10 stitches, SC 37], Sl St to beginning stitch, Ch 1 [60]

**24.** SC 13, HDC 10, SC 37, Sl St to beginning stitch, Ch 1 [60]

> The HDC 10 instruction in Row 24 is worked into the Ch 10 from Row 23.

**25.** SC 13, HDC 10, SC 37, Sl St to beginning stitch, Ch 1 [60]

**26.** Ch 2, starting in the first BLO stitch from Row 22 and continuing working into the leftover BLO of the stitches (and full stitches) from Row 22 as instructed, BLO [SC 13], SC 10, BLO [SC 37], Sl St to beginning stitch, Ch 1 [60]

**27–28.** (2 rows of) SC 60, Sl St to beginning stitch, Ch 1 [60]

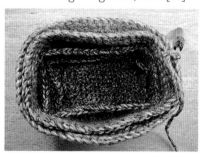

**29.** SC 60 through both Row 28 and Row 25 at the same time, Sl St to beginning stitch, Ch 1 [60]

**30.** SC 60, Sl St to beginning stitch, Ch 1 [60]

**31.** Ch 8, Skip 6 stitches, BLO [Sl St], Ch 1, Skip 3 stitches, BLO [Sl St], Ch 18, Skip 14 stitches, BLO [Sl St], Ch 1, Skip 3 stitches, BLO [Sl St], Ch 10, Skip 6 stitches, BLO [Sl St], Ch 1, Skip 3 stitches, BLO [Sl St], Ch 18, Skip 14 stitches, BLO [Sl St], Ch 1, Skip 2 stitches, BLO [Sl St], Ch 3, Skip the last remaining stitch; continue working rows as normal, ignoring the chain sections and slip stitches and keeping them on the inside of your work

In Row 32, work into all stitches in Row 30 as normal, ignoring all the stitches from Row 31.

**32–37.** (6 rows of) SC 60, Sl St to beginning stitch, Ch 1 [60]

**38.** SC 8, Triple SC Dec, SC 16, Triple SC Dec, SC 8, Triple SC Dec, SC 16, Triple SC Dec, continue in spiral, *do not "Sl St, Ch 1"* [52]

> To make a Triple SC Dec, work a decrease stitch across 3 stitches.

**39.** SC 7, Triple SC Dec, SC 14, Triple SC Dec, SC 6, Triple SC Dec, SC 14, Triple SC Dec [44]

> Row 39 overlaps itself by 1 stitch. This and all stitch counts reflect the number of stitches available to work into in the next row.

**40.** SC 5, Triple SC Dec, SC 12, Triple SC Dec, SC 4, Triple SC Dec, SC 12, Triple SC Dec [36]

> Row 40 overlaps itself by 1 stitch.

After you've completed Row 40, insert safety eyes between Row 31 and Row 32. Safety eye size and placement are up to your discretion; the following are guidelines only. Generalized photos of what these options look like can be found on page 28.

For two 30 mm eyes, insert with approximately 7 stitch spaces between the posts.

For three eyes (two 30 mm and one 40 mm), insert with approximately 5 stitch spaces between each post.

For one or two 40 mm eyes, insert with approximately 7 stitch spaces between the posts.

You could also skip inserting a safety eye and follow the crocheted eye instruction options, including a 2D Medium or Large Eye, an Eye Bump, or an Eye Stalk.

Plastic canvas as an inner body wall support is optional; for more information, see page 102.

Glass gems are optional (for more information, see page 28). Stuff the Body with fiberfill and continue to stuff as you go.

**41.** SC 3, Triple SC Dec, SC 10, Triple SC Dec, SC 2, Triple SC Dec, SC 10, Triple SC Dec [28]

Row 41 overlaps itself by 1 stitch.

**42.** SC, Triple SC Dec, SC 8, Triple SC Dec x 2, SC 8, Triple SC Dec [20]

Row 42 overlaps itself by 1 stitch.

Fasten off with a 12 in/30.5 cm yarn tail.

## Assembly

**1.** Finish stuffing the body; shape the stuffing inside the body as needed to fill out the shaping of the crochet work.

**2.** Finalize the eye options—if you are attaching safety eyes, make sure you have attached them at this point.

**3.** Using the yarn tail, sew shut the top opening of the body, as shown; weave in ends.

**4.** Add any extra details—ears, horns, limbs, etc.—you want to the body!

# SQUARE WITH OVERBITE AND LEGS (MAKE 1)

***Approximately 8.5 in/21.5 cm tall, 5.5 in/14 cm wide, 3 in/7.5 cm deep***

***Body Color Yarn: Approximately 175 yd/160 m worsted/medium weight yarn***

This Monster Body is worked from the bottom of the Feet to the top of the Body.

**1.** SC 6 in Magic Circle, Sl St to beginning stitch, Ch 1 [6]

**2.** Inc x 6, Sl St to beginning stitch, Ch 1 [12]

**3.** (SC, Inc) x 6, Sl St to beginning stitch, Ch 1 [18]

**4.** (SC, Inc, SC) x 6, Sl St to beginning stitch, Ch 1 [24]

**5.** (SC 3, Inc) x 6, Sl St to beginning stitch, Ch 1 [30]

**6.** BLO [SC 30], Sl St to beginning stitch, Ch 1 [30]

**7–9.** (3 rows of) SC 30, Sl St to beginning stitch, Ch 1 [30]

**10.** SC 11, Dec x 4, SC 11, Sl St to beginning stitch, Ch 1 [26]

**11.** SC 10, Dec, SC 2, Dec, SC 10, Sl St to beginning stitch, Ch 1 [24]

**12–13.** (2 rows of) SC 24, Sl St to beginning stitch, Ch 1 [24]

**14.** (SC 3, Inc) x 6, Sl St to beginning stitch, Ch 1 [30]

**15.** SC 30, Sl St to beginning stitch, Ch 1 [30]

**16.** SC 30, Sl St to beginning stitch [30]

Fasten off the first leg with a short yarn tail.

Mark the 25th stitch of the final row of the first leg for reference in Row 17.

Repeat instructions for Rows 1 through 16 for the second leg, do not fasten off, and continue to Row 17.

> It is optional to add flat reinforcement to the bottom of the inside of the foot; see page 49 for details.

**17.** Ch 1, SC 8, working into the marked stitch on the first leg, SC 30, continuing into the next available stitch on the second leg, SC 22, Sl St to beginning stitch, Ch 1 [60]

> This row (18) and all rows like it (Rows 25, 32, and 42) are optional but recommended. They create scaffolding inside the Monster Body to reinforce the square shaping. These rows will not be visible when the Body is complete. If you skip these rows, when the piece is stuffed, it will have a much rounder shape. None of the Slip Stitches in these rows are worked into any of the chain stitches.
>
> If you choose to skip these rows, you will still need to follow the first two instructions from Row 18 (Ch 11, Skip 9 stitches) to shift the start of the next row.
>
> In Row 18 (and 25, 32, and 42), you will make 8 or 9 Slip Stitches and a number of chains, but there is no stitch count associated with the row, because you will not work into any of these stitches again.

**18.** Ch 11, Skip 9 stitches, BLO [Sl St] (*this stitch is the new start of the next row*), Ch 7, Skip 5 stitches, BLO [Sl St], Ch 1, Skip 3 stitches, BLO [Sl St], Ch 10, Skip 6 stitches, BLO [Sl St], Ch 1, Skip 3 stitches, BLO [Sl St], Ch 18, Skip 14 stitches, BLO [Sl St], Ch 1, Skip 3 stitches, BLO [Sl St], Ch 10, Skip 6 stitches, BLO [Sl St], Ch 1, Skip 3 stitches, BLO [Sl St], Ch 11, Skip the next 9 stitches; continue working rows as normal, ignoring the chain sections and slip stitches and keeping them on the inside of your work

In Row 19, work into all stitches in Row 17 as normal (starting into the same stitch that you first Slip Stitched into in this row), ignoring all the stitches from Row 18.

**19–24.** (6 rows of) SC 60, Sl St to beginning stitch, Ch 1 [60]

> In Row 19, be careful not to crochet into the "Sl St, Ch 1" join from Row 17.

**25.** Ch 9, Skip 7 stitches, BLO [Sl St], Ch 1, Skip 3 stitches, BLO [Sl St], Ch 10, Skip 6 stitches, BLO [Sl St], Ch 1, Skip 3 stitches, BLO [Sl St], Ch 18, Skip 14 stitches, BLO [Sl St], Ch 1, Skip 3 stitches, BLO [Sl St], Ch 10, Skip 6 stitches, BLO [Sl St], Ch 1, Skip 3 stitches, BLO [Sl St], Ch 9, Skip 7 stitches; continue working rows as normal, ignoring the chain sections and slip stitches and keeping them on the inside of your work

In Row 26, work into all stitches in Row 24 as normal, ignoring all the stitches from Row 25.

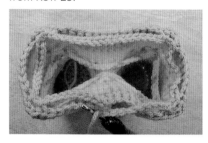

**26–31.** (6 rows of) SC 60, Sl St to beginning stitch, Ch 1 [60]

**32.** Ch 10, Skip 8 stitches, BLO [Sl St], Ch 1, Skip 3 stitches, BLO [Sl St], Ch 10, Skip 6 stitches, BLO [Sl St], Ch 1, Skip 3 stitches, BLO [Sl St], Ch 18, Skip 14 stitches, BLO [Sl St], Ch 1, Skip 3 stitches, BLO [Sl St], Ch 10, Skip 6 stitches, BLO [Sl St], Ch 1, Skip 3 stitches, BLO [Sl St], Ch 9, skip the remaining 6 stitches; continue working rows as normal, ignoring the chain sections and slip stitches and keeping them on the inside of your work

In Row 33, work into all stitches in Row 31 as normal, ignoring all the stitches from Row 32.

**33.** SC 60, Sl St to beginning stitch, Ch 1 [60]

**34.** FLO [SC 26, Ch 10, Skip 10 stitches, SC 24], Sl St to beginning stitch, Ch 1 [60]

**35.** SC 26, HDC 10, SC 24, Sl St to beginning stitch, Ch 1 [60]

> The HDC 10 instruction in Row 35 is worked into the Ch 10 instruction from Row 34.

**36.** SC 26, HDC 10, SC 24, Sl St to beginning stitch, Ch 1 [60]

**37.** Ch 2, starting in the first BLO stitch from Row 33 and continuing working into the leftover BLO of the stitches (and full stitches) from Row 33 as instructed, BLO [SC 26], SC 10, BLO [SC 24], Sl St to beginning stitch, Ch 1 [60]

**38–39.** (2 rows of) SC 60, Sl St to beginning stitch, Ch 1 [60]

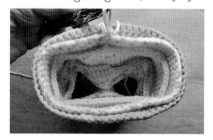

**40.** SC 60 through both Row 36 and Row 39 at the same time, Sl St to beginning stitch, Ch 1 [60]

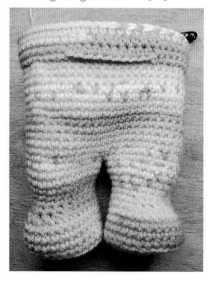

**41.** SC 60, Sl St to beginning stitch, Ch 1 [60]

**42.** Ch 11, Skip 9 stitches, BLO [Sl St], Ch 1, Skip 3 stitches, BLO [Sl St], Ch 10, Skip 6 stitches, BLO [Sl St], Ch 1, Skip 3 stitches, BLO [Sl St], Ch 18, Skip 14 stitches, BLO [Sl St], Ch 1, Skip 3 stitches, BLO [Sl St], Ch 10, Skip 6 stitches, BLO [Sl St], Ch 1, Skip 3 stitches, BLO [Sl St], Ch 9, Skip the remaining 5 stitches; continue working rows as normal, ignoring the chain sections and slip stitches and keeping them on the inside of your work

In Row 43, work into all stitches in Row 41 as normal, ignoring all the stitches from Row 42.

**43–48.** (6 rows of) SC 60, Sl St to beginning stitch, Ch 1 [60]

**49.** SC 10, Triple SC Dec, SC 8, Triple SC Dec, SC 16, Triple SC Dec, SC 8, Triple SC Dec, SC 6, Sl St to beginning stitch, Ch 1 [52]

> To make a Triple SC Dec, work a decrease stitch across 3 stitches.

**50.** SC 9, Triple SC Dec, SC 6, Triple SC Dec, SC 14, Triple SC Dec, SC 6, Triple SC Dec, SC 5, Sl St to beginning stitch, Ch 1 [44]

**51.** SC 8, Triple SC Dec, SC 4, Triple SC Dec, SC 12, Triple SC Dec, SC 4, Triple SC Dec, SC 4, Sl St to beginning stitch, Ch 1 [36]

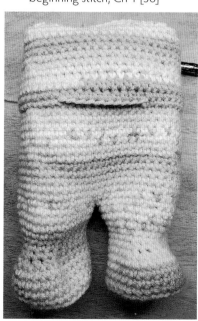

After you've completed Row 51, insert safety eyes between Row 43 and Row 44. Safety eye size and placement are up to your discretion; the following are guidelines only. Generalized photos of what these options look like can be found on page 28.

For two 30 mm eyes, insert with approximately 7 stitch spaces between the posts.

For three eyes (two 30 mm and one 40 mm), insert with approximately 5 stitch spaces between each post.

For one or two 40 mm eyes, insert with approximately 7 stitch spaces between the posts.

You could also skip inserting a safety eye and follow the crocheted eye instruction options, including a 2D Medium or Large Eye, an Eye Bump, or an Eye Stalk.

> Plastic canvas as an inner body wall support is optional; for more information, see page 102.

> Glass gems are optional (for more information, see page 28). Stuff the Body with fiberfill and continue to stuff as you go.

**52.** SC 7, Triple SC Dec, SC 2, Triple SC Dec, SC 10, Triple SC Dec, SC 2, Triple SC Dec, SC 3, Sl St to beginning stitch, Ch 1 [28]

**53.** SC 6, Triple SC Dec x 2, SC 8, Triple SC Dec x 2, SC 2, Sl St to beginning stitch [20]

Fasten off with a 24 in/61 cm yarn tail.

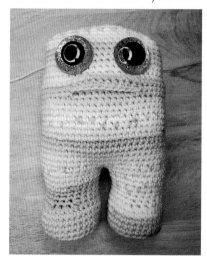

## Assembly

**1.** Finish stuffing the body; shape the stuffing inside the body as needed to fill out the shaping of the crochet work.

**2.** Finalize the eye options—if you are attaching the safety eyes, make sure you have attached them at this point.

**3.** Using the yarn tail, sew shut the top opening of the body, as shown. Also sew the hole between the legs (if necessary); weave in ends.

**4.** Add any extra details—ears, horns, limbs, etc.—you want to the body!

Square with Overbite and Legs, Wide Flat-ended Short Limbs, Circle Folded Ears, Curly Spritz Hair, Squared Teeth

If you want to add metal spikes to any part of your Monster, go to page 172 for tips on how to do that.

**Square with No Mouth and No Legs, Medium Rounded Underbite, Cute Mitten Limbs, Cute Footed Limbs, Spiky Ears, Large Antlers, Four Humanlike Teeth**

If you want to add metal spikes to any part of your Monster, go to page 172 for tips on how to do that.

# SQUARE WITH NO MOUTH AND NO LEGS (MAKE 1)

*Approximately 6.5 in/16.5 cm tall, 5.5 in/14 cm wide, 3 in/7.5 cm deep*

*Body Color Yarn: Approximately 115 yd/105.25 m worsted/medium weight yarn*

This Monster Body is worked from the bottom to the top.

**1.** Ch 11, starting in the second Ch from hook, SC 9, Inc, continue to crochet around to the other side of the starting chain stitches, SC 8, SC in the same Ch stitch as the first SC in this row, Sl St to beginning stitch, Ch 1 [20]

**2.** (Inc, SC 8, Inc) x 2, Sl St to beginning stitch, Ch 1 [24]

**3.** (Inc x 2, SC 8, Inc x 2) x 2, Sl St to beginning stitch, Ch 1 [32]

**4.** (SC, SC & HDC, HDC & SC, SC 10, SC & HDC, HDC & SC, SC) x 2, Sl St to beginning stitch, Ch 1 [40]

**5.** (SC 2, SC & HDC, HDC & SC, SC 12, SC & HDC, HDC & SC, SC 2) x 2, Sl St to beginning stitch, Ch 1 [48]

**6.** (SC 3, SC & HDC, HDC & SC, SC 14, SC & HDC, HDC & SC, SC 3) x 2, Sl St to beginning stitch, Ch 1 [56]

**7.** (SC 5, <Dec>, SC 18, <Dec>, SC 5) x 2, Sl St to beginning stitch, Ch 1 [60]

"<Dec>" is a stitch that is defined in the Glossary.

**8–13.** (6 rows of) SC 60, Sl St to beginning stitch, Ch 1 [60]

This row (14) and all rows like it (Rows 21 and 28) are optional but recommended. They create scaffolding inside the Monster Body to reinforce the square shaping. These rows will not be visible when the Body is complete. If you skip these rows, when the piece is stuffed, it will have a much rounder shape. None of the Slip Stitches in these rows are worked into any of the chain stitches.

In Row 14 (and 21 and 28), you will make 8 Slip Stitches and a number of chains, but there is no stitch count associated with the row, because you will not work into any of these stitches again.

**14.** Ch 6, Skip 4 stitches, BLO [Sl St], Ch 1, Skip 3 stitches, BLO [Sl St], Ch 18, Skip 14 stitches, BLO [Sl St], Ch 1, Skip 3 stitches, BLO [Sl St], Ch 10, Skip 6 stitches, BLO [Sl St], Ch 1, Skip 3 stitches, BLO [Sl St], Ch 18, Skip 14 stitches, BLO [Sl St], Ch 1, Skip 3 stitches, BLO [Sl St], Ch 6, Skip the remaining 2 stitches; continue working rows as normal, ignoring the chain sections and slip stitches and keeping them on the inside of your work

In Row 15, work into all stitches in Row 13 as normal, ignoring all the stitches from Row 14.

**15–20.** (6 rows of) SC 60, Sl St to beginning stitch, Ch 1 [60]

**21.** Ch 7, Skip 5 stitches, BLO [Sl St], Ch 1, Skip 3 stitches, BLO [Sl St], Ch 18, Skip 14 stitches, BLO [Sl St], Ch 1, Skip 3 stitches, BLO [Sl St], Ch 10, Skip 6 stitches, BLO [Sl St], Ch 1, Skip 3 stitches, BLO [Sl St], Ch 18, Skip 14 stitches, BLO [Sl St], Ch 1, Skip 3 stitches, BLO [Sl St], Ch 3, Skip the remaining stitch; continue working rows as normal, ignoring the chain sections and slip stitches and keeping them on the inside of your work

In Row 22, work into all stitches in Row 20 as normal, ignoring all the stitches from Row 21.

**22–27.** (6 rows of) SC 60, Sl St to beginning stitch, Ch 1 [60]

**28.** Ch 8, Skip 6 stitches, BLO [Sl St], Ch 1, Skip 3 stitches, BLO [Sl St], Ch 18, Skip 14 stitches, BLO [Sl St], Ch 1, Skip 3 stitches, BLO [Sl St], Ch 10, Skip 6 stitches, BLO [Sl St], Ch 1, Skip 3 stitches, BLO [Sl St], Ch 18, Skip 14 stitches, BLO [Sl St], Ch 1, Skip 3 stitches, BLO [Sl St], Ch 3; continue working rows as normal, ignoring the chain sections and slip stitches and keeping them on the inside of your work

In Row 29, work into all stitches in Row 27 as normal, ignoring all the stitches from Row 28.

**29–34.** (6 rows of) SC 60, Sl St to beginning stitch, Ch 1 [60]

**35.** SC 8, Triple SC Dec, SC 16, Triple SC Dec, SC 8, Triple SC Dec, SC 16, Triple SC Dec, continue in spiral [52]

> To make a Triple SC Dec, work a decrease stitch across 3 stitches.

**36.** SC 7, Triple SC Dec, SC 14, Triple SC Dec, SC 6, Triple SC Dec, SC 14, Triple SC Dec [44]

> Row 36 overlaps itself by 1 stitch. This and all stitch counts reflect the number of stitches available to work into in the next row.

**37.** SC 5, Triple SC Dec, SC 12, Triple SC Dec, SC 4, Triple SC Dec, SC 12, Triple SC Dec [36]

> Row 37 overlaps itself by 1 stitch.

> After you've completed Row 37, insert safety eyes between Row 26 and Row 27. Safety eye size and placement are up to your discretion; the following are guidelines only. Generalized photos of what these options look like can be found on page 28.
>
> For two 30 mm eyes, insert with approximately 7 stitch spaces between the posts.
>
> For three eyes (two 30 mm and one 40 mm), insert with approximately 5 stitch spaces between each post.
>
> For one or two 40 mm eyes, insert with approximately 7 stitch spaces between the posts.
>
> You could also skip inserting a safety eye and follow the crocheted eye instruction options, including a 2D Medium or Large Eye, an Eye Bump, or an Eye Stalk.

Plastic canvas as an inner body wall support is optional; for more information, see page 102.

Glass gems are optional (for more information, see page 28). Stuff the Body with fiberfill and continue to stuff as you go.

**38.** SC 3, Triple SC Dec, SC 10, Triple SC Dec, SC 2, Triple SC Dec, SC 10, Triple SC Dec [28]

Row 38 overlaps itself by 1 stitch.

**39.** SC, Triple SC Dec, SC 8, Triple SC Dec x 2, SC 8, Triple SC Dec [20]

Row 39 overlaps itself by 1 stitch.

Fasten off with a 12 in/30.5 cm yarn tail.

## Assembly

**1.** Finish stuffing the body; shape the stuffing inside the body as needed to fill out the shaping of the crochet work.

**2.** Finalize the eye options—if you are attaching safety eyes, make sure you have attached them at this point.

**3.** Using the yarn tail, sew shut the top opening of the body, as shown; weave in ends.

**4.** Add any extra details—ears, horns, limbs, etc.—you want to the body!

# SQUARE WITH NO MOUTH AND LEGS (MAKE 1)

*Approximately 8.5 in/21.5 cm tall, 5.5 in/14 cm wide, 3 in/7.5 cm deep*

*Body Color Yarn: 150 yd/137.25 m worsted/medium weight yarn*

This Monster Body is worked from the bottom of the Feet to the top of the Body.

**1.** SC 6 in Magic Circle, Sl St to beginning stitch, Ch 1 [6]

**2.** Inc x 6, Sl St to beginning stitch, Ch 1 [12]

**3.** (SC, Inc) x 6, Sl St to beginning stitch, Ch 1 [18]

**4.** (SC, Inc, SC) x 6, Sl St to beginning stitch, Ch 1 [24]

**5.** (SC 3, Inc) x 6, Sl St to beginning stitch, Ch 1 [30]

**6.** BLO [SC 30], Sl St to beginning stitch, Ch 1 [30]

**7-9.** (3 rows of) SC 30, Sl St to beginning stitch, Ch 1 [30]

**10.** SC 11, Dec x 4, SC 11, Sl St to beginning stitch, Ch 1 [26]

**11.** SC 10, Dec, SC 2, Dec, SC 10, Sl St to beginning stitch, Ch 1 [24]

**12-13.** (2 rows of) SC 24, Sl St to beginning stitch, Ch 1 [24]

**14.** (SC 3, Inc) x 6, Sl St to beginning stitch, Ch 1 [30]

**15.** SC 30, Sl St to beginning stitch, Ch 1 [30]

**16.** SC 30, Sl St to beginning stitch [30]

Fasten off the first leg with a short yarn tail.

Mark the 25th stitch of the final row of the first leg for reference in Row 17.

Repeat instructions for Rows 1 through 16 for the second leg, do not fasten off, and continue to Row 17.

It is optional to add flat reinforcement to the bottom of the inside of the foot; see page 49 for details.

**17.** SC 8, working into the marked stitch on the first leg, SC 30, continuing into the next available stitch on the second leg, SC 22, Sl St to beginning stitch, Ch 1 [60]

This row (18) and all rows like it (Rows 25, 32, and 39) are optional but recommended. They create scaffolding inside the Monster Body to reinforce the square shaping. These rows will not be visible when the Body is complete. If you skip these rows, when the piece is stuffed, it will have a much rounder shape. None of the Slip Stitches in these rows are worked into any of the chain stitches.

If you choose to skip these rows, you will still need to follow the first two instructions from Row 18 (Ch 11, Skip 9 stitches) to shift the start of the next row.

In Row 18 (and 25, 32, and 39), you will make 8 or 9 Slip Stitches and a number of chains, but there is no stitch count associated with the row, because you will not work into any of these stitches again.

**18.** Ch 11, Skip 9 stitches, BLO [Sl St] (*this stitch is the new start of the next row*), Ch 7, Skip 5 stitches, BLO [Sl St], Ch 1, Skip 3 stitches, BLO [Sl St], Ch 10, Skip 6 stitches, BLO [Sl St], Ch 1, Skip 3 stitches, BLO [Sl St], Ch 18, Skip 14 stitches, BLO [Sl St], Ch 1, Skip 3 stitches, BLO [Sl St], Ch 10, Skip 6 stitches, BLO [Sl St], Ch 1, Skip 3 stitches, BLO [Sl St], Ch 11, Skip the next 8 stitches; continue working rows as normal, ignoring the chain sections and slip stitches and keeping them on the inside of your work

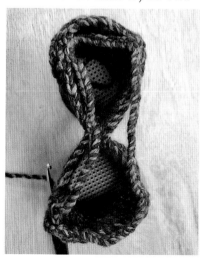 

In Row 19, work into all stitches in Row 17 as normal (starting into the same stitch that you first Slip Stitched into in this row), ignoring all the stitches from Row 18.

**19–24.** (6 rows of) SC 60, Sl St to beginning stitch, Ch 1 [60]

In Row 19, be careful not to crochet into the "Sl St, Ch 1" join from Row 17.

**25.** Ch 9, Skip 7 stitches, BLO [Sl St], Ch 1, Skip 3 stitches, BLO [Sl St], Ch 10, Skip 6 stitches, BLO [Sl St], Ch 1, Skip 3 stitches, BLO [Sl St], Ch 18, Skip 14 stitches, BLO [Sl St], Ch 1, Skip 3 stitches, BLO [Sl St], Ch 10, Skip 6 stitches, BLO [Sl St], Ch 1, Skip 3 stitches, BLO [Sl St], Ch 9, Skip 7 stitches; continue working rows as normal, ignoring the chain sections and slip stitches and keeping them on the inside of your work

In Row 26, work into all stitches in Row 24 as normal, ignoring all the stitches from Row 25.

**26–31.** (6 rows of) SC 60, Sl St to beginning stitch, Ch 1 [60]

**32.** Ch 10, Skip 8 stitches, BLO [Sl St], Ch 1, Skip 3 stitches, BLO [Sl St], Ch 10, Skip 6 stitches, BLO [Sl St], Ch 1, Skip 3 stitches, BLO [Sl St], Ch 18, Skip 14 stitches, BLO [Sl St], Ch 1, Skip 3 stitches, BLO [Sl St], Ch 10, Skip 6 stitches, BLO [Sl St], Ch 1, Skip 3 stitches, BLO [Sl St], Ch 9, skip the remaining 6 stitches; continue working rows as normal, ignoring the chain sections and slip stitches and keeping them on the inside of your work

In Row 33, work into all stitches in Row 31 as normal, ignoring all the stitches from Row 32.

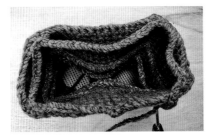

**33–38.** (6 rows of) SC 60, Sl St to beginning stitch, Ch 1 [60]

**39.** Ch 11, Skip 9 stitches, BLO [Sl St], Ch 1, Skip 3 stitches, BLO [Sl St], Ch 10, Skip 6 stitches, BLO [Sl St], Ch 1, Skip 3 stitches, BLO [Sl St], Ch 18, Skip 14 stitches, BLO [Sl St], Ch 1, Skip 3 stitches, BLO [Sl St], Ch 10, Skip 6 stitches, BLO [Sl St], Ch 1, Skip 3 stitches, BLO [Sl St], Ch 9, Skip the remaining 5 stitches; continue working rows as normal, ignoring the chain sections and slip stitches and keeping them on the inside of your work

In Row 40, work into all stitches in Row 38 as normal, ignoring all the stitches from Row 39.

**40–45.** (6 rows of) SC 60, Sl St to beginning stitch, Ch 1 [60]

**46.** SC 10, Triple SC Dec, SC 8, Triple SC Dec, SC 16, Triple SC Dec, SC 8, Triple SC Dec, SC 6, Sl St to beginning stitch, Ch 1 [52]

To work a Triple SC Dec, work a decrease stitch across 3 stitches.

**47.** SC 9, Triple SC Dec, SC 6, Triple SC Dec, SC 14, Triple SC Dec, SC 6, Triple SC Dec, SC 5, Sl St to beginning stitch, Ch 1 [44]

**48.** SC 8, Triple SC Dec, SC 4, Triple SC Dec, SC 12, Triple SC Dec, SC 4, Triple SC Dec, SC 4, Sl St to beginning stitch, Ch 1 [36]

Square with No Mouth and Legs, Small Rounded Overbite, Wide Flat-ended Long Limbs, Large Curved Horns, Four Humanlike Teeth

After you've completed Row 48, insert safety eyes between Row 37 and Row 38. Safety eye size and placement are up to your discretion; the following are guidelines only. Generalized photos of what these options look like can be found on page 28.

For two 30 mm eyes, insert with approximately 7 stitch spaces between the posts.

For three eyes (two 30 mm and one 40 mm), insert with approximately 5 stitch spaces between each post.

For one or two 40 mm eyes, insert with approximately 7 stitch spaces between the posts.

You could also skip inserting a safety eye and follow the crocheted eye instruction options, including a 2D Medium or Large Eye, an Eye Bump, or an Eye Stalk.

Plastic canvas as an inner body wall support is optional; for more information, see page 102.

Glass gems are optional (for more information, see page 28). Stuff the Body with fiberfill and continue to stuff as you go.

49. SC 7, Triple SC Dec, SC 2, Triple SC Dec, SC 10, Triple SC Dec, SC 2, Triple SC Dec, SC 3, Sl St to beginning stitch, Ch 1 [28]

50. SC 6, Triple SC Dec x 2, SC 8, Triple SC Dec x 2, SC 2, Sl St to beginning stitch [20]

Fasten off with a 24 in/61 cm yarn tail.

## Assembly

1. Finish stuffing the body; shape the stuffing inside the body as needed to fill out the shaping of the crochet work.

2. Finalize the eye options—if you are attaching safety eyes, make sure you have attached them at this point.

3. Use the yarn tail to sew the top opening of the body shut, as shown. Also sew the hole between the legs (if necessary). Weave in ends.

4. Add any extra details—ears, horns, limbs, etc.—you want to the body!

# Eyeball Monster Bodies

## EYEBALL MONSTER MAIN BODY/EYE WITH CROCHETED IRIS AND PUPIL (MAKE 1)

*Approximately 4 in/10 cm in diameter*

*Black (Pupil) Yarn: Approximately 2 yd/1.75 m worsted/medium weight yarn*

*Iris Color #1 Yarn: Approximately 2 yd/1.75 m worsted/medium weight yarn*

*Iris Color #2 Yarn: Approximately 3 yd/2.75 m worsted/medium weight yarn*

*Optional Iris Color #3 Yarn: Approximately 3 yd/2.75 m worsted/medium weight yarn*

*White Yarn: Approximately 27 yd/24.75 m worsted/medium weight yarn*

1. Starting with Black Color Yarn, SC 6 in Magic Circle, Sl St to beginning stitch, Ch 1 [6]

It is optional to wait to close the Magic Circle tightly until after working Row 2.

2. Still working into the Magic Circle, work 12 Spike Stitch SC, Sl St to beginning stitch, fasten off with a short yarn tail [12]

Eyeball Monster Main Body/Eye with Crocheted Iris and Pupil, Eyeball Monster Eyelid, Spider Legs

**3.** Attach the Iris Color #1 to the BLO of the first stitch of Row 2, BLO [(SC, Inc) x 6], Sl St to beginning stitch, fasten off with a short yarn tail [18]

Before you fasten off Iris Color #1, it is optional to Slip Stitch around the base of Row 3 into the same Row 2 stitches that you worked into when making Row 3. This will create a cleaner line to delineate the iris and the pupil. It is entirely optional and increases the difficulty of the Spike Stitches in Row 4 (these can be changed to a normal SC if this step is too difficult).

**4.** Attach Iris Color #2 Yarn to the first stitch of Row 3, (SC, Spike Stitch SC, Inc) x 6, Sl St to beginning stitch, fasten off with a short yarn tail [24]

The Spike Stitches in this row will be worked 1 row down into the same stitch that you worked each increase in Row 3.

**5.** Attach the White Yarn to the BLO of the first stitch of Row 4, BLO [(SC 3, Inc) x 6], Sl St to beginning stitch, Ch 1 [30]
OR
Attach Iris Color #3 yarn to the first stitch of Row 4, (Spike Stitch SC, SC, Spike Stitch SC, Inc) x 6, Sl St to beginning stitch, fasten off with a short yarn tail [30]

> The Spike Stitches in this row will be worked 1 row down into the same stitch as the first SC in the repeated pattern of stitches in Row 4 and the same stitch as the increases in the repeated pattern of stitches in Row 4.

**6.** Either continue with the White Yarn or attach the White Yarn to the BLO of the first stitch of Row 5 and work in the BLO [(SC 2, Inc, SC 2) x 6], Sl St to beginning stitch, Ch 1 [36]

**7.** (SC 5, Inc) x 6, Sl St to beginning stitch, Ch 1 [42]

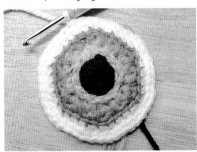

**8–15.** (8 rows of) SC 42, Sl St to beginning stitch, Ch 1 [42]

**16.** (SC 5, Dec) x 6, Sl St to beginning stitch, Ch 1 [36]

**17.** (SC 2, Dec, SC 2) x 6, Sl St to beginning stitch, Ch 1 [30]

**18.** (SC 3, Dec) x 6, Sl St to beginning stitch, Ch 1 [24]

**19.** (SC, Dec, SC) x 6, Sl St to beginning stitch, Ch 1 [18]

> At this point stuff the piece medium-firm with fiberfill. Make sure that you fill out the shape into a smooth round sphere, and do not allow lumps.

**20.** (SC, Dec) x 6, Sl St to beginning stitch, Ch 1 [12]

**21.** Dec x 6, Sl St to beginning stitch [6]

Fasten off with a 12 in/30.5 cm yarn tail.

## Assembly

**1.** Use the yarn tail to sew shut the hole at the back of the eyeball; weave in ends.

**2.** From here, proceed to the Eyeball Monster Eyelid on the next page.

# EYEBALL MONSTER MAIN BODY/EYE WITH SAFETY EYE (MAKE 1)

*Approximately 4 in/10 cm in diameter*

*White Yarn: Approximately 36 yd/33 m worsted/medium weight yarn*

*40 mm or 50 mm safety eye*

**1.** SC 6 in Magic Circle, Sl St to beginning stitch, Ch 1 [6]

**2.** Inc x 6, Sl St to beginning stitch, Ch 1 [12]

**3.** (SC, Inc) x 6, Sl St to beginning stitch, Ch 1 [18]

**4.** (SC, Inc, SC) x 6, Sl St to beginning stitch, Ch 1 [24]

**5.** (SC 3, Inc) x 6, Sl St to beginning stitch, Ch 1 [30]

**6.** (SC 2, Inc, SC 2) x 6, Sl St to beginning stitch, Ch 1 [36]

**7.** (SC 5, Inc) x 6, Sl St to beginning stitch, Ch 1 [42]

**8–15.** (8 rows of) SC 42, Sl St to beginning stitch, Ch 1 [42]

**16.** (SC 5, Dec) x 6, Sl St to beginning stitch, Ch 1 [36]

**17.** (SC 2, Dec, SC 2) x 6, Sl St to beginning stitch, Ch 1 [30]

**18.** (SC 3, Dec) x 6, Sl St to beginning stitch, Ch 1 [24]

**19.** (SC, Dec, SC) x 6, Sl St to beginning stitch, Ch 1 [18]

At this point insert the 40 mm or 50 mm safety eye into the Magic Circle of the eyeball and attach it in place. Then stuff the piece medium-firm with fiberfill. Make sure you fill out the shape into a smooth round sphere, and do not allow lumps.

**20.** (SC, Dec) x 6, Sl St to beginning stitch, Ch 1 [12]

**21.** Dec x 6, Sl St to beginning stitch [6]

Fasten off with a 12 in/30.5 cm yarn tail.

### Assembly

**1.** Use the yarn tail to sew shut the hole at the back of the eyeball; weave in ends.

**2.** From here, proceed on to the Eyeball Monster Eyelid (below).

# EYEBALL MONSTER EYELID (MAKE 1 FOR EITHER EYEBALL MONSTER WITH CROCHETED IRIS/PUPIL OR SAFETY EYE)

*Approximately 4.25 in/11 cm in diameter*

*Eyelid Color Yarn: Approximately 56 yd/51.25 m worsted/medium weight yarn*

### Part 1 (Make 1)

**1.** SC 6 in Magic Circle, Sl St to beginning stitch, Ch 1 [6]

**2.** Inc x 6, Sl St to beginning stitch, Ch 1 [12]

**3.** (SC, Inc) x 6, Sl St to beginning stitch, Ch 1 [18]

**4.** (SC, Inc, SC) x 6, Sl St to beginning stitch, Ch 1 [24]

**5.** (SC 3, Inc) x 6, Sl St to beginning stitch, Ch 1 [30]

**6.** (SC 2, Inc, SC 2) x 6, Sl St to beginning stitch, Ch 1 [36]

**7.** (SC 5, Inc) x 6, Sl St to beginning stitch, Ch 1 [42]

**8.** (SC 10, Inc, SC 10) x 2, Sl St to beginning stitch, Ch 1 [44]

**9–11.** (3 rows of) SC 44, Sl St to beginning stitch, Ch 1 [44]

**12.** SC 11, Ch 22, Skip 22 stitches, SC 11, Sl St to beginning stitch, Ch 1 [22]

Put a stitch marker into the first Ch stitch in this row, for reference on where to attach the yarn in Part 2.

**13.** SC 44, Sl St to beginning stitch, Ch 1 [44]

The SC 44 in Row 13 are worked into the SC stitches from Row 12 and the Ch stitches from Row 12 but are not worked into the stitches you skip in Row 12.

**14–15.** (2 rows of) SC 44, Sl St to beginning stitch, Ch 1 [44]

**16.** (SC 10, Dec, SC 10) x 2, Sl St to beginning stitch, Ch 1 [42]

**17.** (SC 5, Dec) x 6, Sl St to beginning stitch, Ch 1 [36]

**18.** (SC 2, Dec, SC 2) x 6, Sl St to beginning stitch, Ch 1 [30]

**19.** (SC 3, Dec) x 6, Sl St to beginning stitch, Ch 1 [24]

**20.** (SC, Dec, SC) x 6, Sl St to beginning stitch, Ch 1 [18]

**21.** (SC, Dec) x 6, Sl St to beginning stitch, Ch 1 [12]

**22.** Dec x 6, Sl St to beginning stitch [6]

Fasten off with a 12 in/30.5 cm yarn tail.

### Part 2 (Make 1)

**1.** Attach yarn to the marked stitch in Row 12 from Part 1 with a 12 in/30.5 cm yarn tail, working along the Ch stitch side of the 22 Ch stitches in Row 12 (working *inside out* by inserting your hook from the inside of the eyelid to the outside to complete the stitches), SC 22 [22]

**2.** Rotate the eyelid to work along the skipped 22 stitches from Row 12 in Part 1, continuing to work inside out, BLO [SC 3, HDC 16, SC 3] [22]

**3.** Rotate the eyelid to work along the stitches you worked in Row 1, BLO [SC 3, HDC 16, SC 3] [22]

**4.** Rotate the eyelid to work along the stitches you worked in Row 2, BLO [Inc, SC 2, HDC 16, SC 2, Inc] [24]

**5.** Rotate the eyelid to work along the stitches you worked in Row 3, BLO [Inc, SC 2, HDC 16, SC 2, Inc], Sl St into the next stitch [24]

Fasten off with an 18 in/45.5 cm yarn tail.

### Assembly

**1.** Insert the Eyeball Monster Main Body/Eye into the Eyelid.

**2.** You can sew the hole in the back of the eyelid shut or you can wait and sew once you have all the limbs/ extra Monster bits pinned and are ready to sew those to attach. As you sew, you will anchor the eyeball inside the eyelid. Then weave in ends.

**3.** Add any extra details—ears, horns, limbs, etc.—you want to the body!

Eyeball Monster Main Body/Eye with Safety Eye, Eyeball Monster Eyelid, Wide Flat-ended Short Limbs, Wide Flat-ended Long Limbs, Small Antlers

If you want to add metal spikes to any part of your Monster, go to page 172 for tips on how to do that.

# EYES

## OPTIONS

**Eyelid for 30 mm Safety Eye...139**

**Thinner Eyelid/Eyebrow for 30 mm Safety Eye...139**

**Eyelid for 40 mm Safety Eye...140**

**Large 2D Crocheted Eye...141**

**Eyelid for Large 2D Crocheted Eye...141**

**Medium 2D Crocheted Eye...142**

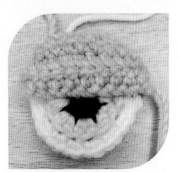

**Eyelid for Medium 2D Crocheted Eye...142**

**Eye Stalks...144**

**Eye Bumps...144**

# EYELID FOR 30 MM SAFETY EYE (MAKE 1 PER EYE)

*Approximately 2 in/5 cm wide by 1 in/2.5 cm tall*

*Body Color Yarn: 3 yd/2.75 m worsted/medium weight yarn per Eyelid*

1. Start with a long enough yarn tail to weave in, Ch 10, Turn, starting in the second Ch from hook, SC 9, Ch 1, Turn [9]
2. BLO [Dec, SC 5, Dec], Ch 1, Turn [7]
3. Dec, SC 3, Dec [5]

Fasten off with an 18 in/45.5 cm yarn tail to use to attach Eyelid and weave in ends.

## Assembly

1. Pin in place over the safety eye.
2. Verify placement. Eyelids can significantly affect the demeanor of your Monster. Make sure you are giving it the expression you desire.
3. Sew in place using the yarn tail to attach it along every edge that is touching the Monster's head/body. Weave in ends.

# THINNER EYELID/EYEBROW FOR 30 MM SAFETY EYE (MAKE 1 PER EYE)

*Approximately 1.5 in/4 cm wide by 0.5 in/1.5 cm tall*

*Body Color Yarn: Approximately 3 yd/2.75 m worsted/medium weight yarn per Eyelid*

1. Start with a long enough yarn tail to weave in, Ch 9, Turn, starting in the second Ch from hook, Sl St, SC, HDC 4, SC, Sl St [8]

Fasten off with an 18 in/45.5 cm yarn tail to use to attach eyelid and weave in ends.

## Assembly

1. Pin in place over the safety eye.

2. Verify placement. Eyelids can significantly affect the demeanor of your Monster. Make sure you are giving it the expression you desire.
3. Sew in place using the yarn tail to attach it along every edge that is touching the Monster's head/body. Weave in ends.

Cylinder with
Open Mouth and No
Legs, Open Mouth with
Humanlike Teeth, Thinner
Eyelid/Eyebrow for 30 mm
Safety Eyes, Cute Mitten Limbs,
Cute Footed Limbs, Teensy
Round Ears, Ridged Spiral
Horns with Accent Color,
Circle Belly

# EYELID FOR 40 MM SAFETY EYE (MAKE 1 PER EYE)

*Approximately 2.5 in/6.5 cm wide by 1 in/2.5 cm tall*

*Body Color Yarn: 4 yd/3.75 m worsted/medium weight yarn per Eyelid*

**1.** Start with a long enough yarn tail to weave in, Ch 11, Turn, starting in the second Ch from hook, SC 10, Ch 1, Turn [10]

**2.** BLO [Dec, SC 6, Dec], Ch 1, Turn [8]

**3.** Dec, SC 4, Dec [6]

Fasten off with an 18 in/45.5 cm yarn tail.

## Assembly

**1.** Pin in place over the safety eye.

**2.** Verify placement. Eyelids can significantly affect the demeanor of your Monster. Make sure you are giving it the expression you desire.

**3.** Sew in place using the yarn tail to attach it along every edge that is touching the Monster's head/body. Weave in ends.

# LARGE 2D CROCHETED EYE (MAKE 1 OR MORE)

*Approximately 2.25 in/5.5 cm in diameter*

*White Yarn: 4 yd/3.75 m worsted/medium weight yarn per Eye*

*Black Yarn: 2 yd/1.75 m worsted/medium weight yarn per Eye*

*Iris Color Yarn: 4 yd/3.75 m worsted/medium weight yarn per Eye*

1. Starting with Black Yarn for the pupil, SC 8 in a Magic Circle, Sl St to beginning stitch, Ch 1 [8]

2. Inc x 8, Sl St to beginning stitch, fasten off with a short yarn tail [16]

3. Attach the Iris Color Yarn to any stitch, (SC, Inc) x 8, Sl St to beginning stitch, Ch 1 [24]

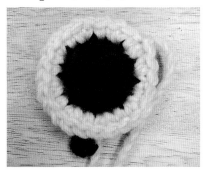

4. (SC, Inc, SC) x 8, Sl St to beginning stitch, fasten off with a short yarn tail [32]

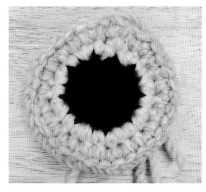

5. Attach the White Yarn to any BLO of any stitch on Row 4, BLO [(SC 3, Inc) x 8], Sl St to beginning stitch, fasten off with a 36 in/91.5 cm yarn tail [40]

6. Use the remaining White Yarn tail to create 1 to 3 "shine" spots on the eye; use the rest of the yarn tail to sew around the outer edge of the eye when attaching to the Body. This step is particularly nice to do if you do not intend to use an eyelid.

## Assembly

1. Pin to attach to the Monster Body.

2. Verify placement.

3. Using the yarn tail, sew the eye along every edge that is touching the Monster's head/body. Weave in ends.

# EYELID FOR LARGE 2D CROCHETED EYE (MAKE 1 PER EYE)

*Approximately 3 in/7.5 cm wide by 1.25 in/3 cm tall*

*Body Color Yarn: 6 yd/5.5 m worsted/medium weight yarn per Eyelid*

1. Start with a long enough yarn tail to weave in, Ch 15, starting in the second Ch from hook, HDC 14, Ch 1, Turn [14]

2. BLO [Dec, SC 10, Dec], Ch 1, Turn [12]

3. Dec, SC 8, Dec, Ch 1, Turn [10]

4. Dec, HDC 6, Dec [8]

Fasten off with an 18 in/45.5 cm yarn tail.

## Assembly

1. Pin in place on the body over the Large 2D Crocheted Eye.

2. Verify placement.

3. Sew in place using the yarn tail to sew along every edge that is touching the Monster's head/body. Weave in ends.

## MEDIUM 2D CROCHETED EYE (MAKE 1 OR MORE)

*Approximately 1.75 in/4.5 cm in diameter*

*White Yarn: 4 yd/3.75 m worsted/medium weight yarn per Eye*

*Black Yarn: 1 yd/1 m worsted/medium weight yarn per Eye*

*Iris Color Yarn: 2 yd/1.75 m worsted/medium weight yarn per Eye*

**1.** Starting with Black Yarn for the pupil, HDC 8 in a Magic Circle, Sl St to beginning stitch, fasten off with a short yarn tail [8]

**2.** Attach the Iris Color Yarn to any stitch, HDC Inc x 8, Sl St to beginning stitch, fasten off with a short yarn tail [16]

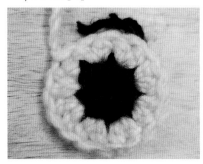

**3.** Attach the White Color Yarn to any BLO of any stitch on Row 2, BLO [Inc x 16], Sl St to beginning stitch, fasten off with a 36 in/ 91.5 cm yarn tail [32]

**4.** Use the remaining White Yarn tail to create 1 to 3 "shine" spots on the eye; use the rest of the yarn tail to sew around the outer edge of the eye when attaching to the Body. This step is particularly nice to do if you do not intend to use an eyelid.

### Assembly

**1.** Pin to the Monster Body; verify placement.

**2.** Use yarn tails to sew the eye to the body and weave in ends.

## EYELID FOR MEDIUM 2D CROCHETED EYE (MAKE 1 PER EYE)

*Approximately 2.5 in/6.5 cm wide by 1.25 in/3 cm tall*

*Body Color Yarn: 6 yd/5.5 m worsted/medium weight yarn per Eyelid*

**1.** Start with a long enough yarn tail to weave in, Ch 12, starting in the second Ch from hook, HDC 11, Ch 1, Turn [11]

**2.** BLO [Dec, SC 7, Dec], Ch 1, Turn [9]

**3.** Dec, SC 5, Dec, Ch 1, Turn [7]

**4.** Dec, HDC 3, Dec [5]

Fasten off with an 18 in/45.5 cm yarn tail.

### Assembly

**1.** Pin in place on the body over the Medium 2D Crocheted Eye.

**2.** Verify placement.

**3.** Sew in place using the yarn tail to sew to attach along every edge that is touching the Monster's head/body. Weave in ends.

Cylinder with Open Mouth and Legs, Open Mouth with Humanlike Teeth, Eye Stalks, Cute Mitten Limbs

# EYE STALKS AND EYE BUMPS (MAKE 1 OR MORE)

*Size for Eye Stalks: Approximately 5 in/13 cm tall, 1.5 in/4 cm wide at the base, 2.5 in/6.5 cm wide at the eye*

*Size for Eye Bumps: Approximately 2.5 in/6.5 cm wide/diameter*

## Choose 1 Eyeball Style:

* **Eyeball Style 1 with Crocheted Iris/Pupil**
  Black Yarn (pupil): Approximately 1 yd/1 m worsted/medium weight yarn per Eye
  Iris Color Yarn: Approximately 2 yd/1.75 m worsted/medium weight yarn per Eye
  White Yarn: Approximately 11 yd/10 m worsted/medium weight yarn per Eye
* **Eyeball Style 2 for Safety Eye**
  White Yarn: Approximately 12 yd/11 m worsted/medium weight yarn per Eye

## Choose Stalk or Bump:

* **Eye Stalk**
  Body Color Yarn: Approximately 25 yd/22.75 m worsted/medium weight yarn per Eye
* **Eye Bump**
  Body Color Yarn: 15 yd/13.75 m worsted/medium weight yarn per Eye Bump Socket

## STYLE 1: Eyeball with Crocheted Iris/Pupil (Make 1 per Eye Stalk or Eye Bump)

**1.** Starting with Black Yarn (pupil yarn color), SC 6 in Magic Circle, Sl St to beginning stitch [6]

Fasten off with a short yarn tail.

**2.** Attach Iris Color Yarn to the BLO of the first stitch of Row 1, BLO [Inc x 6], Sl St to beginning stitch [12]

Fasten off with a short yarn tail.

**3.** Attach White Yarn to the BLO of the first stitch of Row 2, BLO [(SC, Inc) x 6], Sl St to beginning stitch, Ch 1 [18]

**4.** (SC, Inc, SC) x 6, Sl St to beginning stitch, Ch 1 [24]

**5–8.** (4 rows of) SC 24, Sl St to beginning stitch, Ch 1 [24]

**9.** (SC, Dec, SC) x 6, Sl St to beginning stitch, Ch 1 [18]

Stuff the eyeball with fiberfill medium-firm to fill out the spherical shape as you finish the crochet work.

**10.** (SC, Dec) x 6, Sl St to beginning stitch, Ch 1 [12]

**11.** Dec x 6, Sl St to beginning stitch [6]

Fasten off with a 12 in/30.5 cm yarn tail.

### STYLE 2: Eyeball for Safety Eye (Make 1 per Eye Stalk or Eye Bump)

1. Starting with White Yarn, SC 6 in Magic Circle, Sl St to beginning stitch, Ch 1 [6]

> Do not pull the Magic Circle too tight, as you will need to insert the safety eye later.

2. Inc x 6, Sl St to beginning stitch, Ch 1 [12]

3. (SC, Inc) x 6, Sl St to beginning stitch, Ch 1 [18]

4. (SC, Inc, SC) x 6, Sl St to beginning stitch, Ch 1 [24]

5–8. (4 rows of) SC 24, Sl St to beginning stitch, Ch 1 [24]

> Insert 24 mm or 30 mm safety eye in the Row 1 Magic Circle. Sinker eyes work best for this purpose, as they sink into and are flush with the work, like a realistic eyeball. 24 mm safety eyes work well with light weight yarn or a light worsted; 30 mm safety eyes work well with worsted/medium weight yarn.

9. (SC, Dec, SC) x 6, Sl St to beginning stitch, Ch 1 [18]

> Stuff the eyeball with fiberfill medium-firm to fill out the spherical shape as you finish the crochet work.

10. (SC, Dec) x 6, Sl St to beginning stitch, Ch 1 [12]

11. Dec x 6, Sl St to beginning stitch [6]

Fasten off with a 12 in/30.5 cm yarn tail.

### Eye Stalk (Make 1 per Eyeball)

1. Starting with a 12–24-in /30.5–61 cm yarn tail, SC 6 in a Magic Circle, Sl St to beginning stitch, Ch 1 [6]

2. Inc x 6, Sl St to beginning stitch, Ch 1 [12]

3. (SC, Inc) x 6, Sl St to beginning stitch, Ch 1 [18]

4. (SC, Inc, SC) x 6, Sl St to beginning stitch, Ch 1 [24]

5. (SC 7, Inc) x 3, Sl St to beginning stitch, Ch 1 [27]

6. SC 27, Sl St to beginning stitch, Ch 1 [27]

7. SC 8, Ch 11, Skip 11 Stitches, SC 8, Sl St to beginning stitch, Ch 1 [27]

8. SC 8, SC 11 into the Ch stitches from Row 7, SC 8, Sl St to beginning stitch, Ch 1 [27]

9. SC 27, Sl St to beginning stitch, Ch 1 [27]

10. (SC 7, Dec) x 3, Sl St to beginning stitch, Ch 1 [24]

11. (SC, Dec, SC) x 6, Sl St to beginning stitch, Ch 1 [18]

12. (SC 2, Dec, SC 2) x 3, Sl St to beginning stitch, Ch 1 [15]

13. (SC 3, Dec) x 3, Sl St to beginning stitch, Ch 1 [12]

14–19. (6 rows of) SC 12, Sl St to beginning stitch, Ch 1 [12]

> If you want an even longer Eye Stalk, you can repeat Row 19 as desired. Alternatively, if you want a shorter Eye Stalk, you can eliminate any number of rows between Row 14 and Row 19.

20. (SC 3, Inc) x 3, Sl St to beginning stitch, Ch 1 [15]

21. (SC 2, Inc, SC 2) x 3, Sl St to beginning stitch [18]

Fasten off with a 24 in/61 cm yarn tail.

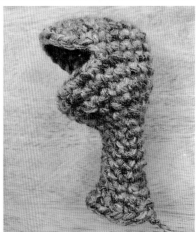

## Assembly

1. Pull the starting yarn tail of the Eye Stalk from the inside to the outside through the Magic Circle area; leave it hanging for now. Use the yarn tail from the Eyeball to sew the hole at the back shut, and weave in this end.

2. Insert the Eyeball into the top of the Eye Stalk and position the pupil side of the Eyeball to be looking out of the Eye Stalk.

3. Stuff the Eye Stalk medium-firm with fiberfill. For added stability, it is optional to insert a wire from the bottom, open side of the Eye Stalk, up into the Eyeball; leave a few inches of wire extending beyond the base of the Eye Stalk. Insert the wire into the body when pinning in place in the next row. This will help the Eye Stalk to be poseable, but it will not be child-safe.

4. Pin the Eye Stalk in place on the top of the Monster Body.

5. Sew to attach to the Body using the yarn tail at the base of the Eye Stalk. Use the Eye Stalk yarn tail from the top of the Eye Stalk to sew the Eyeball inside the Eye Stalk so it is not removable. Weave in ends.

## Eye Bump Socket (Make 1 per Eye Bump)

1. With Body Color Yarn, SC 6 in a Magic Circle, Sl St to beginning stitch, Ch 1 [6]

2. Inc x 6, Sl St to beginning stitch, Ch 1 [12]

3. (SC, Inc) x 6, Sl St to beginning stitch, Ch 1 [18]

4. (SC, Inc, SC) x 6, Sl St to beginning stitch, Ch 1 [24]

5. (SC 7, Inc) x 3, Sl St to beginning stitch, Ch 1 [27]

6–8. (3 rows of) SC 27, Sl St to beginning stitch, Ch 1 [27]

9. (SC 7, Dec) x 3, Sl St to beginning stitch [24]

Fasten off with a 24 in/61 cm yarn tail.

## Assembly

**1.** Sew the hole in the back of the Eyeball shut with the Eyeball's yarn tail and weave in the end.

**2.** Insert the Eyeball into the Eye Socket.

**3.** Pin the Eyeball and Socket to the top of the Monster's Body/head.

**4.** Using the yarn tail from the Eye Socket, sew the Eyeball and Socket to the Monster by using small whipstitches the whole way around the Eye Socket where it touches the Monster's Body, and anchor the Eyeball in place in the Socket; weave in the end.

Blob Body with No Mouth, 2D Open Mouth in Round Shape with Fangs (Upper), Eye Bumps, Medium Tongue, Row of Spikes

# MOUTHS FOR NO-MOUTH BODIES

## OPTIONS

2D Open Mouth: Round...151

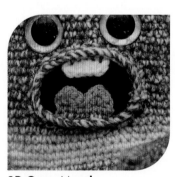

2D Open Mouth: Lima Bean...151

2D Open Mouth: Rectangular...151

Medium Rounded Overbite or Underbite...156

Small Rounded Overbite or Underbite...157

If you want to add metal spikes to any part of your Monster, go to page 172 for tips on how to do that.

Egg Shape with No Mouth and No Legs, 2D Open Mouth in Round Shape with Two Fangs (Upper) and Tongue (Lower), Eye Stalks, Four-toed Crouching Frog Rear Legs

Square with No Mouth and No Legs, 2D Open Mouth in Lima Bean Shape with Straight Row of Teeth (Upper) and Tongue (Lower), Small Nubbins Limbs, Nubbin Footed Limbs, Cat Ears, Medium Slight Curved Striped Horns

# 2D OPEN MOUTHS: ROUND, LIMA BEAN, OR RECTANGULAR, WITH TEETH OR TONGUE (MAKE 1)

*Round Mouth is approximately 3 in/7.5 cm wide, 2.75 in/7 cm tall*

*Lima Bean Mouth is approximately 3 in/7.5 cm wide, 2.25 in/5.5 cm tall*

*Rectangular Mouth is approximately 3 in/7.5 cm wide, 2.5 in/6.5 cm tall*

**Choose to make a Part 1:** Round Mouth, Lima Bean Mouth, or Rectangular Mouth.

### Part 1: Round Mouth

**Black Yarn: Approximately 7 yd/ 6.5 m worsted/medium weight yarn per Mouth**

1. Starting with a short yarn tail, SC 6 in a Magic Circle, Sl St to beginning stitch, Ch 1 [6]
2. Inc x 6, Sl St to beginning stitch, Ch 1 [12]
3. (SC, Inc) x 6, Sl St to beginning stitch, Ch 1 [18]
4. (SC, Inc, SC) x 6, Sl St to beginning stitch, Ch 1 [24]
5. (SC 3, Inc) x 6, Sl St to beginning stitch [30]

Fasten off with a 24 in/61 cm yarn tail.

### Part 1: Lima Bean Mouth

**Black Yarn: Approximately 7 yd/ 6.5 m worsted/medium weight yarn per Mouth**

1. Starting with a short yarn tail, Ch 9, starting in the second Ch from hook, SC 2, HDC Inc, HDC 2, HDC Inc, SC, Inc, continue to crochet around to the other side of the starting chain, SC 2, Dec, SC 2, SC in the same stitch as the first SC in this row, Sl St to beginning stitch, Ch 1 [17]
2. Inc, HDC 8, Inc x 2, SC 5, Inc, Sl St to beginning stitch, Ch 1 [21]
3. Inc, SC, HDC 2, HDC Inc, HDC, <HDC Dec>, HDC, HDC Inc, HDC 2, SC, Inc, HDC Inc x 3, SC 3, HDC Inc x 3, Sl St to beginning stitch, Ch 1 [32]

Fasten off with a 24 in/61 cm yarn tail.

### Part 1: Rectangular Mouth

**Black Yarn: Approximately 6 yd/ 5.5 m worsted/medium weight yarn per Mouth**

1. Starting with a short yarn tail, Ch 10, starting in the second Ch from hook, SC 9, Ch 1, Turn [9]
2-6. (5 rows of) SC 9, Ch 1, Turn [9]

OC means Original Chain and refers to the starting chain from Row 1.

**7.** SC 8, Inc, continue to crochet down the side of the piece, SC once per row for a total of 5 SC, continue to crochet across the opposite side of the OC, Inc, SC 7, Inc, continue to crochet up the side of the piece toward the start of this row, SC once per row for a total of 5 SC, SC in the same stitch as the first SC from this row, Sl St to beginning stitch [32]

Fasten off with a 24 in/61 cm yarn tail.

**Choose to make a Part 2:** Two Fang Teeth, Humanlike Teeth, or Straight Line of Teeth for use along the top/upper edge of the Mouth.

### Part 2: Two Fang Teeth (Upper)

**_White Yarn: Approximately 1 yd/ 1 m worsted/medium weight yarn per piece_**

**1.** Ch 4, starting in the second Ch from hook, Sl St 2, SC, Ch 6, Turn [3]

**2.** Starting in the second Ch from hook, Sl St 2, SC [3]

Fasten off with a 12 in/30.5 cm yarn tail.

### Part 2: Humanlike Teeth (Upper)

**_White Yarn: Approximately 1 yd/ 1 m worsted/medium weight yarn per piece_**

**1.** Ch 7, starting in the third Ch from hook, SC, Ch 1, Sl St in the same Ch as your last SC, Sl St in the next Ch, Ch 1, HDC in the same Ch as your last Sl St, Ch 1, Sl St in the same Ch as your last HDC, Sl St in the next available Ch) x 2, Ch 1, HDC in the same Ch as your last Sl St, Ch 1, Sl St in the same Ch as your last HDC, Sl St in the next available Ch, Ch 1, SC in the same Ch as your last Sl St, Ch 1, Sl St in the same Ch as your last SC [12]

Fasten off with a 12 in/30.5 cm yarn tail.

### Part 2: Straight Line of Teeth (Upper)

**_White Yarn: Approximately 2 yd/1.75 m worsted/medium weight yarn per piece_**

**1.** Starting with a short yarn tail, Ch 6, starting in the second Ch from hook, SC, HDC 3, SC, Sl St in the same Ch stitch as the last SC [6]

Fasten off with a 12 in/30.5 cm yarn tail.

**Choose to make a Part 3:** Tongue, Two Fang Teeth, or Humanlike Teeth for use along the bottom/lower edge of the Mouth.

### Part 3: Tongue (Lower)

**Tongue Color Yarn: Approximately 2 yd/1.75 m worsted/medium weight yarn per piece**

1. Starting with a short yarn tail, Ch 8, starting in the second Ch from hook, SC 7, Ch 1, Turn [7]
2. Skip 1 stitch, work 4 HDC in the next available stitch, Skip 1 stitch, Sl St, Skip 1 stitch, work 4 HDC in the next available stitch, Sl St [10]

Fasten off with a 12 in/30.5 cm yarn tail.

### Part 3: Two Fang Teeth (Lower)

**White Yarn: Approximately 2 yd/1.75 m worsted/medium weight yarn per piece**

1. Starting with a short yarn tail, Ch 4, starting in the second Ch from hook, Sl St 2, SC, Ch 8, Turn [3]
2. Starting in the second Ch from hook, Sl St 2, SC [3]

Fasten off with a 12 in/30.5 cm yarn tail.

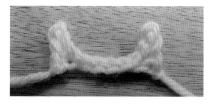

### Part 3: Humanlike Teeth (Lower)

**White Yarn: Approximately 2 yd/1.75 m worsted/medium weight yarn per piece**

1. Ch 9, starting in the third Ch from hook, SC, (Ch 1, Sl St in the same Ch as your last SC, (Sl St in the next available Ch) x 2, Ch 1, SC in the same Ch as your last Sl St) x 3, Ch 1, Sl St in the same chain as your last SC [14]

Fasten off with a 12 in/30.5 cm yarn tail.

Cylinder with No Mouth and Legs, 2D Open Mouth in Rectangular Shape with Humanlike Teeth (Upper and Lower), Eye Stalks, Bulb-ended Short Limbs

## Part 4: Outline for Round Mouth Using Body Color Yarn

### Body Color Yarn: Approximately 7 yd/6.5 m worsted/medium weight yarn per Mouth

1. With a long enough yarn tail to weave in later, attach the Body Color Yarn to the FLO of the first stitch of the final row of the Mouth/Part 1, starting in the same stitch, FLO [SC 5, holding one upper Part 2 piece against Part 1, SC 5 through both parts at the same time, continuing into Part 1 only, SC 9, holding one of the lower Part 3 pieces against the current piece, SC 7 through both parts at the same time, continuing into Part 1 only, SC 4], Sl St to beginning stitch, Ch 1 [30]

You will be crocheting through the OC of Parts 2 and 3 when joining them to Part 1. The short yarn tails from Parts 2 and 3 can be crocheted over when working Part 4. You can also hide them behind the mouth all together, when sewing to attach, without needing to specifically weave them in.

As you work Row 2 and Row 3, be careful to keep your tension even and on the slightly looser side. Do not make these Slip Stitches tight, as that would warp the shape of the Mouth and make it difficult to sew it flat to the Monster's head.

2. FLO [Sl St 30], Sl St to beginning stitch, Ch 1 [30]

3. Working into the BLO of Part 4 Row 1, BLO [Sl St 30], Sl St to beginning stitch [30]

Fasten off with a 36 in/91.5 cm yarn tail.

## Part 4: Outline for Lima Bean Mouth Using Body Color Yarn

***Body Color Yarn: Approximately 5 yd/4.5 m worsted/medium weight yarn per Mouth***

**1.** Attach the Body Color Yarn to the FLO of the first stitch of the final row of Mouth/Part 1, starting in the same stitch, FLO [SC 6, holding one upper Part 2 piece against Part 1, SC 5 through both parts at the same time, continuing into Part 1 only, SC 10, holding one lower Part 3 piece against the current piece, SC 7 through both parts at the same time, continuing into Part 1 only, SC 4], Sl St to beginning stitch, Ch 1 [32]

> You will be crocheting through the OC of Parts 2 and 3 when joining them to Part 1. The short yarn tails from Parts 2 and 3 can be crocheted over when working Part 4. You can also hide them behind the mouth all together, when sewing to attach, without needing to specifically weave them in.

**2.** FLO [Sl St 32], Sl St to beginning stitch, Ch 1 [32]

> As you work Row 2 and Row 3, be careful to keep your tension even and on the slightly looser side. Do not make these Slip Stitches tight, as that would warp the shape of the Mouth and make it difficult to sew it flat to the Monster's head.

**3.** Working into the BLO of Part 4 Row 1, BLO [Sl St 32], Sl St to beginning stitch [32]

Fasten off with a 36 in/91.5 cm yarn tail.

## Part 4: Outline for Rectangular Mouth Using Body Color Yarn

***Body Color Yarn: Approximately 5 yd/4.5 m worsted/medium weight yarn per Mouth***

**1.** Attach the Body Color Yarn to the FLO of the first stitch of the final row of the Mouth/Part 1, starting in the same stitch, FLO [SC 2, holding one upper Part 2 piece against Part 1, SC 5 through both parts at the same time, continuing into Part 1 only, SC 10, holding one lower Part 3 piece against the current piece, SC 7 through both parts at the same time, continuing into Part 1 only, SC 8], Sl St to beginning stitch, Ch 1 [32]

> You will be crocheting through the OC of Parts 2 and 3 when joining them to Part 1. The short yarn tails from Parts 2 and 3 can be crocheted over when working Part 4. You can also hide them behind the mouth all together, when sewing to attach, without needing to specifically weave them in.

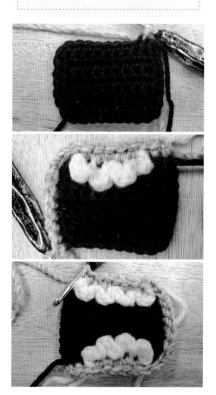

**2.** FLO [Sl St 32], Sl St to beginning stitch, Ch 1 [32]

> As you work Row 2 and Row 3, be careful to keep your tension even and on the slightly looser side. Do not make these Slip Stitches tight, as that would warp the shape of the Mouth and make it difficult to sew it flat to the Monster's head.

**3.** Working into the BLO of Part 4 Row 1, BLO [Sl St 32], Sl St to beginning stitch [32]

Fasten off with a 36 in/91.5 cm yarn tail.

## Assembly for All Shape Mouths

**1.** Use the Part 2 (upper) yarn tail to anchor and sew Part 2 to Part 1. Weave in or knot the end on the back of the Mouth piece.

**2.** Use the Part 3 (lower) yarn tail to sew and anchor Part 3 to Part 1. Weave in or knot the end on the back of the Mouth piece.

**3.** Pin the Mouth to attach to the Monster Body.

**4.** Once you are satisfied with placement, use the Mouth (Black) yarn tail to attach the black center of the Mouth to the Monster Body and anchor it in place.

**5.** Use the Body Color Yarn tail to sew to attach around the outer edge of the piece; weave in ends.

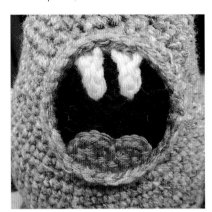

# MEDIUM ROUNDED OVERBITE OR UNDERBITE (MAKE 1)

*Approximately 3.5 in/9 cm wide, 2 in/5 cm tall*

*Body Color Yarn: Approximately 8 yd/7.25 m worsted/medium weight yarn per mouth*

**1.** Starting with a short yarn tail, SC 6 in a Magic Circle, Sl St to beginning stitch, Ch 1 [6]

**2.** Inc x 6, Sl St to beginning stitch, Ch 1 [12]

**3.** (SC, Inc) x 6, Sl St to beginning stitch, Ch 1 [18]

**4.** (SC 5, Inc) x 3, Sl St to beginning stitch, Ch 1 [21]

**5.** (SC 3, Inc, SC 3) x 3, Sl St to beginning stitch, Ch 1 [24]

**6.** Crocheting just half a row, (SC, Inc) x 6 [18]

Fasten off with a 24 in/61 cm yarn tail.

## Assembly

**1.** Fold the piece in half, pressing it flat so that Row 6 is visible along the front edge of the mouth.

**2.** Pin to attach to the Monster's face/body as an underbite or overbite with Row 6 being the side of the Mouth that will be sewn to the Body, and the folded edge acting as the lip for the underbite or the overbite. When sewing to the Body, sew only along Row 6, leaving the fold of the Mouth unsewn. Weave in ends.

# SMALL ROUNDED OVERBITE OR UNDERBITE (MAKE 1)

*Approximately 3 in/7.5 cm wide, 1.5 in/4 cm tall*

*Body Color Yarn: 7 yd/6.5 m worsted/medium weight yarn*

**1.** Starting with a short yarn tail, SC 6 in a Magic Circle, Sl St to beginning stitch, Ch 1 [6]

**2.** Inc x 6, Sl St to beginning stitch, Ch 1 [12]

**3.** (SC, Inc) x 6, Sl St to beginning stitch, Ch 1 [18]

**4.** (SC 5, Inc) x 3, Sl St to beginning stitch, Ch 1 [21]

**5.** Stitching only a partial row, SC 3, Inc, SC 6, Inc [13]

Fasten off with a 24 in/61 cm yarn tail.

### Assembly

**1.** Fold the piece in half, pressing it flat so Row 5 is visible along the front edge of the Mouth.

**2.** Pin to attach to the Monster's face/body as an underbite or overbite with Row 5 being the side of the Mouth that will be sewn to the Body and the folded edge acting as the lip for the underbite or the overbite. When sewing to the Body, sew only along Row 5, leaving the fold of the Mouth unsewn.

Sphere with No Mouth, Medium Rounded Underbite, Short Arms with Two Fingers, Tiny Little Footed Legs, Medium Curved Horns, Individual Small Short Fangs, Long Thin Tongue

**Square with No Mouth and Legs, Small Rounded Overbite, Wide Flat-ended Long Limbs, Large Curved Horns, Four Humanlike Teeth**

# FEET

## OPTIONS

Rounded Feet...162

Big-toed Feet...164

Large Rounded Feet...165

Pointy-toed Feet...167

Small Feet with Tiny Nubbin Toes...168

For more information on how to add metal spikes to any of these Feet options, go to page 172 for tips on how to do that.

Egg Shape with Overbite and No Legs, Small Short Limbs, Rounded Feet, Small Half Circle Ears, Mohawk, Small Tongue

# ROUNDED FEET (MAKE 2)

*Approximately 3.25 in/8.5 cm long from base to tip, 1.5 in/4 cm wide at the base, 2 in/5 cm wide at the widest part*

*Main Body Color Yarn: Approximately 13 yd/12 m worsted/medium weight yarn per Foot*

**1.** Ch 5, Turn, starting in the second Ch from hook, SC 3, Triple SC Inc in the last Ch stitch, keep crocheting around to the opposite side of the OC stitches, SC 2, Inc in the same stitch as the first SC you worked in this row, Sl St to beginning stitch, Ch 1 [10]

**2.** (SC 4, Inc) x 2, Sl St to beginning stitch, Ch 1 [12]

**3.** (SC 3, Inc) x 3, Sl St to beginning stitch, Ch 1 [15]

**4–6.** (3 rows of) SC 15, Sl St to beginning stitch, Ch 1 [15]

**7.** (SC 4, Inc) x 3, Sl St to beginning stitch, Ch 1 [18]

**8–10.** (3 rows of) SC 18, Sl St to beginning stitch, Ch 1 [18]

**11.** (SC 5, Inc) x 3, Sl St to beginning stitch, Ch 1 [21]

**12.** SC 21, Sl St to beginning stitch, Ch 1 [21]

**13.** (SC 5, Dec) x 3, Sl St to beginning stitch, Ch 1 [18]

> Stuff the piece medium-firm with fiberfill.

**14.** (SC, Dec) x 6, Sl St to beginning stitch, Ch 1 [12]

**15.** Dec x 6, Sl St to beginning stitch [6]

Fasten off with a 24 in/61 cm yarn tail.

This photo shows the side of the foot with the Sl St, Ch 1 join seam.

## Assembly

**1.** Use the yarn tail to sew the hole shut.

**2.** Pin the Foot in place on the bottom of the Monster's Body.

**3.** Once you are satisfied with placement, sew the Foot to the Body with the remaining yarn tail; weave in ends.

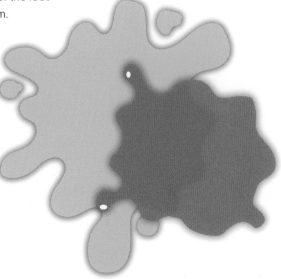

Egg Shape with Underbite and No Legs, Small Short Limbs, Big-toed Feet, Big Round Horns, Two Small Fangs

# BIG-TOED FEET (MAKE 2)

*Approximately 5.5 in/14 cm long from heel to toe, 4.5 in/11.5 cm wide across the toes, 2.25 in/5.5 cm wide across the heel, 1 in/2.5 cm tall*

*Main Body Color Yarn: Approximately 72 yd/65.75 m worsted/medium weight yarn per Foot*

## Part 1: Big Toe (Make 1 per Foot)

1. SC 6 in Magic Circle, Sl St to beginning stitch, Ch 1 [6]
2. (SC, Inc) x 3, Sl St to beginning stitch, Ch 1 [9]
3. (SC, Inc, SC) x 3, Sl St to beginning stitch, Ch 1 [12]
4–6. (3 rows of) SC 12, Sl St to beginning stitch, Ch 1 [12]
7. (SC, Dec, SC) x 3, Sl St to beginning stitch, Ch 1 [9]
8. SC 9, Sl St to beginning stitch [9]

Fasten off with a short yarn tail.

## Part 2: Small Toes and Foot

Make 3 Small Toes per Foot, Rows 1–6, and then complete the Foot following the rest of the instructions.

1. SC 6 in Magic Circle, Sl St to beginning stitch, Ch 1 [6]
2. (SC, Inc) x 3, Sl St to beginning stitch, Ch 1 [9]
3–5. (3 rows of) SC 9, Sl St to beginning stitch, Ch 1 [9]
6. (SC, Dec) x 3, Sl St to beginning stitch [6]

For the First and Second Small Toe, fasten off with a short yarn tail.

For the Third Small Toe, continue to Row 7 in the next column.

7. Ch 1, SC 2, starting into the first stitch on the next Small Toe, SC 3, starting into the first stitch on the next Small Toe, SC 3, starting into the first stitch on the Big Toe, SC 9, continuing into the next available stitch on the closest Small Toe, SC 3, continuing into the next available stitch on the next Small Toe, SC 3, continuing into the next available stitch on the last Small Toe, SC 4, Sl St to beginning stitch, Ch 1 [27]

> Do not crochet into the "Sl St, Ch 1" join space on any of the toes.

8–9. (2 rows of) SC 27, Sl St to beginning stitch, Ch 1 [27]
10. (SC 7, Dec) x 3, Sl St to beginning stitch, Ch 1 [24]

11–12. (2 rows of) SC 24, Sl St to beginning stitch, Ch 1 [24]
13. (SC 3, Dec, SC 3) x 3, Sl St to beginning stitch, Ch 1 [21]
14–15. (2 rows of) SC 21, Sl St to beginning stitch, Ch 1 [21]
16. (SC 5, Dec) x 3, Sl St to beginning stitch, Ch 1 [18]

> Stuff the Toes and front of the Foot with fiberfill medium-firm. It is optional to include some kind of weight(s) in the Foot to help with stability. Stuff the rest of the Foot lightly as you crochet.

17–18. (2 rows of) SC 18, Sl St to beginning stitch, Ch 1 [18]
19. (SC, Dec) x 6, Sl St to beginning stitch, Ch 1 [12]
20. Dec x 6, Sl St to beginning stitch [6]

Fasten off with a 24 in/61 cm yarn tail.

## Assembly

1. Use the yarn tail to sew the hole shut.

2. Pin the Foot in place on the bottom of the Monster's Body.

3. Once you are satisfied with placement, sew the Foot to the Body with the remaining yarn tail; weave in ends.

# LARGE ROUNDED FEET (MAKE 2)

***Approximately 4 in/10 cm long from heel to toes, 3.5 in/9 cm at the widest part of the foot, 2 in/5 cm wide at the heel***

***Main Body Color Yarn: Approximately 28 yd/25.5 m worsted/medium weight yarn per Foot***

1. Ch 9, Turn, starting in the second Ch from hook, SC 7, Triple SC Inc in the last Ch stitch, keep crocheting around to the opposite side of the OC stitches, SC 6, Inc in the same stitch as the first SC you worked in this row, Sl St to beginning stitch, Ch 1 [18]

2. (SC 8, Inc) x 2, Sl St to beginning stitch, Ch 1 [20]

3. (SC 2, Inc, SC 2) x 4, Sl St to beginning stitch, Ch 1 [24]

4. SC 24, Sl St to beginning stitch, Ch 1 [24]

5. (SC 3, Inc) x 6, Sl St to beginning stitch, Ch 1 [30]

6–9. (4 rows of) SC 30, Sl St to beginning stitch, Ch 1 [30]

10. (SC 4, Dec, SC 4) x 3, Sl St to beginning stitch, Ch 1 [27]

11. SC 27, Sl St to beginning stitch, Ch 1 [27]

12. (SC 7, Dec) x 3, Sl St to beginning stitch, Ch 1 [24]

13. SC 24, Sl St to beginning stitch, Ch 1 [24]

14. (SC 3, Dec, SC 3) x 3, Sl St to beginning stitch, Ch 1 [21]

15. SC 21, Sl St to beginning stitch, Ch 1 [21]

16. (SC 5, Dec) x 3, Sl St to beginning stitch, Ch 1 [18]

17. SC 18, Sl St to beginning stitch, Ch 1 [18]

> Stuff the piece medium-firm with fiberfill.

18. SC 18, Sl St to beginning stitch [18]

Fasten off with a 24 in/61 cm yarn tail.

Continue to assembly on the next page.

## Assembly

**1.** Press the foot flat, as shown.

**2.** Use the yarn tail to sew the open end of the foot shut.

**3.** It is optional to use an accent color to sew 2 lines along the front of the foot to create the impression of having 3 toes, as shown.

**4.** Pin in place on the bottom of the Monster Body.

**5.** Once you are satisfied with placement, sew to attach using the yarn tail and weave in ends.

Egg Shape with Open Mouth and No Legs, Open Mouth with Buck Teeth (Lower), Small Short Rounded Limbs, Large Rounded Feet, Triangular Scales, Curved Dragon/Dinosaur Tail, Fin Ears, Large Ridged Belly

# POINTY-TOED FEET (MAKE 2)

*Approximately 5.5 in/14 cm long from base to toes, 2 in/5 cm wide at the base, 4 in/10 cm wide at the toes, toes are 1.5 in/4 cm long from base to tip*

*Main Body Color Yarn: Approximately 30 yd/27.5 m worsted/medium weight yarn per Foot*

Make 3 Small Toes per Foot, Rows 1–7, and then complete the foot following the rest of the instructions.

1. SC 4 in Magic Circle, Sl St to beginning stitch, Ch 1 [4]
2. (SC, Inc) x 2, Sl St to beginning stitch, Ch 1 [6]
3. SC 6, Sl St to beginning stitch, Ch 1 [6]
4. (SC, Inc, SC) x 2, Sl St to beginning stitch, Ch 1 [8]
5. SC 8, Sl St to beginning stitch, Ch 1 [8]
6. (SC 3, Inc) x 2, Sl St to beginning stitch, Ch 1 [10]
7. SC 10, Sl St to beginning stitch [10]

For the first and second Small Toe, fasten off after Row 7 with a short yarn tail.

For the third Small Toe, continue to Row 8.

If you want to add metal spikes to these Toes, go to page 172 for tips on how to do that.

8. Ch 1, SC 3, starting in the first stitch of Toe 2, SC 5, starting in the first stitch of Toe 1, SC 10, continuing into the next available stitch on Toe 2, SC 5, continuing into the next available stitch on Toe 3, SC 7, Sl St to beginning stitch, Ch 1 [30]

Do not crochet into the "Sl St, Ch 1" join space on any of the Toes.

9–10. (2 rows of) SC 30, Sl St to beginning stitch, Ch 1 [30]
11. (SC 4, Dec, SC 4) x 3, Sl St to beginning stitch, Ch 1 [27]
12. SC 27, Sl St to beginning stitch, Ch 1 [27]
13. (SC 7, Dec) x 3, Sl St to beginning stitch, Ch 1 [24]
14. SC 24, Sl St to beginning stitch, Ch 1 [24]
15. (SC 3, Dec, SC 3) x 3, Sl St to beginning stitch, Ch 1 [21]
16. SC 21, Sl St to beginning stitch, Ch 1 [21]
17. (SC 5, Dec) x 3, Sl St to beginning stitch, Ch 1 [18]

Stuff the Toes and front of the Foot with fiberfill medium-firm. Stuff the rest of the Foot lightly as you crochet.

18. SC 18, Sl St to beginning stitch, Ch 1 [18]

19. (SC 2, Dec, SC 2) x 3, Sl St to beginning stitch, Ch 1 [15]
20. SC 15, Sl St to beginning stitch, Ch 1 [15]
21. (SC 3, Dec) x 3, Sl St to beginning stitch, Ch 1 [12]
22. Dec x 6, Sl St to beginning stitch [6]

Fasten off with a 24 in/61 cm yarn tail.

## Assembly

1. Use the yarn tail to sew the hole shut.
2. Pin the Foot in place on the bottom of the Monster's Body.

3. Once you are satisfied with placement, sew the Foot to the Body with the remaining yarn tail; weave in ends.

# SMALL FEET WITH TINY NUBBIN TOES (MAKE 2)

*Approximately 0.75 in/2 cm long from base to the sole of the foot, 2 in/5 cm wide at the sole of the foot, 1.25 in/3 cm wide at the base of the foot*

*Main Body Color Yarn: Approximately 18 yd/16.5 m worsted/medium weight yarn per Foot*

1. SC 6 in Magic Circle, Sl St to beginning stitch, Ch 1 [6]

2. Inc x 6, Sl St to beginning stitch, Ch 1 [12]

3. (SC, Inc) x 6, Sl St to beginning stitch, Ch 1 [18]

4. (SC, Inc, SC) x 6, Sl St to beginning stitch, Ch 1 [24]

5. SC 8, (Bobble, SC) x 4, SC 8, Sl St to beginning stitch, Ch 1 [24]

Work the Bobble as follows:

YO, insert your hook into the next available stitch, YO, pull up,

YO, pull through 2 loops,

YO, insert your hook into the same stitch, YO, pull up,

YO, pull through 2 loops,

YO, insert your hook into the same stitch, YO, pull up,

YO, pull through 2 loops,

YO, insert your hook into the same stitch, YO, pull up,

YO, pull through 2 loops,

YO, pull through all remaining loops

6. SC 24, Sl St to beginning stitch, Ch 1 [24]

7. SC 8, Dec x 4, SC 8, Sl St to beginning stitch, Ch 1 [20]

8. SC 6, Dec x 4, SC 6, Sl St to beginning stitch, Ch 1 [16]

9–10. (2 rows of) SC 16, Sl St to beginning stitch, Ch 1 [16]

Fasten off with an 18 in/45.5 cm yarn tail.

## Assembly

1. Stuff the Foot medium-firm with fiberfill.

2. Pin in place on the Monster's Body.

3. Once you are satisfied with placement, sew to attach the Foot using the yarn tail; weave in ends.

If you want to add metal spikes to any part of your Monster, go to page 172 for tips on how to do that.

Sphere with Overbite, Small Short Limbs, Pointy-toed Feet, Medium Curved Horns, Two Small Uneven Pointy Fangs

Eyeball Monster Main Body/Eye with Safety Eye, Eyeball Monster Eyelid, Small Feet with Tiny Nubbin Toes, Tiny Curved Horns

# LIMBS

## OPTIONS

**Short Rounded Limbs...174**

**Long Rounded Limbs...174**

**Three-fingered Hand with Elbow and Arm...177**

**Two-toed Feet with Knees and Legs...180**

**Four-toed Crouching Frog Rear Legs...185**

**Spider Legs...188**

**Small Cone Limbs...193**

**Large Cone Limbs...194**

**Wide Flat-ended Short Limbs...196**

**Wide Flat-ended Long Limbs...197**

**Three-fingered Wide Limbs...198**

**Bulb-ended Short Limbs...200**

**Bulb-ended Long Limbs...202**

**Cute Mitten Limbs...202**

**Cute Footed Limbs...205**

**Small Nubbins Limbs...208**

**Large Nubbins Limbs...209**

**Nubbin Footed Limbs...211**

**Large-footed Bent Limbs...212**

**Small Short Limbs...215**

**Small Short Rounded Limbs...216**

**Crouching Rounded Hind Legs...218**

**Curved Arms...219**

**Tiny Little Arms...221**

**Thick Short Arms with Claws...223**

**Thin Arms with Two Fingers...224**

**Short Arms with Two Fingers...227**

**Three-toed Dangling Legs...229**

**Squarish Short Limbs...232**

**Squarish Long Limbs...232**

**Tiny Little Footed Legs...233**

**ALL LIMBS -** It is entirely optional to use metal spikes that screw in place as claws on the ends of any Toes or Fingers. This step should be done before you get too far along on the Toes/Fingers. To use metal spikes as claws, place the screw through the inside of the magic circle at the end of the Toe or Finger, and twist the spike (claw) onto the end of the screw. Tighten it as much as possible. Once it is fully placed, you can cement it in place by putting some craft glue inside the Toe/Finger on top of the screw head to fasten it more permanently. If the screw won't stay in place because the stitches are too open, you can use a washer, or you can fashion a washer from a small piece of plastic canvas, to prevent the screw from slipping through the stitches. Note that use of metal spikes makes the Monster unsafe for children.

Egg Shape with Underbite and No Legs, Short Rounded Limbs, Feet with Big Toes, Big Round Horns, Individual Medium Fangs

# SHORT ROUNDED LIMBS (MAKE 2)

*(RECOMMENDED AS ARMS OR SHORTER LEGS)*

*Approximately 6 in/15 cm long, 2 in/5 cm wide at the widest point, 1 in/2.5 cm wide at the base*

*Main Body Color Yarn: Approximately 20 yd/18.25 m worsted/medium weight yarn per Limb*

1. SC 6 in Magic Circle, Sl St to beginning stitch, Ch 1 [6]

2. Inc x 6, Sl St to beginning stitch, Ch 1 [12]

3. (SC, Inc) x 6, Sl St to beginning stitch, Ch 1 [18]

4–8. (5 rows of) SC 18, Sl St to beginning stitch, Ch 1 [18]

9. (SC, Dec) x 6, Sl St to beginning stitch, Ch 1 [12]

10–13. (4 rows of) SC 12, Sl St to beginning stitch, Ch 1 [12]

> Stuff the piece medium-firm with fiberfill.

14. (SC 2, Dec, SC 2) x 2, Sl St to beginning stitch, Ch 1 [10]

15–17. (3 rows of) SC 10, Sl St to beginning stitch, Ch 1 [10]

18. (SC 3, Dec) x 2, Sl St to beginning stitch, Ch 1 [8]

19–23. (5 rows of) SC 8, Sl St to beginning stitch, Ch 1 [8]

24. SC 8, Sl St to beginning stitch [8]

Fasten off with a 24 in/61 cm yarn tail.

## Assembly

1. Stuff the end of the limb medium-firm with fiberfill, but leave the upper part of the limb lightly stuffed or not stuffed at all.

2. Pin in place on the body.

3. Once you are satisfied with placement, sew to the body using the yarn tail; weave in ends.

# LONG ROUNDED LIMBS (MAKE 2)

*(RECOMMENDED AS LEGS OR EXTRA-LONG ARMS)*

*Approximately 8 in/20.5 cm long, 2.25 in/5.5 cm wide at the widest point, 1.25 in/3 cm wide at the base*

*Main Body Color Yarn: Approximately 34 yd/31 m worsted/medium weight yarn per Limb*

1. SC 6 in Magic Circle, Sl St to beginning stitch, Ch 1 [6]

2. Inc x 6, Sl St to beginning stitch, Ch 1 [12]

3. (SC, Inc) x 6, Sl St to beginning stitch, Ch 1 [18]

4. (SC, Inc, SC) x 6, Sl St to beginning stitch, Ch 1 [24]

5–10. (6 rows of) SC 24, Sl St to beginning stitch, Ch 1 [24]

11. (SC 2, Dec, SC 2) x 4, Sl St to beginning stitch, Ch 1 [20]

12–13. (2 rows of) SC 20, Sl St to beginning stitch, Ch 1 [20]

14. (SC 3, Dec) x 4, Sl St to beginning stitch, Ch 1 [16]

15–16. (2 rows of) SC 16, Sl St to beginning stitch, Ch 1 [16]

> Stuff the piece medium-firm with fiberfill and continue to stuff as you crochet. For a floppier limb, leave the upper end of the limb unstuffed or only lightly stuffed.

17. (SC, Dec, SC) x 4, Sl St to beginning stitch, Ch 1 [12]

18–32. (15 rows of) SC 12, Sl St to beginning stitch, Ch 1 [12]

**33.** SC 12, Sl St to beginning stitch [12]

Fasten off with a 24 in/61 cm yarn tail.

## Assembly

**1.** Finish stuffing with fiberfill.

**2.** Pin in place on the Monster Body.

**3.** Once you are satisfied with placement, sew to to the Body using the yarn tail.

**4.** Weave in ends.

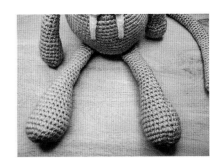

**Egg Shape with Overbite and No Legs, Short Rounded Limbs, Long Rounded Limbs, Cat Tail, Cat Ears, Two Walrus Tusks, Muzzle for Egg Shape Body with Overbite, Tiny Pointed Claws**

Cylinder with No Mouth and No Legs, 2D Open Mouth in Lima Bean Shape with Straight Teeth (Upper) and Tongue (Lower), Eye Stalks, Three-fingered Hand with Elbow and Arm, Two-toed Feet with Knees and Legs

If you want to add metal spikes to any part of your Monster, go to page 172 for tips on how to do that.

# THREE-FINGERED HAND WITH ELBOW AND ARM (MAKE 2)

*Approximately 10 in/25.5 cm long from base to fingertip, 1 in/2.5 cm wide at base*

*Main Body Color Yarn: Approximately 50 yd/45.75 m worsted/medium weight yarn total for 2 Arms*

*Optional: Strong wire*

## Part 1: Elbow (Make 1 per Arm)

1. SC 6 in Magic Circle, Sl St to beginning stitch, Ch 1 [6]
2. (SC, Inc) x 3, Sl St to beginning stitch [9]

Fasten off with a short yarn tail.

## Part 2: Thumb (Make 1 per Arm)

1. SC 6 in Magic Circle, Sl St to beginning stitch, Ch 1 [6]
2. (SC, Inc, SC) x 2, Sl St to beginning stitch, Ch 1 [8]
3. SC 8, Sl St to beginning stitch, Ch 1 [8]
4. (SC, Dec, SC) x 2, Sl St to beginning stitch, Ch 1 [6]
5. SC 4, Dec, Sl St to beginning stitch, Ch 1 [5]
6. SC 5, Sl St to beginning stitch, Ch 1 [5]
7. SC 5, Sl St to beginning stitch [5]

Fasten off with a short yarn tail.

## Part 3: Finger, Hand, and Arm (Make 2 Fingers per Arm, Rows 1–8, and then complete the Arm following the rest of the instructions.)

1. SC 6 in Magic Circle, Sl St to beginning stitch, Ch 1 [6]
2. (SC, Inc, SC) x 2, Sl St to beginning stitch, Ch 1 [8]
3. SC 8, Sl St to beginning stitch, Ch 1 [8]
4. (SC, Dec, SC) x 2, Sl St to beginning stitch, Ch 1 [6]
5. SC 4, Dec, Sl St to beginning stitch, Ch 1 [5]
6–7. (2 rows of) SC 5, Sl St to beginning stitch, Ch 1 [5]
8. SC 5, Sl St to beginning stitch [5]

Fasten off the first Finger with a short yarn tail.

Repeat Rows 1–8 for the second Finger, and then Ch 1 and continue on to Row 9 for the rest of the Hand/Arm instructions.

> If you want to add metal spikes to these Fingers, go to page 172 for tips on how to do that.

9. SC, starting in the first stitch on the first Finger, SC 5 around the first Finger, continuing into the first available stitch on the second Finger, SC 4, Sl St to beginning stitch, Ch 1 [10]

> In this row you will work into the available stitches by inserting your hook as normal from the right side/outside to the inside/wrong side to complete your stitches. Be careful not to work into the "Sl St, Ch 1" join space.

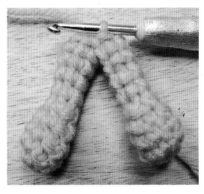

10. SC 10, Sl St to beginning stitch, Ch 1 [10]

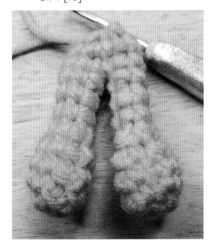

**11.** SC 5, hold the Thumb piece against your current row (right sides together), working through both pieces at the same time, SC 2, and then, working into the current row only, SC 3, Sl St to beginning stitch, Ch 1 [10]

When you work through the Thumb in this row, you will insert your hook through the inside/wrong side to the outside/right side of the Thumb and then through the outside/right side to the inside/wrong side of the Hand. Be careful not to work into the "Sl St, Ch 1" join space.

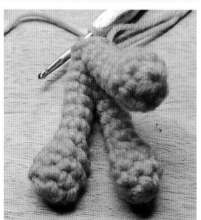

**12.** SC 5, working into the Thumb SC 3, continuing into the Hand SC 3, Sl St to beginning stitch, Ch 1 [11]

In this row you will work around the available stitches by inserting your hook as normal from the right side/outside to the inside/wrong side to complete your stitches. Ignore the stitches from the previous row that were used to connect the Thumb to the Hand. Be careful not to work into the "Sl St, Ch 1" join space.

**13.** Dec, SC 9, continue in Spiral (do not Sl St or Ch 1 join) [10]

**14.** SC 10 [10]

**15.** SC 3, Dec, SC 2, Dec, SC [8]

**16–27.** (12 rows of) SC 8 [8]

**28.** SC 3, hold the Elbow piece against your current row (right sides together), working through both pieces at the same time, SC 3, SC 2 through the arm only [8]

When you work through the Elbow in this row, you will insert your hook through the inside/wrong side to the outside/right side of the Elbow and then through the outside/right side to the inside/wrong side of the Arm. See this video for more information on this technique: https://youtu.be/paLzIAi--vk

**29.** SC 2, start a decrease in the last available stitch on the Arm and complete the decrease in the first available stitch on the Elbow, SC 4, start a decrease in the last available stitch on the Elbow and complete the decrease in the first available stitch on the Arm, SC [9]

> In this row you will work into the available stitches by inserting your hook as normal from the right side/outside to the inside/ wrong side to complete your stitches. Ignore the stitches from the previous row that were used to connect the Elbow to the Arm.

**30–44.** (15 rows of) SC 9 [9]

Fasten off with an 18 in/45.5 cm yarn tail.

## Assembly

**1.** For assembly without wire, stuff the Arm lightly with fiberfill, and pin to attach to the Body of the Monster. Once you are satisfied with placement, sew to attach with a yarn tail. Weave in ends. All wire instructions are optional. If you add wire, the piece will no longer be safe for small children. Take 2 pieces of wire (18 in/45.5 cm paper-wrapped stem wire or similar recommended; err on the side of heavier wire if you want the limbs to be poseable), bend the end over on itself by an inch or two, secure it to itself with duct tape on the first piece of wire. Cut the second wire in half and repeat the same instruction (bend the end over on itself, secure with duct tape) to both of those shorter wire pieces.

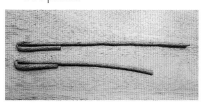

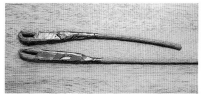

**2.** Line up one of the shorter pieces with the longest piece of wire. Make sure the folded ends of the wire are the same height and secure the two wires to each other with duct tape. These wires will be inserted into the two longest Fingers.

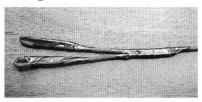

**3.** Insert these wires into the two longest Fingers in the Hand.

**4.** Take the last short wire, scrunch up the crocheted arm to make it as short as possible on the wires you've inserted all the way into the two longest Fingers, and insert the remaining wire so that it goes into the "thumb" of the Hand. Keeping the Arm scrunched up on the wire, use duct tape to secure the thumb wire to the rest of the Arm wire. Pull the Arm back in place over the wire.

**5.** Trim the longest wire to be slightly shorter than the Monster Body you will insert the wire into. For the large Eyeball Monster Body, that means no longer than about 3 in/7.5 cm.

**6.** Insert the arm wire into the Body; repeat for the second Arm. Pin in place.

**7.** Sew to attach once you have finalized placement; weave in yarn tails.

# TWO-TOED FEET WITH KNEES AND LEGS (MAKE 2)

*Approximately 10 in/25.5 cm long from base to toe, 1 in/2.5 cm wide at base*

*Main Body Color Yarn: Approximately 52 yd/47.5 m worsted/medium weight yarn total for 2 Legs*

*Optional: Strong wire*

### Part 1: Knee (Make 1 per Leg)

**1.** SC 6 in Magic Circle, Sl St to beginning stitch, Ch 1 [6]

**2.** Inc x 6, Sl St to beginning stitch [12]

Fasten off with a short yarn tail.

### Part 2: Heel (Make 1 per Leg)

**1.** SC 6 in Magic Circle, Sl St to beginning stitch, Ch 1 [6]

**2.** Inc x 6, Sl St to beginning stitch [12]

Fasten off with a short yarn tail.

## Part 3: Toe, Foot, and Leg (Make 2 Toes per Leg, Rows 1–4, and then complete the Leg following the rest of the instructions.)

**1.** SC 5 in Magic Circle, Sl St to beginning stitch, Ch 1 [5]

**2.** SC 2, Inc, SC 2, Sl St to beginning stitch, Ch 1 [6]

**3.** SC 6, Sl St to beginning stitch, Ch 1 [6]

**4.** SC 3, <Dec>, SC 3, Sl St to beginning stitch [7]

> "<Dec>" is a stitch that is defined in the Glossary.

Fasten off the first Toe with a short yarn tail.

For the second Toe, repeat Rows 1–4, and then Ch 1, and continue on to Row 5 for the rest of the Foot/Leg instructions.

**5.** SC 2, working into the 6th stitch on the first Toe and continuing around, SC 2, Inc, SC 4, continuing into the first available stitch on the second Toe, SC 4, Inc, Sl St to beginning stitch, Ch 1 [16]

> In Row 5, you will work into the available stitches by inserting your hook as normal from the right side/outside to the inside/wrong side to complete your stitches. Be careful not to work into the "Sl St, Ch 1" join space.

**6–7.** (2 rows of) SC 16, Sl St to beginning stitch, Ch 1 [16]

**8.** SC 6, Dec, SC 5, Dec, SC, Sl St to beginning stitch, Ch 1 [14]

**9.** SC 14, Sl St to beginning stitch, Ch 1 [14]

**10.** Hold the Heel piece against your current row (right sides together), SC 4 through both pieces at the same time, SC 9 through the foot/current row only, *do not* Sl St or Ch 1, continue in spiral [13]

> Row 10 ends 1 stitch early. You will make 13 stitches in Row 10, but you will have 14 stitches available to work into in Row 11.

> If you want to add metal spikes to these Limbs, go to page 172 for tips on how to do that.

> When you work into a Heel piece, insert your hook into the wrong side/inside of the Heel piece first; then insert your hook into the right side/outside of the limb next and complete a SC through both at the same time. Do not work into the Sl St join from the joint piece. See this video for more information on this technique: https://youtu.be/paLzIAi--vk

**11.** Start a decrease in the last available stitch on the Foot and complete the decrease in the first available stitch on the Heel, SC 6, start a decrease in the last available stitch on the Heel, and complete the decrease in the first available stitch on the Foot, SC 8 [16]

> In Row 11, you will work into the available stitches by inserting your hook as normal from the right side/outside to the inside/wrong side to complete your stitches. Ignore the stitches from the previous row that were used to connect the Heel to the Foot. Be careful not to work into the "Sl St, Ch 1" join space.

**12.** Dec, SC 4, Dec, SC 8 [14]

**13.** Dec, SC 3, Dec, SC 7 [12]

**14.** SC, 2 Dec in 3 SC, SC 8 [11]

**15.** SC, Dec, SC 8 [10]

**16–27.** (12 rows of) SC 10 [10]

**28.** SC 9, hold the Knee piece against your current work (right sides together), working through both pieces at the same time, SC 2 [10]

> Row 28 goes 1 stitch beyond where it started. You work 11 stitches in Row 28, but there are only 10 to crochet into for Row 29. This technique is repeated in this pattern.

> When you work through the Knee in this row, you will insert your hook through the inside/wrong side to the outside/right side of the Knee, and then through the outside/right side to the inside/wrong side of the Leg. Be careful not to work into the "Sl St, Ch 1" join space.

**29.** SC 7, start a decrease in the last available stitch on the Leg and complete the decrease in the first available stitch on the Knee, SC 8, start a decrease in the last available stitch on the Knee and complete the decrease in the first available stitch on the Leg [16]

> Row 29 goes 1 stitch beyond where it started.

> In Row 29, you will work into the available stitches by inserting your hook as normal from the right side/outside to the inside/wrong side to complete your stitches. Ignore the stitches from the previous row that were used to connect the Knee to the Leg.

**30.** (SC 6, Dec) x 2 [14]

**31.** SC 6, Dec, SC 4, Dec [12]

**32–43.** (12 rows of) SC 12 [12]

**44.** SC 9 [–9] [12]

> Yes, Row 44 does say to SC 9; this sets you up at a good spot for attaching the Leg to the Body.

Fasten off with an 18 in/45.5 cm yarn tail.

## Assembly

**1.** *Optional:* Take 1 piece of wire (18 in/45.5 cm paper-wrapped stem wire or similar recommended; err on the side of heavier wire if you want the limbs to be poseable). Bend the end of the wire over on itself to create a teardrop shape that will fit inside the foot area; secure it to itself with duct tape. (Please note that the use of wire makes the piece unsafe for children.)

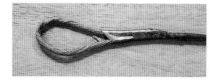

**2.** Stuff the end of the foot lightly with fiberfill. It is a simple thing to stuff into long small places like this if you use hemostats/forceps to pinch a small amount of stuffing and deposit it inside the foot.

**3.** Once you have stuffed the toes/end of the foot lightly with fiberfill, you can optionally insert the wire loop into the leg all the way down into the foot. You can bend the wire at the ankle and knee of the leg to match the leg shaping.

**4.** It is optional to stuff the rest of the leg with fiberfill around the wire (if you are using wire). Do not overstuff. Stuff medium/lightly. You just want to fill out the shape. Do not change the shape or warp it; if you overstuff, you will not be able to easily pose the leg. The legs you see on the Monsters in the photos *are* stuffed.

**5.** If you used wire, trim the wire that exits the Leg slightly shorter than the Monster Body you will be inserting the wire into. For the large Eyeball Monster Body, that means no longer than about 3 in/7.5 cm.

**6.** You can insert the Leg wire into the Monster Body wherever you want to place it. Repeat for the second leg. Pin in place.

**7.** Sew to attach with yarn tails. Weave in ends.

**Eyeball Monster Main Body/Eye with Crocheted Iris and Pupil, Eyeball Monster Eyelid, Two-toed Feet with Knees and Legs, Medium Curved Horns**

**Egg Shape with No Mouth and Legs, Eye Stalks, 2D Open Mouth in Round Shape with Fang Teeth (Upper) and Tongue (Lower), Four-toed Crouching Frog Rear Legs**

If you want to add metal spikes to any part of your Monster, go to page 172 for tips on how to do that.

# FOUR-TOED CROUCHING FROG REAR LEGS (MAKE 2)

*Approximately 4 in/10 cm wide across the toes, 5.5 in/14 cm tall from ground to top of the knee, 5.5 in/14 cm long from joint to joint, 5.5 in/14 cm long from joint to toes, 5 in/13 cm long from knee to base*

*Main Body Color Yarn: Approximately 45 yd/41 m worsted/medium weight yarn per Leg*

### Part 1: Toes and Leg (Make 4 Toes, Rows 1–5, and 1 Leg per limb)

1. SC 5 in Magic Circle, Sl St to beginning stitch, Ch 1 [5]

2. SC 5, Sl St to beginning stitch, Ch 1 [5]

3. SC 2, Inc, SC 2, Sl St to beginning stitch, Ch 1 [6]

4. SC 6, Sl St to beginning stitch, Ch 1 [6]

5. SC 3, <Dec>, SC 3, Sl St to beginning stitch [7]

> "<Dec>" is a stitch that is defined in the Glossary.

Repeat Rows 1–5 to make 4 Toes. Fasten off the first 3 Toes with a short yarn tail. Ch 1 and continue to Row 6 for Toe 4.

6. SC 2, starting into the 6th stitch on another Toe, SC 7, continuing into the next available stitch on the current (fourth) toe, SC 5, Sl St to beginning stitch, Ch 1 [14]

> Be careful not to crochet into the "Sl St, Ch 1" join space on either Toe.

7. SC, Dec, SC 2, starting into the 6th stitch on another Toe, SC 7, continuing into the next available stitch from Row 6, SC 3, Dec, SC 3, starting into the third stitch on the last Toe, SC 7, continuing into the next available stitch from Row 6, SC, Sl St to beginning stitch, Ch 1 [26]

8. 2 Dec in 3 SC, Dec, SC 5, Dec, SC, 2 Dec in 3 SC, SC, Dec, SC 5, Dec, Sl St to beginning stitch, Ch 1 [20]

9. Dec, SC 8, Dec, SC 8, Sl St to beginning stitch, Ch 1 [18]

10. SC 7, Dec, SC, Dec, SC 6, Sl St to beginning stitch, Ch 1 [16]

11. Inc, SC 6, 2 Dec in 3 SC, SC 6, Sl St to beginning stitch, Ch 1 [16]

12. (Dec, SC 6) x 2, Sl St to beginning stitch, Ch 1 [14]

13. SC 14, Sl St to beginning stitch, Ch 1 [14]

14. SC 3, 2 Dec in 3 SC, SC 4, 2 Dec in 3 SC, SC, Sl St to beginning stitch, Ch 1 [12]

15–18. (4 rows of) SC 12, Sl St to beginning stitch, Ch 1 [12]

> If you want to add metal spikes to these Toes, go to page 172 for tips on how to do that.

**19.** SC 9, Ch 12, & SC, SC 3, Sl St to beginning stitch, Ch 1 [13]

Place a stitch marker into the final Ch stitch of the Ch 12 in Row 19. The "& SC" will be worked into the same stitch as the last of the SC 9. Make sure you do not twist the chain when you anchor it to Row 18 with the "& SC." In the following row, you will work into all the SC and Ch stitches from Row 19. Also take note of the stitch you worked the "& SC" into—you will work into this stitch again in Row 1, Part 2 (mark this stitch if you'll have trouble finding it later). This technique will also be used in Part 2, Row 11.

Start to stuff the Toes, Foot, and Leg and continue to stuff with fiberfill as you go. A tool like hemostats can assist with stuffing hard to reach places. If you wish to add wire to the Leg, you can wait until assembly to stuff.

**20.** SC 25, Sl St to beginning stitch, Ch 1 [25]
**21.** SC 4, (SC 3, Dec) x 4, SC, Sl St to beginning stitch, Ch 1 [21]
**22.** SC 4, (SC, Dec, SC) x 4, SC, Sl St to beginning stitch, Ch 1 [17]
**23.** SC 4, (SC, Dec) x 4, SC, Sl St to beginning stitch, Ch 1 [13]
**24.** SC, (SC, Dec) x 4, Sl St to beginning stitch, Ch 1 [9]
**25.** (SC, Dec) x 3, Sl St to beginning stitch [6]

Fasten off with a 12 in/30.5 cm yarn tail to use to sew the hole shut.

## Part 2

**1.** Attach the yarn to the marked Ch stitch from Row 19, Part 1, SC 12, Inc into the same stitch that you worked the "& SC" in Row 19, Part 1, Sl St to beginning stitch, Ch 1 [14]

**2–10.** (9 rows of) SC 14, Sl St to beginning stitch, Ch 1 [14]
**11.** SC 7, Ch 13, & SC, SC 7, Sl St to beginning stitch, Ch 1 [15]

Place a stitch marker into the final Ch stitch of the Ch 13 in this row. Also take note of the stitch that you worked the "& SC" into—you will work into these stitches again in Row 1, Part 3.

12. SC 28, Sl St to beginning stitch, Ch 1 [28]

13. (SC 5, Dec) x 4, Sl St to beginning stitch, Ch 1 [24]

14. (SC 2, Dec, SC 2) x 4, Sl St to beginning stitch, Ch 1 [20]

15. (SC 3, Dec) x 4, Sl St to beginning stitch, Ch 1 [16]

16. (SC, Dec, SC) x 4, Sl St to beginning stitch, Ch 1 [12]

17. (SC, Dec) x 4, Sl St to beginning stitch, Ch 1 [8]

18. (SC, Dec) x 2, SC 2, Sl St to beginning stitch [6]

Fasten off with a 12 in/30.5 cm yarn tail to use to sew the hole shut. You may continue to stuff the Leg medium-firm to this point, or, if you are adding wire to the Leg, you can wait to stuff until assembly.

## Part 3

1. Attach the yarn to the marked Ch stitch from Row 11, Part 2, SC 13 in Ch stitches, Inc in the same stitch that you worked the "& SC" into in Row 11, Part 2, Sl St to the beginning stitch, Ch 1 [15]

2. (SC 2, Inc, SC 2) x 3, Sl St to beginning stitch, Ch 1 [18]

3. SC 18, Sl St to beginning stitch, Ch 1 [18]

4. (SC 4, Inc, SC 4) x 2, Sl St to beginning stitch, Ch 1 [20]

5–9. (5 rows of) SC 20, Sl St to beginning stitch, Ch 1 [20]

10. (SC 9, Inc) x 2, Sl St to beginning stitch, Ch 1 [22]

11–13. (3 rows of) SC 22, Sl St to beginning stitch, Ch 1 [22]

> Omit the Ch 1 on the final row.

Fasten off with an 18 in/45.5 cm yarn tail.

## Assembly

1. If you are not using wire, stuff the Leg medium-firm up to the last 1–2 in/2.5–5 cm of the Leg. At that last bit before the opening of the Leg, leave it lightly stuffed (or not stuffed at all), as shown. This part of the Leg will be pressed and stretched against the Monster's Body. If you are using wire, add wire before stuffing.

2. Wire is optional but helps to achieve the shape and poseability of the Leg. (Please note that the use of wire makes the piece unsafe for children.) If you choose to use wire, I recommend 18 in/45.5 cm paper-wrapped stem wire or similar (err on the side of heavier wire). Take one piece of wire and bend the end over on itself by an inch or two. Secure it to itself with duct tape.

   Insert the looped end of the wire through the Leg into the Foot. Force the wire to exit through the inner Thigh of the Leg. Create one left-oriented Leg and one right-oriented Leg.

3. Trim the wire that exits the inner Thigh to be slightly shorter than the Monster Body you will be inserting the wire into. As an example, for the large Eyeball Monster Body, that means no longer than about 3 in/7.5 cm.

4. Insert the wires of the Legs into the Monster Body to create a frog-looking leg configuration.

5. Pin the Legs to the Body. The ends of the Legs/thighs can overlap each other in the very back of the Body.

6. Use the yarn tails to sew the Magic Circle holes shut on the Legs and sew the Legs to the Body. Use small whipstitches to sew the Legs to the Body everywhere the Legs touch the Body. Do not be afraid to sew the Legs into position so the Monster sits firmly and securely on a flat surface. Weave in ends.

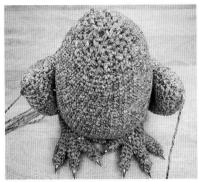

# SPIDER LEGS (MAKE 4, 6, OR 8)

*Approximately 9 in/23 cm long from base to tip, 1 in/2.5 cm wide at base*

*Main Body Color Yarn: Approximately 28 yd/25.5 m worsted/medium weight yarn per Leg*

*Optional but recommended: Strong wire*

### Part 1: Knee (Make 2 per Leg)

1. SC 6 in Magic Circle, Sl St to beginning stitch, Ch 1 [6]

2. Inc x 6, Sl St to beginning stitch [12]

Fasten off with a short yarn tail.

### Part 2: Leg (Make 1 per Leg)

1. SC 5 in Magic Circle, Sl St to beginning stitch, Ch 1 [5]

2. SC 5, Sl St to beginning stitch, Ch 1 [5]

3. SC 4, Inc, Sl St to beginning stitch, Ch 1 [6]

4. SC 6, Sl St to beginning stitch, Ch 1 [6]

5. SC 5, Inc, Sl St to beginning stitch, Ch 1 [7]

6. SC 7, Sl St to beginning stitch, Ch 1 [7]

7. SC 6, Inc, Sl St to beginning stitch, Ch 1 [8]

8. SC 8, Sl St to beginning stitch, Ch 1 [8]

9. SC 7, Inc, Sl St to beginning stitch, Ch 1 [9]

10. SC 9, Sl St to beginning stitch, Ch 1 [9]

11. SC 8, Inc, Sl St to beginning stitch, Ch 1 [10]

12. SC 10, Sl St to beginning stitch, Ch 1 [10]

13. SC 9, Inc, Sl St to beginning stitch, Ch 1 [11]

14. SC 11, Sl St to beginning stitch, Ch 1 [11]

15. SC 10, Inc, Sl St to beginning stitch, Ch 1 [12]

16. SC 12, Sl St to beginning stitch, Ch 1 [12]

**17.** SC 4, hold the first Knee against the current work, SC 4 through both the Knee and the current work at the same time, SC 4, Sl St to beginning stitch, Ch 1 [12]

> When you work into a joint piece (as in Rows 17 and 28), insert your hook into the wrong side/inside of the joint piece first; then insert your hook into the right side/outside of the limb next and complete a SC through both at the same time. Do not work into the Sl St join from the joint piece. See this video for more information on this technique: https://youtu.be/paLzIAi--vk

**18.** Dec, SC, start a decrease in the last available stitch on the Leg and complete the decrease in the first available stitch on the Knee, SC 6, start a decrease in the last available stitch on the Knee and complete the decrease in the first available stitch on the Leg, SC, Dec, Sl St to beginning stitch, Ch 1 [12]

> In Row 18 and Row 29, you will work through the available stitches in both the Leg and the Knee by inserting your hook as normal from the right side/outside to the inside/wrong side to complete your stitches. Ignore the stitches from the previous row that were used to connect the Knee to the Leg. Be careful not to work into the "Sl St, Ch 1" join space.

**19.** SC 2, Dec, SC 4, Dec, SC 2, Sl St to beginning stitch, Ch 1 [10]

**20.** Inc, SC, Dec, SC 2, Dec, SC, Inc, Sl St to beginning stitch, Ch 1 [10]

**21.** SC 4, Dec, SC 4, Sl St to beginning stitch, Ch 1 [9]

**22–26.** (5 rows of) SC 9, Sl St to beginning stitch, Ch 1 [9]

**27.** SC, Inc, SC 7, Sl St to beginning stitch, Ch 1 [10]

**28.** SC 5, hold the second Knee against the current work, SC 4 through both the Knee and the current work at the same time, SC, Sl St to beginning stitch, Ch 1 [10]

**29.** SC, Dec, SC, start a decrease in the last available stitch on the Leg and complete the decrease in the first available stitch on the Knee, SC 6, start a decrease in the last available stitch on the Knee and complete the decrease in the first available stitch on the Leg, Sl St to beginning stitch, Ch 1 [11]

**30.** SC 3, Dec, SC 4, Dec, Sl St to beginning stitch, Ch 1 [9]

**31.** Inc, SC, Inc, SC, Dec x 2, SC, Sl St to beginning stitch, Ch 1 [9]

**32–34.** (3 rows of) SC 9, Sl St to beginning stitch, Ch 1 [9]

**35.** SC 2, Dec, SC 5, Sl St to beginning stitch, Ch 1 [8]

**36–38.** (3 rows of) SC 8, Sl St to beginning stitch, Ch 1 [8]

Do not Ch 1 on the final repeat of these instructions.

Fasten off with a 12 in/30.5 cm yarn tail.

## Assembly

You do not need to include wire if you want the Legs to just contain stuffing. If you don't want to stuff them at all, you can do that. They will not support the weight of the Body or be poseable without wire. With wire, they are not safe for a small child.

**1.** You will need one wire per Leg. Bend one of the wires over on itself and secure it to itself with strips of duct tape, as shown. This is so that the end of the wire that will slide all the way into the tip of the spider Leg won't be sharp and won't escape through any holes in the stitchwork.

**2.** Slide each Leg onto a wire.

**3.** Insert the Leg's wire into the Monster's Body where you want the Leg to extend from. Each Leg needs only one wire, but each wire should enter the Monster's Body and exit the Body on the opposite side from where it entered, which should also line up with another Leg's entry point. This will enable you to tape and twist the wires together to make the wired legs stronger and more stable. The stability is increased even more if you intermix the different wires instead of pairing only opposite leg wires with each other. See the configurations below for how to insert wire through a round Body, such as the Eyeball Monster. Each color indicates a separate wire.

If you are using 8 legs, here are two potential configurations of wire:

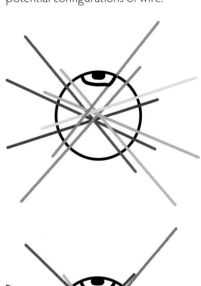

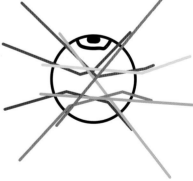

If you are using 6 legs, here are two potential configurations of wire:

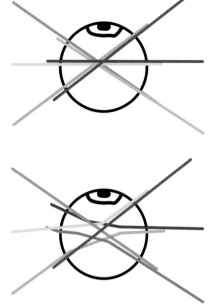

If you are using 4 legs, here are two potential configurations of wire:

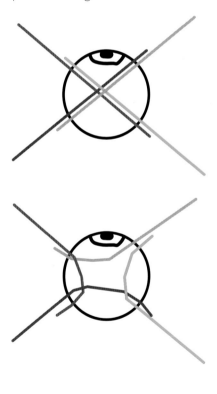

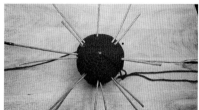

**4.** After you have inserted all the required wires through the Body, you now need to secure each wire to one other wire for stability. To guarantee that you have enough wire to fill out the Leg and you aren't compromising on lengths, slide one Leg over the wire you are ready to attach. Push the wire onto the Leg as far as you can to fill the Leg with the wire's length. Stop when the Leg is very slightly stretched by the wire. You now have discovered the exact length of that one wire and its position through the Body.

Repeat this process for the next wire that you will attach to the wire you just measured, and once you have

confirmed those wire lengths, wrap the wires in duct tape to attach them to each other. This process becomes more complex if you are doing a more stable design, but it is doable. Once the Legs are stable and pinned to attach to the Body on the wires, use the yarn tails to sew the Legs to attach to the Body using small whipstitches around the edge of the leg as it touches the Body. Weave in ends.

**5.** Use the wire to pose your creature.

Eyeball
Monster
Main Body/Eye
with Crocheted Iris
and Pupil, Eyeball
Monster Eyelid,
Spider Legs

# SMALL CONE LIMBS (MAKE 2)

*(RECOMMENDED AS ARMS OR SMALL LEGS)*

*Approximately 6 in/15 cm long, 2 in/5 cm wide at the widest point, 1 in/2.5 cm wide at the base*

*Main Body Color Yarn: Approximately 23 yd/21 m worsted/medium weight yarn per Limb*

*Accent Color Yarn: Approximately 4 yd/3.75 m worsted/medium weight yarn per Limb*

### Part 1: Bottom Circle (Make 1 per Limb)

**1.** With Accent Color, SC 6 in Magic Circle, Sl St to beginning stitch, Ch 1 [6]

**2.** Inc x 6, Sl St to beginning stitch, Ch 1 [12]

**3.** (SC, Inc) x 6, Sl St to beginning stitch, Ch 1 [18]

**4.** (SC, Inc, SC) x 6, Sl St to beginning stitch [24]

Fasten off with a short yarn tail.

### Part 2: Limb (Make 1 per Limb)

**1.** Attach the Main Body Color yarn to any BLO of Row 4 of Part 1, BLO [SC 24], Sl St to beginning stitch, Ch 1 [24]

> Be careful not to work into the Sl St join of Row 4 of Part 1 when working Row 1 of Part 2.

**2–3.** (2 rows of) SC 24, Sl St to beginning stitch, Ch 1 [24]

**4.** (SC 5, Dec, SC 5) x 2, Sl St to beginning stitch, Ch 1 [22]

**5–6.** (2 rows of) SC 22, Sl St to beginning stitch, Ch 1 [22]

**7.** (SC 9, Dec) x 2, Sl St to beginning stitch, Ch 1 [20]

**8–9.** (2 rows of) SC 20, Sl St to beginning stitch, Ch 1 [20]

**10.** (SC 4, Dec, SC 4) x 2, Sl St to beginning stitch, Ch 1 [18]

**11–12.** (2 rows of) SC 18, Sl St to beginning stitch, Ch 1 [18]

**13.** (SC 7, Dec) x 2, Sl St to beginning stitch, Ch 1 [16]

**14–15.** (2 rows of) SC 16, Sl St to beginning stitch, Ch 1 [16]

**16.** (SC 3, Dec, SC 3) x 2, Sl St to beginning stitch, Ch 1 [14]

**17–18.** (2 rows of) SC 14, Sl St to beginning stitch, Ch 1 [14]

**19.** (SC 5, Dec) x 2, Sl St to beginning stitch, Ch 1 [12]

**20–21.** (2 rows of) SC 12, Sl St to beginning stitch, Ch 1 [12]

**22.** (SC 2, Dec, SC 2) x 2, Sl St to beginning stitch, Ch 1 [10]

**23.** SC 10, Sl St to beginning stitch, Ch 1 [10]

**24.** SC 10, Sl St to beginning stitch [10]

Fasten off with a 12 in/30.5 cm yarn tail.

### Assembly

**1.** Stuff the end of the limb medium-firm with fiberfill; stuff lightly or not at all in the upper part of the limb.

**2.** Pin in place on the Body.

**3.** Once you are satisfied with placement, sew to the body using the yarn tail; weave in ends.

# LARGE CONE LIMBS (MAKE 2)

*(RECOMMENDED AS LEGS OR VERY LONG ARMS)*

*Approximately 9 in/23 cm long, 2 in/5 cm wide at the base, 3 in/7.5 cm wide at the widest point*

*Main Body Color yarn: Approximately 50 yd/45.75 m worsted/medium weight yarn per Limb*

*Accent Color Yarn: Approximately 5 yd/4.5 m worsted/medium weight yarn per Limb*

## Part 1: Bottom Circle (Make 1 per Limb)

**1.** With Accent Color Yarn, SC 6 in Magic Circle, Sl St to beginning stitch, Ch 1 [6]

**2.** Inc x 6, Sl St to beginning stitch, Ch 1 [12]

**3.** (SC, Inc) x 6, Sl St to beginning stitch, Ch 1 [18]

**4.** (SC, Inc, SC) x 6, Sl St to beginning stitch, Ch 1 [24]

**5.** (SC 3, Inc) x 6, Sl St to beginning stitch [30]

Fasten off with a short yarn tail.

## Part 2: Limb (Make 1 per Limb)

**1.** Attach the Body Color Yarn to any BLO of Row 5 of Part 1, BLO [SC 30], Sl St to beginning stitch, Ch 1 [30]

> Be careful not to work into the Sl St join of Row 5 of Part 1 when working Row 1 of Part 2.

**2–3.** (2 rows of) SC 30, Sl St to beginning stitch, Ch 1 [30]

**4.** (SC 13, Dec) x 2, Sl St to beginning stitch, Ch 1 [28]

**5–6.** (2 rows of) SC 28, Sl St to beginning stitch, Ch 1 [28]

**7.** (SC 6, Dec, SC 6) x 2, Sl St to beginning stitch, Ch 1 [26]

**8–9.** (2 rows of) SC 26, Sl St to beginning stitch, Ch 1 [26]

**10.** (SC 11, Dec) x 2, Sl St to beginning stitch, Ch 1 [24]

**11–12.** (2 rows of) SC 24, Sl St to beginning stitch, Ch 1 [24]

**13.** (SC 5, Dec, SC 5) x 2, Sl St to beginning stitch, Ch 1 [22]

**14–15.** (2 rows of) SC 22, Sl St to beginning stitch, Ch 1 [22]

**16.** (SC 9, Dec) x 2, Sl St to beginning stitch, Ch 1 [20]

**17–18.** (2 rows of) SC 20, Sl St to beginning stitch, Ch 1 [20]

**19.** (SC 4, Dec, SC 4) x 2, Sl St to beginning stitch, Ch 1 [18]

**20–21.** (2 rows of) SC 18, Sl St to beginning stitch, Ch 1 [18]

**22.** (SC 7, Dec) x 2, Sl St to beginning stitch, Ch 1 [16]

**23–24.** (2 rows of) SC 16, Sl St to beginning stitch, Ch 1 [16]

**25.** (SC 3, Dec, SC 3) x 2, Sl St to beginning stitch, Ch 1 [14]

**26–27.** (2 rows of) SC 14, Sl St to beginning stitch, Ch 1 [14]

**28.** (SC 5, Dec) x 2, Sl St to beginning stitch, Ch 1 [12]

**29–32.** (4 rows of) SC 12, Sl St to beginning stitch, Ch 1 [12]

**33.** SC 12, Sl St to beginning stitch [12]

Fasten off with a 12 in/30.5 cm yarn tail.

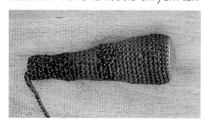

## Assembly

**1.** Stuff the end of the limb medium-firm with fiberfill; stuff lightly or not at all in the upper part of the limb.

**2.** Pin in place on the Body.

**3.** Once you are satisfied with placement, sew to the Body using the yarn tail; weave in ends.

**4.** Use the accent color to add toe stitches to the base of the limb, if desired. It is optional to go to page 334 for instructions on how to embroider claws.

Eyeball Monster Main Body/Eye with Safety Eye, Eyeball Monster Eyelid, Wide Flat-ended Short Limbs, Wide Flat-ended Long Limbs, Small Antlers

Cylinder with Open Mouth and Legs, Open Mouth with Short Row of Small Teeth (Lower), Small Cone Limbs, Short Bunny Ears

Square with No Mouth and Legs, Small Rounded Overbite, Wide Flat-ended Long Limbs, Large Curved Horns, Four Humanlike Teeth

Sphere with Underbite, Thinner Eyelid/Eyebrow for 30 mm Safety Eyes, Bulb-ended Short Limbs, Bulb-ended Long Limbs, Thin L-shaped Horns, Squared Teeth

# WIDE FLAT-ENDED SHORT LIMBS (MAKE 2)

*(RECOMMENDED FOR ARMS OR VERY SHORT LEGS)*

*Approximately 6 in/15 cm long, 3 in/7.5 cm wide at the end, 1 in/2.5 cm wide at the base*

*Main Body Color Yarn: Approximately 30 yd/27.5 m worsted/medium weight yarn per Limb*

**1.** Ch 13, starting in the second Ch from hook, SC 11, Inc, continue to crochet around to the other side of the starting chain, SC 10, SC in the same Ch as your first SC in this row, Sl St to beginning stitch, Ch 1 [24]

**2-3.** (2 rows of) SC 24, Sl St to beginning stitch, Ch 1 [24]

**4.** (SC 5, Dec, SC 5) x 2, Sl St to beginning stitch, Ch 1 [22]

**5-6.** (2 rows of) SC 22, Sl St to beginning stitch, Ch 1 [22]

**7.** (SC 9, Dec) x 2, Sl St to beginning stitch, Ch 1 [20]

**8.** SC 20, Sl St to beginning stitch, Ch 1 [20]

**9.** (SC 4, Dec, SC 4) x 2, Sl St to beginning stitch, Ch 1 [18]

**10.** SC 18, Sl St to beginning stitch, Ch 1 [18]

**11.** (SC 7, Dec) x 2, Sl St to beginning stitch, Ch 1 [16]

**12.** SC 16, Sl St to beginning stitch, Ch 1 [16]

**13.** (SC 3, Dec, SC 3) x 2, Sl St to beginning stitch, Ch 1 [14]

**14.** SC 14, Sl St to beginning stitch, Ch 1 [14]

**15.** (SC 5, Dec) x 2, Sl St to beginning stitch, Ch 1 [12]

**16-17.** (2 rows of) SC 12, Sl St to beginning stitch, Ch 1 [12]

**18.** (SC 2, Dec, SC 2) x 2, Sl St to beginning stitch, Ch 1 [10]

**19-24.** (6 rows of) SC 10, Sl St to beginning stitch, Ch 1 [10]

> Do not Ch 1 on your final repeat of these instructions.

Fasten off with a 12 in/30.5 cm yarn tail.

## Assembly

**1.** Stuff the end of the limb medium-firm with fiberfill; stuff lightly or not at all in the upper part of the limb.

**2.** Pin in place on the Body.

**3.** Once you are satisfied with placement, sew to the Body using the yarn tail; weave in ends. It is optional to go to page 334 for instructions on how to embroider claws.

# WIDE FLAT-ENDED LONG LIMBS (MAKE 2)

### (RECOMMENDED FOR LEGS OR VERY LONG ARMS)

**Approximately 8 in/20.5 cm long, 4 in/10 cm wide at the end, 1.5 in/4 cm wide at the base**

**Main Body Color Yarn: Approximately 50 yd/45.75 m worsted/medium weight yarn per Limb**

**1.** Ch 16, starting in the second Ch from hook, SC 14, Inc, continue to crochet around to the other side of the starting chain, SC 13, SC in the same Ch as your first SC in this row, Sl St to beginning stitch, Ch 1 [30]

**2–3.** (2 rows of) SC 30, Sl St to beginning stitch, Ch 1 [30]

**4.** (SC 13, Dec) x 2, Sl St to beginning stitch, Ch 1 [28]

**5–6.** (2 rows of) SC 28, Sl St to beginning stitch, Ch 1 [28]

**7.** (SC 6, Dec, SC 6) x 2, Sl St to beginning stitch, Ch 1 [26]

**8–9.** (2 rows of) SC 26, Sl St to beginning stitch, Ch 1 [26]

**10.** (SC 11, Dec) x 2, Sl St to beginning stitch, Ch 1 [24]

**11–12.** (2 rows of) SC 24, Sl St to beginning stitch, Ch 1 [24]

**13.** (SC 5, Dec, SC 5) x 2, Sl St to beginning stitch, Ch 1 [22]

**14–15.** (2 rows of) SC 22, Sl St to beginning stitch, Ch 1 [22]

**16.** (SC 9, Dec) x 2, Sl St to beginning stitch, Ch 1 [20]

**17–18.** (2 rows of) SC 20, Sl St to beginning stitch, Ch 1 [20]

**19.** (SC 4, Dec, SC 4) x 2, Sl St to beginning stitch, Ch 1 [18]

**20–21.** (2 rows of) SC 18, Sl St to beginning stitch, Ch 1 [18]

**22.** (SC 7, Dec) x 2, Sl St to beginning stitch, Ch 1 [16]

**23–24.** (2 rows of) SC 16, Sl St to beginning stitch, Ch 1 [16]

**25.** (SC 3, Dec, SC 3) x 2, Sl St to beginning stitch, Ch 1 [14]

**26–27.** (2 rows of) SC 14, Sl St to beginning stitch, Ch 1 [14]

**28.** (SC 5, Dec) x 2, Sl St to beginning stitch, Ch 1 [12]

**29–33.** (5 rows of) SC 12, Sl St to beginning stitch, Ch 1 [12]

> Do not Ch 1 on your final repeat of these instructions.

Fasten off with a 12 in/30.5 cm yarn tail.

## Assembly

**1.** Stuff the end of the limb medium-firm with fiberfill; stuff lightly or not at all in the upper part of the limb.

**2.** Pin in place on the Body.

**3.** Once you are satisfied with placement, sew to the Body using the yarn tail; weave in ends.

# THREE-FINGERED WIDE LIMBS (MAKE 2)

*(RECOMMENDED FOR ARMS)*

**Approximately 7 in/18 cm long, 1 in/2.5 cm wide at the base**

**Main Body Color Yarn: Approximately 40 yd/36.5 m worsted/medium weight yarn per limb**

### Part 1: Thumb (Make 1 per Limb)

**1.** SC 6 in Magic Circle, Sl St to beginning stitch, Ch 1 [6]

**2.** (SC, Inc) x 3, Sl St to beginning stitch, Ch 1 [9]

**3–5.** (3 rows of) SC 9, Sl St to beginning stitch, Ch 1 [9]

**6.** SC 9, Sl St to beginning stitch [9]

Fasten off with a short yarn tail.

### Part 2: Fingers and Arm (Make 2 Fingers, Rows 1–7, and one Arm per Limb)

**1.** SC 6 in Magic Circle, Sl St to beginning stitch, Ch 1 [6]

**2.** (SC, Inc) x 3, Sl St to beginning stitch, Ch 1 [9]

**3–6.** (4 rows of) SC 9, Sl St to beginning stitch, Ch 1 [9]

**7.** SC 9, Sl St to beginning stitch [9]

Fasten off the first Finger with a short yarn tail.

Repeat Rows 1–7 for the second Finger and then proceed to Row 8.

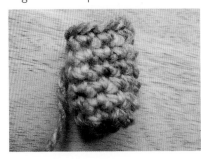

**8.** Ch 1, SC 5, working into a stitch on the Part 2 First Finger, SC 9 around, continuing into the next available stitch on the current work/second Finger, SC 4, Sl St to beginning stitch, Ch 1 [18]

> Be careful not to crochet into the "Sl St, Ch 1" join.

9. SC 4, hold the Thumb piece against the current work (right side to right side), complete a SC through both pieces at the same time, working through the next available stitch on both pieces at the same time SC again, continuing into the next available stitch on the current piece, SC 12, Sl St to beginning stitch, Ch 1 [18]

When you work through the Thumb in this row, you will insert your hook through the inside/wrong side to the outside/right side of the Thumb and then through the outside/right side to the inside/wrong side of the Hand. Be careful not to work into the "Sl St, Ch 1" join space.

10. SC 4, starting into the next available stitch on the Thumb, SC 7, continuing into the next available stitch on the current work, SC 12, Sl St to beginning stitch, Ch 1 [23]

In this row you will work around the available stitches by inserting your hook as normal from the right side/outside to the inside/wrong side to complete your stitches. Ignore the stitches that were used to connect the Thumb with the current work. Be careful not to work into the "Sl St, Ch 1" join space.

## Assembly

1. Stuff the end of the limb medium-firm with fiberfill; stuff lightly or not at all in the upper part of the limb.

2. Pin in place on the Body.

3. Once you are satisfied with placement, sew to the Body using the yarn tail; weave in ends.

11. SC 23, Sl St to beginning stitch, Ch 1 [23]

12. SC 3, Dec, SC 5, Dec, SC 11, Sl St to beginning stitch, Ch 1 [21]

13. (SC 5, Dec) x 3, Sl St to beginning stitch, Ch 1 [18]

14. SC 18, Sl St to beginning stitch, Ch 1 [18]

15. (SC 2, Dec, SC 2) x 3, Sl St to beginning stitch, Ch 1 [15]

16–17. (2 rows of) SC 15, Sl St to beginning stitch, Ch 1 [15]

18. (SC 3, Dec) x 3, Sl St to beginning stitch, Ch 1 [12]

19–21. (3 rows of) SC 12, Sl St to beginning stitch, Ch 1 [12]

22. (SC, Dec, SC) x 3, Sl St to beginning stitch, Ch 1 [9]

23–30. (8 rows of) SC 9, Sl St to beginning stitch, Ch 1 [9]

Do not Ch 1 on your final repeat of these instructions.

Fasten off with an 18 in/45.5 cm yarn tail.

# BULB-ENDED SHORT LIMBS (MAKE 2)

## (RECOMMENDED FOR ARMS OR VERY SHORT LEGS)

*Approximately 6 in/15 cm long, 2 in/5 cm wide at the widest point, 1.5 in/4 cm wide at the base*

*Main Body Color Yarn: Approximately 26 yd/23.75 m worsted/medium weight yarn per Limb*

1. SC 6 in Magic Circle, Sl St to beginning stitch, Ch 1 [6]

2. Inc x 6, Sl St to beginning stitch, Ch 1 [12]

3. (SC, Inc) x 6, Sl St to beginning stitch, Ch 1 [18]

4. (SC, Inc, SC) x 6, Sl St to beginning stitch, Ch 1 [24]

5-9. (5 rows of) SC 24, Sl St to beginning stitch, Ch 1 [24]

10. (SC, Dec, SC) x 6, Sl St to beginning stitch, Ch 1 [18]

11-12. (2 rows of) SC 18, Sl St to beginning stitch, Ch 1 [18]

13. (SC, Dec) x 6, Sl St to beginning stitch, Ch 1 [12]

14-27. (14 rows of) SC 12, Sl St to beginning stitch, Ch 1 [12]

28. SC 12, Sl St to beginning stitch [12]

Fasten off with an 18 in/45.5 cm yarn tail.

## Assembly

1. Stuff the end of the limb medium-firm with fiberfill; stuff lightly or not at all in the upper part of the limb.

2. Pin in place on the Body.

3. Once you are satisfied with placement, sew to the Body using the yarn tail; weave in ends.

Cylinder with
No Mouth and
Legs, 2D Open Mouth
in Rectangular Shape
with Humanlike Teeth
(Upper and Lower), Eye
Stalks, Bulb-ended
Short Limbs

# BULB-ENDED LONG LIMBS (MAKE 2)

*(RECOMMENDED FOR LEGS OR VERY LONG ARMS)*

*Approximately 8 in/20.5 cm long, 2.5 in/6.5 cm wide at the widest point, 1.5 in/4 cm wide at the base*

*Main Body Color Yarn: Approximately 32 yd/29.25 m cm worsted/medium weight yarn per Limb*

**I.** SC 6 in Magic Circle, Sl St to beginning stitch, Ch 1 [6]

**2.** Inc x 6, Sl St to beginning stitch, Ch 1 [12]

**3.** (SC, Inc) x 6, Sl St to beginning stitch, Ch 1 [18]

**4.** (SC, Inc, SC) x 6, Sl St to beginning stitch, Ch 1 [24]

**5.** (SC 3, Inc) x 6, Sl St to beginning stitch, Ch 1 [30]

**6-10.** (5 rows of) SC 30, Sl St to beginning stitch, Ch 1 [30]

**II.** (SC 3, Dec) x 6, Sl St to beginning stitch, Ch 1 [24]

**12-13.** (2 rows of) SC 24, Sl St to beginning stitch, Ch 1 [24]

**14.** (SC, Dec, SC) x 6, Sl St to beginning stitch, Ch 1 [18]

**15.** SC 18, Sl St to beginning stitch, Ch 1 [18]

**16.** (SC, Dec) x 6, Sl St to beginning stitch, Ch 1 [12]

**17-33.** (17 rows of) SC 12, Sl St to beginning stitch, Ch 1 [12]

**34.** SC 12, Sl St to beginning stitch [12]

Fasten off with an 18 in/45.5 cm yarn tail.

## Assembly

**I.** Stuff the end of the limb medium-firm with fiberfill; stuff lightly or not at all in the upper part of the limb.

**2.** Pin in place on the Body.

**3.** Once you are satisfied with placement, sew to the Body using the yarn tail; weave in ends.

# CUTE MITTEN LIMBS (MAKE 2)

*(RECOMMENDED FOR ARMS)*

There are multiple options in this Limb's instructions. You can make a short Limb with no Elbow and a straight Arm. You can make a longer Limb with an elbow bend.

*With an Elbow is approximately 9 in/23 cm long, 1.25 in/3 cm wide at the base; without an Elbow is approximately 6.5 in/16.5 cm long*

*Main Body Color Yarn, version with Elbow: Approximately 35 yd/32 m worsted/medium weight yarn per Limb*

*Main Body Color Yarn, version with no Elbow: Approximately 28 yd/25.5 m worsted/medium weight yarn per Limb*

## Optional: Elbow for a Longer Limb (Make 1 per Limb)

**I.** SC 6 in Magic Circle, Sl St to beginning stitch, Ch 1 [6]

**2.** Inc x 6, Sl St to beginning stitch [12]

Fasten off with a short yarn tail.

## Part 1: Thumb (Make 1 per Limb)

**I.** SC 6 in Magic Circle, Sl St to beginning stitch, Ch 1 [6]

**2.** (Inc, SC, Inc) x 2, Sl St to beginning stitch, Ch 1 [10]

**3-4.** (2 rows of) SC 10, Sl St to beginning stitch, Ch 1 [10]

**5.** (SC 3, Dec) x 2, Sl St to beginning stitch, Ch 1 [8]

**6.** SC 8, Sl St to beginning stitch [8]

Fasten off with a short yarn tail.

Sphere with Open Mouth, Open Mouth with Pointy Teeth, Cute Mitten Limbs, Cute Footed Limbs, Skinny Curved Horns

## Part 2: Mitten Hand and Arm (Make 1 per Limb)

**1.** Ch 7, starting in the second Ch from Hook, SC 5, Inc, continue to crochet around to the other side of the OC stitches, SC 4, SC in the same Ch stitch as the first SC of this row, Sl St to beginning stitch, Ch 1 [12]

**2.** (SC, Inc) x 6, Sl St to beginning stitch, Ch 1 [18]

**3–8.** (6 rows of) SC 18, Sl St to beginning stitch, Ch 1 [18]

**9.** SC 8, hold the Thumb against the current work (right side to right side), complete a SC through both pieces at the same time, working through the next available stitch on both pieces at the same time make another SC, continuing into the next available stitch on Part 2, SC 8, Sl St to beginning stitch, Ch 1 [18]

> When you work through the Thumb in this row, you will insert your hook through the inside/wrong side to the outside/right side of the Thumb and then through the outside/right side to the inside/wrong side of the Hand. Be careful not to work into the "Sl St, Ch 1" join space.

**10.** SC 7, start a decrease in the last available stitch on the current piece and complete the decrease in the first available stitch on the Thumb, SC 4 around the Thumb, start a decrease in the last available stitch on the Thumb and complete the decrease in the first available stitch on the Hand, continuing into the next available stitch on the Hand, SC 7, Sl St to beginning stitch, Ch 1 [20]

> In this row you will work around the available stitches by inserting your hook as normal from the right side/outside to the inside/wrong side to complete your stitches. Ignore the stitches that were used to connect the Thumb with the Hand. Be careful not to work into the "Sl St, Ch 1" join space.

> If you want to add metal spikes to these Mitten Hands, go to page 172 for tips on how to do that.

**11.** (SC 3, Dec) x 4, Sl St to beginning stitch, Ch 1 [16]

**12.** SC 16, Sl St to beginning stitch, Ch 1 [16]

**13.** (SC 3, Dec, SC 3) x 2, Sl St to beginning stitch, Ch 1 [14]

**14–15.** (2 rows of) SC 14, Sl St to beginning stitch, Ch 1 [14]

**16.** (SC 5, Dec) x 2, Sl St to beginning stitch, Ch 1 [12]

**17–19.** (3 rows of) SC 12, Sl St to beginning stitch, Ch 1 [12]

**20.** (SC 2, Dec, SC 2) x 2, Sl St to beginning stitch, Ch 1 [10]

> Follow Rows 21–26 for a short, straight arm. For a longer arm, work only 3 rows of SC 10 (creating Rows 21–23) and then skip to the optional Row 24 instruction to incorporate an elbow joint and make the arm longer.

**21–26.** (6 rows of) SC 10, Sl St to beginning stitch, Ch 1 [10]

> Do not Ch 1 on your final repeat of these instructions if you are fastening off for a short straight arm.

For a short straight Arm, fasten off with a 12 in/30.5 cm yarn tail.

### Optional Elbow Joint

**24.** SC, hold the Elbow against the current work (right side to right side), complete a SC through both pieces at the same time, working through the next available stitch on both pieces at the same time SC 2, continuing into the next available stitch on your current work, SC 6, Sl St to beginning stitch, Ch 1 [10]

When you work through the Elbow in this row, you will insert your hook through the inside/wrong side to the outside/right side of the Elbow and then through the outside/right side to the inside/wrong side of the Arm. Be careful not to work into the "Sl St, Ch 1" join space. See this video for more information on this technique: https://youtu.be/paLzIAi--vk

**25.** Start a decrease in the first available stitch of the Arm and complete the decrease in the first available stitch of the Elbow, SC 7 around the Elbow, start a decrease in the last available stitch on the Elbow and complete the decrease in the first available stitch on the Arm, continuing into the next available stitch on the Arm, SC 5, Sl St to beginning stitch, Ch 1 [14]

In this row you will work around the available stitches by inserting your hook as normal from the right side/outside to the inside/wrong side to complete your stitches. Ignore the stitches that were used to connect the Elbow with the Arm. Be careful not to work into the "Sl St, Ch 1" join space.

**26.** (SC, Dec, SC, Dec, SC) x 2, Sl St to beginning stitch, Ch 1 [10]

**27–37.** (11 rows of) SC 10, Sl St to beginning stitch, Ch 1 [10]

Do not Ch 1 on your final repeat of these instructions.

Fasten off with a 24 in/61 cm yarn tail.

### Assembly

**1.** Stuff the end of the limb medium-firm with fiberfill; stuff lightly or not at all in the upper part of the limb.

**2.** Pin in place on the Body.

**3.** Once you are satisfied with placement, sew to the Body using the yarn tail; weave in ends.

# CUTE FOOTED LIMBS (MAKE 2)

*(RECOMMENDED FOR LEGS)*

There are multiple options in this Limb's instructions. You can make a short Limb with no Knee and a straight Leg. You can make a longer Limb with a Knee bend.

*With a Knee is approximately 8 in/20.5 cm long, 2 in/5 cm wide at the base, 3 in/7.5 cm from heel to toe; without a Knee it is approximately 4 in/10 cm long*

*Main Body Color Yarn, version with Knee: Approximately 38 yd/34.75 m worsted/medium weight yarn per Limb*

*Main Body Color yarn, short version/no Knee: Approximately 25 yd/22.75 m worsted/medium weight yarn per Limb*

### Optional: Make 1 Knee per Limb for a Long, Dangling Leg

**1.** SC 6 in Magic Circle, Sl St to beginning stitch, Ch 1 [6]

**2.** Inc x 6, Sl St to beginning stitch [12]

Fasten off with a short yarn tail.

## Limb

**1.** Ch 7, starting in the second Ch from hook, SC 5, Inc, continue to crochet around to the other side of the OC stitches, SC 4, SC in the same chain stitch as the first SC of this row, Sl St to beginning stitch, Ch 1 [12]

**2.** (Inc, SC 4, Inc) x 2, Sl St to beginning stitch, Ch 1 [16]

**3.** (Inc x 2, SC 4, Inc x 2) x 2, Sl St to beginning stitch, Ch 1 [24]

**4.** (SC, Inc) x 2, SC 4, (Inc, SC) x 2, (SC, Inc) x 2, SC 4, (Inc, SC) x 2, Sl St to beginning stitch, Ch 1 [32]

**5–6.** (2 rows of) SC 32, Sl St to beginning stitch, Ch 1 [32]

**7.** SC 8, (SC, Dec, SC) x 4, SC 8, Sl St to beginning stitch, Ch 1 [28]

**8.** SC 6, (SC, Dec, SC) x 4, SC 6, Sl St to beginning stitch, Ch 1 [24]

**9.** SC 4, (SC, Dec, SC) x 4, SC 4, Sl St to beginning stitch, Ch 1 [20]

**10.** SC 2, (SC, Dec, SC) x 4, SC 2, Sl St to beginning stitch, Ch 1 [16]

**11–18.** (8 rows of) SC 16, Sl St to beginning stitch, Ch 1 [16]

You can fasten off here for a short Foot/Leg with no Knee, or you can continue to Row 19 to make the Leg longer, dangly, and with a Knee.

**19–22.** (4 rows of) SC 16, Sl St to beginning stitch, Ch 1 [16]

**23.** SC 10, hold the Knee piece against your current work (right side to right side), complete a SC through both pieces at the same time, working through the next available stitches on both pieces at the same time SC 2, continuing into the next available stitch on your current work, SC 3, Sl St to beginning stitch, Ch 1 [16]

> When you work through the Knee in this row, you will insert your hook through the inside/wrong side to the outside/right side of the Knee, and then through the outside/right side to the inside/wrong side of the Foot. Be careful not to work into the "Sl St, Ch 1" join space. See this video for more information on this technique: https://youtu.be/paLzIAi--vk

**24.** SC 9, start a decrease in the last available stitch on the Leg and complete the decrease in the first available stitch on the Knee, SC 7 around the Knee, start a decrease in the last available stitch on the Knee and complete the decrease in the first available stitch on the Leg, continuing into the next available stitch on the Leg, SC 2, Sl St to beginning stitch, Ch 1 [20]

> In Row 24, you will work around the available stitches by inserting your hook as normal from the right side/outside to the inside/wrong side to complete your stitches. Ignore the stitches that were used to connect the Knee with the Leg. Be careful not to work into the "Sl St, Ch 1" join space.

**25.** (SC 3, Dec) x 4, Sl St to beginning stitch, Ch 1 [16]

**26–35.** (10 rows of) SC 16, Sl St to beginning stitch, Ch 1 [16]

Leave off the "Ch 1" on the final row.

Fasten off with a 24 in/61 cm yarn tail.

**Square with No Mouth and No Legs, Medium Rounded Underbite, Cute Mitten Limbs, Cute Footed Limbs, Spiky Ears, Large Antlers, Four Humanlike Teeth**

If you want to add metal spikes to any part of your Monster, go to page 172 for tips on how to do that.

## Assembly

**1.** Stuff the end of the limb medium-firm with fiberfill; stuff lightly or not at all in the upper part of the limb.

**2.** Pin in place on the Body.

**3.** Once you are satisfied with placement, sew to the Body using the yarn tail; weave in ends.

# SMALL NUBBINS LIMBS (MAKE 2)

*(RECOMMENDED FOR ARMS OR SMALL LEGS)*

**Approximately 6 in/15 cm long, 1.25 in/3 cm wide at base**

**Main Body Color Yarn: Approximately 17 yd/15.5 m worsted/medium weight yarn per Limb**

**1.** Ch 8, starting in the second Ch from hook, SC 6, Inc, continue to crochet around to the other side of the starting chain, (Bobble, SC) x 2, Bobble, SC in the same stitch as the first SC of this row, Sl St to beginning stitch, Ch 1 [14]

A Bobble is worked as follows:

YO, insert the hook into the next available stitch,

YO, pull up,

YO, pull through 2 loops,

(YO twice, Insert the hook into the same stitch, YO, pull up, YO, pull through 2 loops, YO, pull through 2 loops) x 3

YO, insert the hook into the same stitch,

YO, pull up,

YO, pull through 2 loops,

YO, pull through all remaining loops

Once you've completed a Bobble, you may need to use your pinky finger or the end of your hook to push the Bobble right side out.

**2–6.** (5 rows of) SC 14, Sl St to beginning stitch, Ch 1 [14]

**7.** (SC 5, Dec) x 2, Sl St to beginning stitch, Ch 1 [12]

**8–12.** (5 rows of) SC 12, Sl St to beginning stitch, Ch 1 [12]

**13.** (SC 2, Dec, SC 2) x 2, Sl St to beginning stitch, Ch 1 [10]

**14–23.** (10 rows of) SC 10, Sl St to beginning stitch, Ch 1 [10]

Leave off the "Ch 1" on the final row.

Fasten off with a 12 in/30.5 cm yarn tail.

## Assembly

**1.** Stuff the end of the limb medium-firm with fiberfill; stuff lightly or not at all in the upper part of the limb.

**2.** Pin in place on the Body.

**3.** Once you are satisfied with placement, sew to the Body using the yarn tail; weave in ends.

**Square with Deep Pocket Underbite and Legs, Small Nubbins Limbs, Double-layer Wedge Folded Ears, Tiny Curved Horns**

# LARGE NUBBINS LIMBS (MAKE 2)

*(RECOMMENDED FOR LONG ARMS OR LEGS)*

**Approximately 7.5 in/19 cm long, 2 in/5 cm wide at the base**

**Main Body Color Yarn:** Approximately 34 yd/31 m worsted/medium weight yarn per Limb

1. Ch 10, starting in the second Ch from Hook, SC 8, Inc, continue to crochet around to the other side of the starting chain, SC 7, SC in the same Ch as your first SC in this row, Sl St to beginning stitch, Ch 1 [18]

2. Inc, SC 7, Inc x 2, (Bobble, SC) x 3, Bobble, Inc, Sl St to beginning stitch, Ch 1 [22]

> The Bobble stitch here is worked the same way as in the Small Nubbins Limbs section on page 208.

3–7. (5 rows of) SC 22, Sl St to beginning stitch, Ch 1 [22]

8. (SC 9, Dec) x 2, Sl St to beginning stitch, Ch 1 [20]

9–13. (5 rows of) SC 20, Sl St to beginning stitch, Ch 1 [20]

14. (SC 4, Dec, SC 4) x 2, Sl St to beginning stitch, Ch 1 [18]

15–18. (4 rows of) SC 18, Sl St to beginning stitch, Ch 1 [18]

19. (SC 7, Dec) x 2, Sl St to beginning stitch, Ch 1 [16]

20–23. (4 rows of) SC 16, Sl St to beginning stitch, Ch 1 [16]

24. (SC 3, Dec, SC 3) x 2, Sl St to beginning stitch, Ch 1 [14]

25–27. (3 rows of) SC 14, Sl St to beginning stitch, Ch 1 [14]

28. (SC 5, Dec) x 2, Sl St to beginning stitch [12]

Fasten off with a 12 in/30.5 cm yarn tail.

## Assembly

1. Stuff the end of the limb medium-firm with fiberfill; stuff lightly or not at all in the upper part of the limb.

2. Pin in place on the Body.

3. Once you are satisfied with placement, sew to the Body using the yarn tail; weave in ends.

**Egg Shape with Open Mouth and No Legs, Open Mouth with Short Row of Small Teeth (Upper and Lower), Three-fingered Wide Limbs, Nubbin Footed Limbs, Long Rounded Striped Tail, Medium Slight Curved Striped Horns, Large Ridged Belly**

# NUBBIN FOOTED LIMBS (MAKE 2)

*(RECOMMENDED FOR LEGS)*

**With a Knee, approximately 9.5 in/24 cm long, 2 in/5 cm wide at base, or approximately 3.5 in/9 cm long without a Knee**

**Main Body Color Yarn, longer version with Knee: Approximately 45 yd/41 m worsted/medium weight yarn per Limb**

**Main Body Color Yarn, shorter version without Knee: Approximately 27 yd/24.75 m worsted/medium weight yarn per Limb**

## Optional: Knee for a Longer Limb (Make 1 per Limb)

**1.** SC 6 in Magic Circle, Sl St to beginning stitch, Ch 1 [6]

**2.** Inc x 6, Sl St to beginning stitch [12]

Fasten off with a short yarn tail.

## Limb

**1.** SC 6 in Magic Circle, Sl St to beginning stitch, Ch 1 [6]

**2.** Inc x 6, Sl St to beginning stitch, Ch 1 [12]

**3.** (SC, Inc) x 6, Sl St to beginning stitch, Ch 1 [18]

**4.** (SC, Inc, SC) x 6, Sl St to beginning stitch, Ch 1 [24]

**5.** (SC 3, Inc) x 6, Sl St to beginning stitch, Ch 1 [30]

**6.** SC 10, (Bobble, SC) x 4, Bobble, SC 11, Sl St to beginning stitch, Ch 1 [30]

> The Bobble stitch here is worked the same way as in the Small Nubbins Limbs section on page 208.

**7.** SC 30, Sl St to beginning stitch, Ch 1 [30]

**8.** SC 7, (SC, Dec, SC) x 4, SC 7, Sl St to beginning stitch, Ch 1 [26]

**9.** SC 5, (SC, Dec, SC) x 4, SC 5, Sl St to beginning stitch, Ch 1 [22]

**10.** SC 3, (SC, Dec, SC) x 4, SC 3, Sl St to beginning stitch, Ch 1 [18]

**11.** SC 5, (SC, Dec, SC) x 2, SC 5, Sl St to beginning stitch, Ch 1 [16]

**12–19.** (8 rows of) SC 16, Sl St to beginning stitch, Ch 1 [16]

You can fasten off here for a short Foot/Leg with no Knee, or you can continue to Row 20 to make the Leg longer, dangly, and with a Knee.

**20–23.** (4 rows of) SC 16, Sl St to beginning stitch, Ch 1 [16]

**24.** SC 10, holding the Knee piece against the Leg (right side to right side), working through both pieces at the same time, SC 3, working into the Leg only SC 3, Sl St to beginning stitch, Ch 1 [16]

> When you work through the Knee in Row 24, you will insert your hook through the inside/wrong side to the outside/right side of the Knee, and then through the outside/right side to the inside/wrong side of the Leg. Be careful not to work into the "Sl St, Ch 1" join space. See this video for more information on this technique: https://youtu.be/paLzIAi--vk

**25.** SC 9, start a decrease in the first available stitch on the Leg and complete the decrease in the first available stitch on the Knee, SC 7 around the Knee, start a decrease in the last available stitch on the Knee and complete the decrease in the first available stitch on the Leg, continuing into the next available stitch on the Leg, SC 2, Sl St to beginning stitch, Ch 1 [20]

> In Row 25, you will work around the available stitches by inserting your hook as normal from the right side/outside to the inside/wrong side to complete your stitches. Ignore the stitches that were used to connect the Knee with the Leg. Be careful not to work into the "Sl St, Ch 1" join space.

**26.** (SC 3, Dec) x 4, Sl St to beginning stitch, Ch 1 [16]

**27–36.** (10 rows of) SC 16, Sl St to beginning stitch, Ch 1 [16]

> Do not Ch 1 on your final repeat of these instructions.

Fasten off with a 24 in/61 cm yarn tail.

## Assembly

**1.** Stuff the end of the limb medium-firm with fiberfill. If you are using a shorter limb, stuff the entire limb. If you are using a longer limb or a limb with a Knee, stuff lightly or not at all in the upper part of the limb.

**2.** Pin in place on the Body.

**3.** Once you are satisfied with placement, sew to attach to the Body using the yarn tail; weave in ends.

# LARGE-FOOTED BENT LIMBS (MAKE 2)

*Longer version with a Knee, approximately 10.5 in/26.5 cm long; without a Knee is approximately 5.5 in/14 cm long, 1.5 in/ 4 cm wide at base, 3.5 in/9 cm from heel to toe*

*Main Body Color Yarn: Approximately 60 yds worsted/ medium weight yarn total per Limb*

## Part 1

**1.** Ch 9, starting in the second Ch from hook, SC 6, HDC, work 4 HDC in the final Ch, continue to crochet around to the other side of the starting chain, HDC, SC 5, SC in the same Ch as the first SC in this row, Sl St to beginning stitch, Ch 1 [18]

**2.** Inc, SC 4, HDC 2, HDC Inc x 4, HDC 2, SC 4, Inc, Sl St to beginning stitch, Ch 1 [24]

**3.** SC, Inc, SC 3, HDC 4, HDC Inc x 6, HDC 4, SC 3, Inc, SC, Sl St to beginning stitch, Ch 1 [32]

**4.** SC, Inc, SC 8, HDC 2, (HDC, HDC Inc) x 4, HDC 2, SC 8, Inc, SC, Sl St to beginning stitch, Ch 1 [38]

**5-8.** (4 rows of) SC 38, Sl St to beginning stitch, Ch 1 [38]

**9.** SC 10, (SC, Dec) x 6, SC 10, Sl St to beginning stitch, Ch 1 [32]

**10.** SC 10, Dec x 6, SC 10, Sl St to beginning stitch, Ch 1 [26]

**11.** SC 4, (SC, Dec) x 6, SC 4, Sl St to beginning stitch, Ch 1 [20]

**12.** (SC 3, Dec) x 4, Sl St to beginning stitch, Ch 1 [16]

**13-24.** (12 rows of) SC 16, Sl St to beginning stitch, Ch 1 [16]

You can end the Limb at any point after Row 13 to create a leg without a knee joint. Fasten off with a 24 in/61 cm yarn tail. To create a longer leg with knee joint, work Rows 13–24 as written and continue to Row 25.

**25.** SC 4, Ch 16, SC 12, Sl St to beginning stitch, Ch 1 [16]

Insert a stitch marker in the last Ch stitch of the Ch 16 in Row 25 for reference in Row 1 of Part 2 for where to attach the yarn. Start stuffing the limb with fiberfill at this point; continue to stuff as you crochet.

**26.** SC 4, SC 16 into the Ch Stitches from Row 25, SC 12, Sl St to beginning stitch, Ch 1 [32]

**27.** SC 32, Sl St to beginning stitch, Ch 1 [32]

**28.** (SC 3, Dec, SC 3) x 4, Sl St to beginning stitch, Ch 1 [28]

**29.** (SC 5, Dec) x 4, Sl St to beginning stitch, Ch 1 [24]

**30.** (SC 2, Dec, SC 2) x 4, Sl St to beginning stitch, Ch 1 [20]

**31.** (SC 3, Dec) x 4, Sl St to beginning stitch, Ch 1 [16]

**32.** (SC, Dec, SC) x 4, Sl St to beginning stitch, Ch 1 [12]

Cylinder with Open Mouth and No Legs, Open Mouth with Buck Teeth (Upper), Short Rounded Limbs, Large-footed Bent Limbs, Medium Curved Horns

**33.** (SC, Dec) x 4, Sl St to beginning stitch, Ch 1 [8]

**34.** Dec x 4, Sl St to beginning stitch [4]

Fasten off with a 12 in/30.5 cm yarn tail.

## Part 2

**1.** Attach the yarn to the marked Ch stitch in Row 25 of Part 1, starting in that stitch, SC 16, Sl St to beginning stitch, Ch 1 [16]

**2–10.** (9 rows of) SC 16, Sl St to beginning stitch, Ch 1 [16]

> Do not Ch 1 on your final repeat of these instructions.

Fasten off with a 24 in/61 cm yarn tail.

## Assembly

**1.** Stuff the limb medium-firm with fiberfill.

**2.** Pin in place on the Body.

**3.** Once you are satisfied with placement, sew to the Body using the yarn tail; weave in ends. Sew the hole shut at the point of the knee joint; weave in the end.

# SMALL SHORT LIMBS (MAKE 2)

*(RECOMMENDED FOR ARMS)*

*Approximately 4.5 in/11.5 cm long from base to tip, 1.75 in/4.5 cm wide at the widest part, 1 in/2.5 cm wide at base*

*Main Body Color Yarn: Approximately 15 yd/13.75 m worsted/medium weight yarn per Limb*

**1.** Ch 9, starting in the second Ch from hook, SC 2, HDC 4, SC, Inc, continue to crochet around to the other side of the OC stitches, SC, HDC 4, SC, SC in the same Ch stitch as the first SC in this row, Sl St to beginning stitch, Ch 1 [16]

**2–3.** (2 rows of) SC 2, HDC 4, SC 4, HDC 4, SC 2, Sl St to beginning stitch, Ch 1 [16]

**4–5.** (2 rows of) SC 16, Sl St to beginning stitch, Ch 1 [16]

**6.** (SC, Dec, SC) x 4, Sl St to beginning stitch, Ch 1 [12]

**7.** (SC, Dec, SC) x 3, Sl St to beginning stitch, Ch 1 [9]

**8–16.** (9 rows of) SC 9, Sl St to beginning stitch, Ch 1 [9]

**17.** SC 9, Sl St to beginning stitch [9]

Fasten off with a 24 in/61 cm yarn tail.

## Assembly

**1.** Stuff the end of the limb medium-firm with fiberfill; stuff lightly or not at all in the upper part of the limb.

**2.** Pin in place on the Body.

**3.** Once you are satisfied with placement, sew to the Body using the yarn tail; weave in ends.

# SMALL SHORT ROUNDED LIMBS (MAKE 2)

*(RECOMMENDED FOR ARMS OR SHORTER LEGS)*

***Approximately 4.5 in/11.5 cm long from base to tip, 1.5 in/4 cm wide at the widest part, 1 in/2.5 cm wide at the base***

***Main Body Color Yarn: Approximately 12 yd/11 m worsted/medium weight yarn per Limb***

**1.** SC 6 in Magic Circle, Sl St to beginning stitch, Ch 1 [6]

**2.** Inc x 6, Sl St to beginning stitch, Ch 1 [12]

**3.** (SC, Inc, SC) x 4, Sl St to beginning stitch, Ch 1 [16]

**4–6.** (3 rows of) SC 16, Sl St to beginning stitch, Ch 1 [16]

**7.** (SC, Dec, SC) x 4, Sl St to beginning stitch, Ch 1 [12]

**8–9.** (2 rows of) SC 12, Sl St to beginning stitch, Ch 1 [12]

Stuff the piece medium-firm with fiberfill.

**10.** (SC 2, Dec, SC 2) x 2, Sl St to beginning stitch, Ch 1 [10]

**11–12.** (2 rows of) SC 10, Sl St to beginning stitch, Ch 1 [10]

**13.** (SC 3, Dec) x 2, Sl St to beginning stitch, Ch 1 [8]

**14–16.** (3 rows of) SC 8, Sl St to beginning stitch, Ch 1 [8]

**17.** SC 8, Sl St to beginning stitch [8]

Fasten off with a 12 in/30.5 cm yarn tail.

## Assembly

**1.** Stuff the end of the limb medium-firm with fiberfill; stuff lightly or not at all in the upper part of the limb.

**2.** Pin in place on the Body.

**3.** Once you are satisfied with placement, sew to the Body using the yarn tail; weave in ends.

Egg Shape with No Mouth and Legs, Small Rounded Overbite, Small Short Limbs, Medium to the Side Curved Horns, Hair Puff, Two Small Fangs (Upper), Nose with Wide Nostrils

If you want to add metal spikes to any part of your Monster, go to page 172 for tips on how to do that.

# CROUCHING ROUNDED HIND LEGS (MAKE 2)

*Approximately 4.5 in/11.5 cm long from toes to back of leg, 4 in/10 cm tall from bottom to top*

*Main Body Color Yarn: Approximately 35 yd/32 m worsted/medium weight yarn per Leg*

## Part 1 (Make 1 per Leg)

1. SC 6 in Magic Circle, Sl St to beginning stitch, Ch 1 [6]

2. Inc x 6, Sl St to beginning stitch, Ch 1 [12]

3. (SC, Inc) x 6, Sl St to beginning stitch, Ch 1 [18]

4. (SC, Inc, SC) x 6, Sl St to beginning stitch, Ch 1 [24]

5. (SC 3, Inc) x 6, Sl St to beginning stitch, Ch 1 [30]

6. SC 30, Sl St to beginning stitch, Ch 1 [30]

7. SC 30, Sl St to beginning stitch [30]

Fasten off with a short yarn tail.

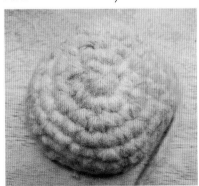

## Part 2 (Make 1 per Leg)

1. SC 6 in Magic Circle, Sl St to beginning stitch, Ch 1 [6]

2. Inc x 6, Sl St to beginning stitch, Ch 1 [12]

3. (SC, Inc) x 6, Sl St to beginning stitch, Ch 1 [18]

4–7. (4 rows of) SC 18, Sl St to beginning stitch, Ch 1 [18]

8. (SC 7, Dec) x 2, Sl St to beginning stitch, Ch 1 [16]

9. SC 16, Sl St to beginning stitch, Ch 1 [16]

10. (SC 3, Dec, SC 3) x 2, Sl St to beginning stitch, Ch 1 [14]

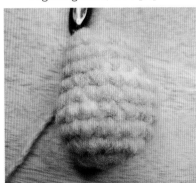

11. SC 7, starting in the first stitch of the final row of Part 1, SC 30, continuing into the next available stitch on Part 2, SC 7, Sl St to beginning stitch, Ch 1 [44]

12. (SC 9, Dec) x 4, Sl St to beginning stitch, Ch 1 [40]

13. (SC 4, Dec, SC 4) x 4, Sl St to beginning stitch, Ch 1 [36]

14. SC 36, Sl St to beginning stitch, Ch 1 [36]

15. (SC 7, Dec) x 4, Sl St to beginning stitch, Ch 1 [32]

16. (SC 3, Dec, SC 3) x 4, Sl St to beginning stitch, Ch 1 [28]

17. SC 28, Sl St to beginning stitch, Ch 1 [28]

18. (SC 5, Dec) x 4, Sl St to beginning stitch, Ch 1 [24]

> Stuff the front of the foot medium-firm with fiberfill; stuff the front of the leg medium-firm with fiberfill. Stuff the rest of the leg very lightly and continue to fill as you crochet. Err on the side of under-stuffing; you want to be able to squash the leg against the body as you sew to attach it.

19. (SC 2, Dec, SC 2) x 4, Sl St to beginning stitch, Ch 1 [20]

20. (SC 3, Dec) x 4, Sl St to beginning stitch, Ch 1 [16]

21. (SC, Dec, SC) x 4, Sl St to beginning stitch, Ch 1 [12]

22. (SC, Dec) x 4, Sl St to beginning stitch [8]

Fasten off with a 24 in/61 cm yarn tail.

### Assembly

**1.** Stuff the end of the limb medium-firm with fiberfill; stuff lightly or not at all in the upper part of the limb.

**2.** Pin in place on the Body, squishing it against the Body a bit as you pin it to attach, as shown.

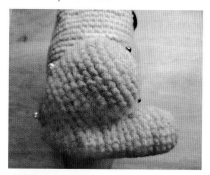

**3.** Once you are satisfied with placement, sew to the Body using the yarn tail with small whipstitches around the entire edge of the limb as it touches the body; weave in ends.

# CURVED ARMS (MAKE 2)

*Approximately 4.5 in/11.5 cm long, 1.5 in/4 cm wide at the widest point, 1 in/2.5 cm wide at base*

*Main Body Color Yarn: Approximately 14 yd/12.75 m worsted/medium weight yarn per Arm*

**1.** SC 6 in Magic Circle, Sl St to beginning stitch, Ch 1 [6]

**2.** Inc x 6, Sl St to beginning stitch, Ch 1 [12]

**3.** (SC 3, Inc) x 3, Sl St to beginning stitch, Ch 1 [15]

**4.** SC 15, Sl St to beginning stitch, Ch 1 [15]

**5.** HDC Dec, SC 6, Inc, SC 6, Sl St to beginning stitch, Ch 1 [15]

**6.** SC 15, Sl St to beginning stitch, Ch 1 [15]

**7.** HDC Dec, SC 6, Inc, SC 6, Sl St to beginning stitch, Ch 1 [15]

**8.** SC 15, Sl St to beginning stitch, Ch 1 [15]

**9.** HDC, HDC Dec, SC 4, Inc, SC 4, HDC Dec, HDC, Sl St to beginning stitch, Ch 1 [14]

**10.** SC 14, Sl St to beginning stitch, Ch 1 [14]

**11.** HDC, HDC Dec, SC 8, HDC Dec, HDC, Sl St to beginning stitch, Ch 1 [12]

**12.** SC 12, Sl St to beginning stitch, Ch 1 [12]

**13.** HDC Dec, Dec, SC 2, <Dec>, SC 2, Dec, HDC Dec, Sl St to beginning stitch, Ch 1 [9]

> "<Dec>" is a stitch that is defined in the Glossary.

**14.** SC 9, Sl St to beginning stitch, Ch 1 [9]

**15.** HDC Dec, SC 2, Inc, SC 2, HDC Dec, Sl St to beginning stitch, Ch 1 [8]

**16.** SC 8, Sl St to beginning stitch, Ch 1 [8]

**17.** HDC Dec, SC, Inc x 2, SC, HDC Dec, Sl St to beginning stitch, Ch 1 [8]

**18.** SC 8, Sl St to beginning stitch

Fasten off with a 24 in/61 cm yarn tail.

> Continue to page 221 for Assembly.

Egg Shape with
Overbite and
Legs, Curved Arms,
Long Bunny Ears,
Squared Teeth

### Assembly

1. Stuff the end of the limb medium-firm with fiberfill; stuff lightly or not at all in the upper part of the limb.

2. Pin in place on the Body.

3. Once you are satisfied with placement, sew to the Body using the yarn tail; weave in ends.

## TINY LITTLE ARMS (MAKE 2)

*Approximately 3.5 in/9 cm long, 1.5 in/4 cm wide at the widest point, 1 in/2.5 cm wide at the base*

*Main Body Color Yarn: Approximately 10 yd/9.25 m worsted/medium weight yarn per Arm*

1. SC 6 in Magic Circle, Sl St to beginning stitch, Ch 1 [6]
2. Inc x 6, Sl St to beginning stitch, Ch 1 [12]
3. (SC 5, Inc) x 2, Sl St to beginning stitch, Ch 1 [14]
4–5. (2 rows of) SC 14, Sl St to beginning stitch, Ch 1 [14]
6. (SC 5, Dec) x 2, Sl St to beginning stitch, Ch 1 [12]

> At this point you can stuff the end of the limb medium-firm with fiberfill. Stuff lightly or not at all in the upper part of the limb as you continue the following rows.

7. (SC 2, Dec, SC 2) x 2, Sl St to beginning stitch, Ch 1 [10]
8. (SC 3, Dec) x 2, Sl St to beginning stitch, Ch 1 [8]
9. (SC, Dec, SC) x 2, Sl St to beginning stitch, Ch 1 [6]
10–13. (4 rows of) SC 6, Sl St to beginning stitch, Ch 1 [6]
14. SC 6, Sl St to beginning stitch [6]

Fasten off with a 24 in/61 cm yarn tail.

### Assembly

1. Pin in place on the Body.

2. Once you are satisfied with placement, sew to the Body using the yarn tail; weave in ends.

Eyeball
Monster
Main Body/Eye with
Crocheted Iris and Pupil,
Eyeball Monster Eyelid,
Tiny Little Arms, Two-toed
Feet with Knees and Legs,
Triangular Scales,
Medium Curved
Horns

# THICK SHORT ARMS WITH CLAWS (MAKE 2)

*Approximately 5.5 in/14 cm long, 2 in/5 cm wide at widest part, 1 in/2.5 cm wide at base*

*Main Body Color Yarn: Approximately 24 yd/22 m worsted/medium weight yarn per Arm*

**1.** SC 6 in Magic Circle, Sl St to beginning stitch, Ch 1 [6]

**2.** (Inc, Ch 4, starting in the second Ch from hook, Sl St, SC 2) x 3, Inc x 2, Ch 4, starting in the second Ch from hook, Sl St, SC 2, Inc, Sl St to beginning stitch, Ch 1 [12]

> All of the "Ch 4, starting in the second Ch from Hook, Sl St, SC 2" instructions create a claw. These claws will not be crocheted into in the following row. Keep them oriented to the outside of the work and skip them in future rows. They are not counted in the stitch count.

**3.** (SC, Inc) x 6, Sl St to beginning stitch, Ch 1 [18]

**4–5.** (2 rows of) SC 18, Sl St to beginning stitch, Ch 1 [18]

**6.** (SC 5, Inc) x 3, Sl St to beginning stitch, Ch 1 [21]

**7–11.** (5 rows of) SC 21, Sl St to beginning stitch, Ch 1 [21]

**12.** (SC 5, Dec) x 3, Sl St to beginning stitch, Ch 1 [18]

**13.** SC 18, Sl St to beginning stitch, Ch 1 [18]

**14.** (SC, Dec) x 6, Sl St to beginning stitch, Ch 1 [12]

> Start to stuff the arm with fiberfill. Stuff this beginning part of the arm medium firmly. Continue to stuff as you crochet. Only stuff the upper part of the arm (Row 17 to Row 22) lightly or not at all.

**15.** Dec x 6, Sl St to beginning stitch, Ch 1 [6]

**16.** SC 6, Sl St to beginning stitch, Ch 1 [6]

**17.** Inc x 6, Sl St to beginning stitch, Ch 1 [12]

**18–21.** (4 rows of) SC 12, Sl St to beginning stitch, Ch 1 [12]

**22.** Dec x 6, Sl St to beginning stitch [6]

Fasten off with a 24 in/61 cm yarn tail.

## Assembly

**1.** Pin in place on the Body.

**2.** Once you are satisfied with placement, sew to the Body using the yarn tail; weave in ends.

# THIN ARMS WITH TWO FINGERS (MAKE 2)

*Approximately 6 in/15 cm long, 2 in/5 cm wide at widest part, 1 in/2.5 cm wide at base*

*Main Body Color Yarn: Approximately 21 yd/19.25 m worsted/medium weight yarn per Arm*

### Part 1: Elbow (Make 1 per Limb)

1. SC 6 in Magic Circle, Sl St to beginning stitch, Ch 1 [6]
2. Inc x 6, Sl St to beginning stitch [12]

Fasten off with a short yarn tail.

### Part 2: Fingers and Arms (Make 2 Fingers, Rows 1–5, and 1 Arm per Limb)

1. SC 6 in Magic Circle, Sl St to beginning stitch, Ch 1 [6]
2–4. (3 rows of) SC 6, Sl St to beginning stitch, Ch 1 [6]
5. SC 6, Sl St to beginning stitch [6]

Fasten off the first Finger with a short yarn tail.

Work Rows 1 through 5 again to make a second Finger, and then proceed to Row 6.

**6.** Ch 1, SC 5, starting into the first stitch on the first Finger, SC 6 around the first Finger, continuing into the last available stitch on the current (second) Finger, SC, Sl St to beginning stitch, Ch 1 [12]

In this row you will work into the available stitches by inserting your hook as normal from the right side/outside to the inside/wrong side to complete your stitches. Be careful not to work into the "Sl St, Ch 1" join space.

**7.** SC 12, Sl St to beginning stitch, Ch 1 [12]

If you want to stuff the arm with fiberfill, you can start to do so now by stuffing the Fingers and continuing to stuff as you crochet. As you work the rest of the piece, leave the upper arm (Row 22 to Row 29) lightly stuffed or not stuffed at all. If you want to use wire in the arm, you can add that later by following the wire instructions for the Three-fingered Hand with Elbow and Arm Assembly instructions (page 179), altering it for only two Fingers.

**8.** SC 4, Dec, SC 4, Dec, Sl St to beginning stitch, Ch 1 [10]

**9.** SC 10, Sl St to beginning stitch, Ch 1 [10]

**10.** SC, Dec, SC 3, Dec, SC 2, Sl St to beginning stitch, Ch 1 [8]

**11–18.** (8 rows of) SC 8, Sl St to beginning stitch, Ch 1 [8]

You can end here for a short arm without an elbow (leave off the Ch 1 on the final repeat). For a longer arm with an elbow, continue to Row 19.

**19.** SC 3, holding the Elbow piece against the current work (right side to right side), working through both pieces at the same time, SC 4, SC through the Arm only [8]

When you work through the Elbow in this row, you will insert your hook through the inside/wrong side to the outside/right side of the Elbow and then through the outside/right side to the inside/wrong side of the Arm.

**20.** SC 2, start a decrease in the last available stitch on the Arm and complete the decrease in the first available stitch on the Elbow, SC 6, start a decrease in the last available stitch on the Elbow and complete the decrease in the last available stitch on the Arm, Sl St to beginning stitch, Ch 1 [10]

In this row you will work into the available stitches by inserting your hook as normal from the right side/outside to the inside/wrong side to complete your stitches. Ignore the stitches from the previous row that were used to connect the Elbow to the Arm. Be careful not to work into the "Sl St, Ch 1" join space.

**21.** SC 2, Dec, SC 4, Dec, Sl St to beginning stitch, Ch 1 [8]

**22–29.** (8 rows of) SC 8, Sl St to beginning stitch, Ch 1 [8]

Leave off the "Ch 1" on the final row.

Fasten off with a 12 in/30.5 cm yarn tail.

## Assembly

**1.** Pin in place on the Body.

**2.** Once you are satisfied with placement, sew to the Body using the yarn tail; weave in ends.

Cylinder with Open Mouth and Legs, Open Mouth with Four Pointed Teeth (Lower), Thin Arms with Two Fingers, Skinny Spikes, Long Reptile Tail, Long Slightly Curved Horns, Embroidered Eyebrows

# SHORT ARMS WITH TWO FINGERS (MAKE 2)

*Approximately 6 in/15 cm long, 2 in/5.0 cm wide at the widest part, 1 in/2.5 cm wide at the base*

*Main Body Color Yarn: Approximately 19 yd/17.5 m worsted/medium weight yarn per Arm*

## Make 2 Fingers (Rows 1–7) and 1 Arm per Limb

**1.** SC 6 in Magic Circle, Sl St to beginning stitch, Ch 1 [6]

**2.** (SC, Inc, SC) x 2, Sl St to beginning stitch, Ch 1 [8]

**3–6.** (4 rows of) SC 8, Sl St to beginning stitch, Ch 1 [8]

**7.** SC 8, Sl St to beginning stitch [8]

Fasten off the first Finger with a short yarn tail.

Work Rows 1 through 7 again to make a second Finger, and then proceed to Row 8.

**8.** Ch 1, SC 8, starting into the first stitch on the first Finger, SC 8 around the first Finger, Sl St to beginning stitch, Ch 1 [16]

In this row you will work into the available stitches by inserting your hook as normal from the right side/outside to the inside/wrong side to complete your stitches. Be careful not to work into the "Sl St, Ch 1" join space.

**9–11.** (3 rows of) SC 16, Sl St to beginning stitch, Ch 1 [16]

If you want to stuff the arm with fiberfill, you can start to do so now by stuffing the Fingers, and continue to stuff as you crochet, leaving the upper arm lightly stuffed or not stuffed at all. If you want to use wire in the arm, you can add that later by following the wire instructions from the Three-fingered Hand with Elbow and Arm (page 179), altering it for two Fingers.

**12.** (SC 3, Dec, SC 3) x 2, Sl St to beginning stitch, Ch 1 [14]

**13–15.** (3 rows of) SC 14, Sl St to beginning stitch, Ch 1 [14]

**16.** (SC 5, Dec) x 2, Sl St to beginning stitch, Ch 1 [12]

**17–19.** (3 rows of) SC 12, Sl St to beginning stitch, Ch 1 [12]

**20.** (SC 2, Dec, SC 2) x 2, Sl St to beginning stitch, Ch 1 [10]

**21–23.** (3 rows of) SC 10, Sl St to beginning stitch, Ch 1 [10]

**24.** (SC 3, Dec) x 2, Sl St to beginning stitch, Ch 1 [8]

**25–26.** (2 rows of) SC 8, Sl St to beginning stitch, Ch 1 [8]

**27.** SC 8, Sl St to beginning stitch [8]

Fasten off with a 12 in/30.5 cm yarn tail.

## Assembly

**1.** Pin in place on the Body.

**2.** Once you are satisfied with placement, sew to the Body using the yarn tail; weave in ends.

Egg Shape with Open Mouth and No Legs, Open Mouth with Buck Teeth (Lower), Small Short Rounded Limbs, Large Rounded Feet, Triangular Scales, Curved Dragon/Dinosaur Tail, Fin Ears, Large Ridged Belly

Square with Deep Pocket Underbite and No Legs, Curved Arms, Crouching Rounded Hind Legs, Rounded Scales, Straight Dragon/Dinosaur Tail, Short Bunny Ears

Eyeball Monster Main Body/Eye with Safety Eye, Eyeball Monster Eyelid, Short Arms with Two Fingers, Two-toed Feet with Knees and Legs, Skinny Curved Horns

Cylinder with Open Mouth and No Legs, Open Mouth with No Teeth Black Hole, Three-toed Dangling Legs (also used as Arms), Long Slightly Curved Horns

# THREE-TOED DANGLING LEGS (MAKE 2)

*(RECOMMENDED FOR LEGS, BUT INSTRUCTIONS ARE ALSO GIVEN FOR A SHORTER VERSION FOR ARMS)*

---

***Approximately 9 in/23 cm long, 1 in/2.5 cm wide at base, 3.5 in/ 9 cm wide across the toes***

***Main Body Color Yarn: Approximately 29 yd/26.5 m worsted/ medium weight yarn per Leg***

### Part 1: Knee Joint (Make 1 per Limb)

**1.** SC 6 in Magic Circle, Sl St to beginning stitch, Ch 1 [6]

**2.** (Inc, SC, Inc) x 2, Sl St to beginning stitch [10]

Fasten off with a short yarn tail.

### Part 2: Toes and Limb (Make 3 Toes, Rows 1–7, and 1 Leg per Limb)

**1.** SC 6 in Magic Circle, Sl St to beginning stitch, Ch 1 [6]

**2.** Inc x 6, Sl St to beginning stitch, Ch 1 [12]

**3.** SC 12, Sl St to beginning stitch, Ch 1 [12]

**4.** Dec x 6, Sl St to beginning stitch, Ch 1 [6]

**5–6.** (2 rows of) SC 6, Sl St to beginning stitch, Ch 1 [6]

**7.** SC 6, Sl St to beginning stitch [6]

Fasten off first and second Toes with a short yarn tail. Do not fasten off third Toe, but proceed to Row 8.

**8.** Ch 1, SC 6, Sl St to beginning stitch, Ch 1 [6]

**9.** SC 2, starting into the first stitch on the first Toe, SC 6, continuing into the next available stitch on the current (third) Toe, SC 3, starting into the first stitch on the second Toe, SC 6, SC in the last available stitch on the current (third) Toe, Sl St to beginning stitch, Ch 1 [18]

> In this row you will work into the available stitches by inserting your hook as normal from the right side/outside to the inside/ wrong side to complete your stitches. Be careful not to work into the "Sl St, Ch 1" join space.

**10.** SC 18, Sl St to beginning stitch, Ch 1 [18]

**11.** (SC 2, Dec, SC 2) x 3, Sl St to beginning stitch, Ch 1 [15]

**12.** SC 15, Sl St to beginning stitch, Ch 1 [15]

> If you want to stuff the limb with fiberfill, you can start to do so now by stuffing the toes, and continue to stuff as you crochet, leaving the upper limb lightly stuffed or not stuffed at all. If you want to use wire in the limb, you can add that later on by following the wire instructions for the Three-fingered Hand with Elbow and Arm (page 179).

**13.** (SC 3, Dec) x 3, Sl St to beginning stitch, Ch 1 [12]

**14.** SC 12, Sl St to beginning stitch, Ch 1 [12]

**15.** (SC 2, Dec, SC 2) x 2, Sl St to beginning stitch, Ch 1 [10]

**16–24.** (9 rows of) SC 10, Sl St to beginning stitch, Ch 1 [10]

> For an Arm, work 6 rows of SC 10, Sl St to beginning stitch, Ch 1, Skip Rows 22–24, and continue with Row 25.

**25.** SC 6, holding the Knee joint against the current piece (right side to right side), complete a SC through both pieces at the same time, working through the next available stitch on both pieces at the same time SC 2, continuing into the next available stitch on the Leg, SC, Sl St to beginning stitch, Ch 1 [10]

When you work through the Knee in this row, you will insert your hook through the inside/wrong side to the outside/right side of the Knee, and then through the outside/right side to the inside/wrong side of the Leg. Be careful not to work into the "Sl St, Ch 1" join space. See this video for more information on this technique: https://youtu.be/paLzIAi--vk

**26.** SC 5, start a decrease in the last available stitch on the Leg and complete the decrease in the first available stitch on the Knee, SC 5 around the Knee, start a decrease in the last available stitch on the Knee and complete the decrease in the first available stitch on the Leg, Sl St to beginning stitch, Ch 1 [12]

In this row you will work around the available stitches by inserting your hook as normal from the right side/outside to the inside/wrong side to complete your stitches. Ignore the stitches that were used to connect the Knee with the current work. Be careful not to work into the "Sl St, Ch 1" join space.

**27.** (SC 2, Dec, SC 2) x 2, Sl St to beginning stitch, Ch 1 [10]

**28–38.** (11 rows of) SC 10, Sl St to beginning stitch, Ch 1 [10]

**39.** SC 10, Sl St to beginning stitch [10]

Fasten off with a 12 in/30.5 cm yarn tail.

### Assembly

**1.** Pin in place on the Body.

**2.** Once you are satisfied with placement, sew to the Body using the yarn tail; weave in ends.

Square with Underbite and No Legs, Squarish Short Limbs, Squarish Long Limbs, Medium Slight Curved Striped Horns, Two Separated Rounded Teeth

## SQUARISH SHORT LIMBS (MAKE 2)

### (RECOMMENDED FOR ARMS OR LEGS)

*Approximately 6 in/15 cm long, 2 in/5 cm wide at the end, 1.25 in/ 3 cm wide at the base*

*Main Body Color Yarn: Approximately 28 yd/25.5 m worsted/ medium weight yarn per Limb*

1. SC 8 in Magic Circle, Sl St to beginning stitch, Ch 1 [8]
2. (SC, HDC Inc) x 4, Sl St to beginning stitch, Ch 1 [12]
3. (SC 2, <HDC Dec>, SC) x 4, Sl St to beginning stitch, Ch 1 [16]

> <Dec> is a stitch that is defined in the glossary. A <HDC Dec> is worked the same way as <Dec> but using a "HDC Dec" instead of just a "Dec."

4. (SC 2, HDC Triple Inc, SC) x 4, Sl St to beginning stitch, Ch 1 [24]
5. BLO [SC 24], Sl St to beginning stitch, Ch 1 [24]
6-7. (2 rows of) SC 24, Sl St to beginning stitch, Ch 1 [24]
8. (SC 3, Dec, SC 3) x 3, Sl St to beginning stitch, Ch 1 [21]
9-11. (3 Rows of) SC 21, Sl St to beginning stitch, Ch 1 [21]
12. (SC 5, Dec) x 3, Sl St to beginning stitch, Ch 1 [18]

13-15. (3 rows of) SC 18, Sl St to beginning stitch, Ch 1 [18]
16. (SC 2, Dec, SC 2) x 3, Sl St to beginning stitch, Ch 1 [15]
17-19. (3 rows of) SC 15, Sl St to beginning stitch, Ch 1 [15]
20. (SC 3, Dec) x 3, Sl St to beginning stitch, Ch 1 [12]
21-23. (3 rows of) SC 12, Sl St to beginning stitch, Ch 1 [12]
24. (SC 2, Dec, SC 2) x 2, Sl St to beginning stitch, Ch 1 [10]
25-26. (2 rows of) SC 10, Sl St to beginning stitch, Ch 1 [10]
27. SC 10, Sl St to beginning stitch [10]

Fasten off with a 12 in/30.5 cm yarn tail.

### Assembly

1. Stuff the limb with fiberfill medium-firm at the bottom of the limb and lighter or not at all at the top.
2. Pin in place on the Body.

3. Once you are satisfied with placement, sew to the Body using the yarn tail; weave in ends.

## SQUARISH LONG LIMBS (MAKE 2)

### (RECOMMENDED FOR LEGS OR VERY LONG ARMS)

*Approximately 8.5 in/21.5 cm long, 2.75 in/7 cm wide at the end, 1.5 in/4 cm wide at the base of the Limb*

*Main Body Color Yarn: Approximately 59 yd/54 m worsted/medium weight yarn per Limb*

1. SC 8 in Magic Circle, Sl St to beginning stitch, Ch 1 [8]
2. (SC, HDC Triple Inc) x 4, Sl St to beginning stitch, Ch 1 [16]
3. (SC 2, HDC Triple Inc, SC) x 4, Sl St to beginning stitch, Ch 1 [24]
4. (SC 3, HDC Triple Inc, SC 2) x 4, Sl St to beginning stitch, Ch 1 [32]
5. (SC 4, HDC Triple Inc, SC 3) x 4, Sl St to beginning stitch, Ch 1 [40]
6. BLO [SC 40], Sl St to beginning stitch, Ch 1 [40]

**7–8.** (2 rows of) SC 40, Sl St to beginning stitch, Ch 1 [40]

> You can include a wide bottle cap or piece of plastic canvas at the bottom of the limb to keep it flat.

**9.** (SC 4, Dec, SC 4) x 4, Sl St to beginning stitch, Ch 1 [36]

**10–12.** (3 rows of) SC 36, Sl St to beginning stitch, Ch 1 [36]

**13.** (SC 7, Dec) x 4, Sl St to beginning stitch, Ch 1 [32]

**14–16.** (3 rows of) SC 32, Sl St to beginning stitch, Ch 1 [32]

**17.** (SC 3, Dec, SC 3) x 4, Sl St to beginning stitch, Ch 1 [28]

**18–20.** (3 rows of) SC 28, Sl St to beginning stitch, Ch 1 [28]

**21.** (SC 5, Dec) x 4, Sl St to beginning stitch, Ch 1 [24]

**22–24.** (3 rows of) SC 24, Sl St to beginning stitch, Ch 1 [24]

**25.** (SC 2, Dec, SC 2) x 4, Sl St to beginning stitch, Ch 1 [20]

**26–28.** (3 rows of) SC 20, Sl St to beginning stitch, Ch 1 [20]

**29.** (SC 3, Dec) x 4, Sl St to beginning stitch, Ch 1 [16]

**30–34.** (5 rows of) SC 16, Sl St to beginning stitch, Ch 1 [16]

**35.** (SC, Dec, SC) x 4, Sl St to beginning stitch, Ch 1 [12]

**36–39.** (4 rows of) SC 12, Sl St to beginning stitch, Ch 1 [12]

**40.** SC 12, Sl St to beginning stitch [12]

Fasten off with a 12 in/30.5 cm yarn tail.

## Assembly

**1.** If desired, you can place a little bit of something weighted at the bottom of the inside of the limb. Stuff the limb with fiberfill medium-firm at the bottom of the limb, lighter or nothing at the top.

**2.** Pin in place on the Body.

**3.** Once you are satisfied with placement, sew to the Body using the yarn tail; weave in ends.

# TINY LITTLE FOOTED LEGS (MAKE 2)

*Approximately 5.5 in/14 cm long, 1.25 in/3 cm at the base, 1.75 in/4.5 cm from heel to toe*

*Main Body Color Yarn: Approximately 16 yd/14.75 m worsted/medium weight yarn per Leg*

### Optional: Knee (Make 1 per Limb if you want your Leg to be long enough to have a Knee/dangle)

**1.** SC 8 in Magic Circle, Sl St to beginning stitch [8]

Fasten off with a short yarn tail.

### Leg

**1.** Ch 6, starting in the second Ch from hook, SC 4, Inc, continue to crochet around to the other side of the OC stitches, SC 3, SC in the same Ch stitch as the first SC of this row, Sl St to beginning stitch, Ch 1 [10]

**2.** Inc, SC 2, HDC Inc x 4, SC 2, Inc, Sl St to beginning stitch, Ch 1 [16]

**3.** BLO [SC 16], Sl St to beginning stitch, Ch 1 [16]

**4.** SC 5, Dec, SC 2, Dec, SC 5, Sl St to beginning stitch, Ch 1 [14]

**5.** SC 5, Dec x 2, SC 5, Sl St to beginning stitch, Ch 1 [12]

**6.** SC 4, Dec x 2, SC 4, Sl St to beginning stitch, Ch 1 [10]

**7.** SC 3, Dec x 2, SC 3, Sl St to beginning stitch, Ch 1 [8]

**8–14.** (7 rows of) SC 8, Sl St to beginning stitch, Ch 1 [8]

You can fasten off here for a short Foot/Leg with no knee (leave off the Ch 1 on the final repeat). For a longer, dangly Leg with a Knee, continue to Row 15.

**15.** SC 4, holding the Knee piece against the current piece (right side to right side), SC 2 through both pieces at the same time, SC 2, Sl St to beginning stitch, Ch 1 [8]

When you work into a joint piece, insert your hook into the wrong side/inside of the joint piece first; then insert your hook into the right side/outside of the limb next, and complete a SC through both at the same time. Do not work into the Sl St join from the joint piece. See this video for more information on this technique: https://youtu.be/paLzIAi--vk

**16.** SC 3, start a decrease in the next available stitch on the Leg and complete the decrease in the first available stitch on the Knee, SC 4 on the Knee only, start a decrease in the last available stitch on the Knee and complete the decrease in the next available stitch on the Leg, SC in the Leg only, Sl St to beginning stitch, Ch 1 [10]

In this row, when you work into the Knee piece you will insert your hook as normal (right side/outside to inside/wrong side). Ignore the stitches that were used to connect the Knee and the Leg in the previous row.

**17–23.** (7 rows of) SC 10, Sl St to beginning stitch, Ch 1 [10]

**24.** SC 10, Sl St to beginning stitch [10]

Fasten off with a 12 in/30.5 cm yarn tail.

## Assembly

**1.** Stuff the limb with fiberfill medium-firm at the bottom of the limb, lighter or nothing at the top. If desired, you can place a little bit of something weighted at the bottom of the inside of the limb.

**2.** Pin in place on the Body.

**3.** Once you are satisfied with placement, sew to the body using the yarn tail; weave in ends.

Sphere with No Mouth, Medium Rounded Underbite, Short Arms with Two Fingers, Tiny Little Footed Legs, Medium Curved Horns, Individual Small Short Fangs, Long Thin Tongue

# BACK SCALES

## OPTIONS

Triangular Scales...238

Rounded Scales...238

Triangular Spikes of
Varying Size...239

Skinny Spikes...240

# TRIANGULAR SCALES (MAKE 1)

*Each triangle scale is approximately 1 in/2.5 cm wide and 1.25 in/ 3 cm tall*

*Accent Color Yarn: Approximately 17 yd/15.5 m worsted/medium weight yarn (this will vary depending on the length of the scale piece)*

1. Ch 5, starting in the second Ch from hook, SC, HDC, DC, Half Trip, Ch 6, Turn [4]

2. Starting in the second Ch from hook, SC, HDC, DC, Half Trip, Ch 6, Turn [4]

Repeat Row 2 as many times as necessary to create a long enough piece to stretch either from the center of the Monster's forehead down the back/spine of the Monster's Body OR from the center of the Monster's forehead down the back/spine of the Monster's Body and along the tail to the tail tip. Leave off the "Ch 6" on the final repeat.

3. *Optional:* Ch 1, turn to work back along the scales you created in the previous rows, (Sl St 4, Ch 2, Sl St in the second Ch from hook, working back down the chain side of the stitches that make up the scale, Sl St 4, Sl St in the chain between the current and next scale). Repeat these instructions up and down each scale you made in the previous rows; leave off the final Sl St instruction on the final scale.

Fasten off with a 48 in/122 cm yarn tail.

## Assembly

1. Pin the scales into position on the Body of the Monster.

2. Once you are satisfied with placement, sew to the Body using the yarn tail; weave in ends.

# ROUNDED SCALES (MAKE 1)

*Each rounded scale is approximately 1.25 in/3 cm wide and 0.75 in/2 cm tall*

*Accent Color Yarn: Approximately 7 yd/6.5 m worsted/medium weight yarn (this will vary depending on the length of the scale piece)*

1. Chain a length equal to the length you want to span with the back scales in a multiple of 6 (for example, if you want the piece to be about 10 to 11 inches long, Ch 54), Turn

2. Starting into the third Ch from hook, work 5 DC into one Ch stitch, Sk 2 Ch stitches, Sl St

3. Sk 2 Ch stitches, work 5 DC into the next available Ch stitch, Sk 2 Ch stitches, Sl St into the next available Ch stitch

Repeat step 3 until you've reached the end of the chain from Row 1.

Fasten off with a long enough yarn tail to be able to attach to the Body (36 in/ 91.5 cm or more).

## Assembly

**1.** Pin the scales in place on the Body of the Monster.

**2.** Once you are satisfied with placement, sew to the Body using the yarn tail; weave in ends.

# TRIANGULAR SPIKES OF VARYING SIZE (MAKE 1)

*Approximately 6.5 in/16.5 cm long, 1 in/2.5 cm tall at the tallest point*

*Accent Color Yarn: Approximately 4 yd/3.75 m worsted/medium weight yarn*

**1.** Starting with a long enough yarn tail to weave in later, Ch 4, Sl St in the second Ch from hook [1]

**2.** Ch 4, starting in the second Ch from hook, Sl St, SC [2]

**3–9.** (7 rows of) Ch 5, starting in the second Ch from hook, Sl St, SC, HDC [3]

**10.** Ch 4, starting in the second Ch from hook, Sl St, SC [2]

**11.** Ch 3, Sl St in the second Ch from hook [1]

**12.** Ch 3, Sl St in the second Ch from hook [1]

**13.** Ch 2, Turn, starting in the second Ch from hook, Sl St all the way back down the length of the base of the spikes (approximately Sl St 33) [≈33]

Fasten off with a 24 in/61 cm yarn tail.

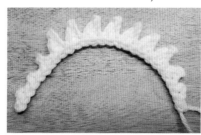

## Assembly

**1.** Pin the scales in place on the Body of the Monster.

**2.** Once you are satisfied with placement, sew to the Body using the yarn tail; weave in ends.

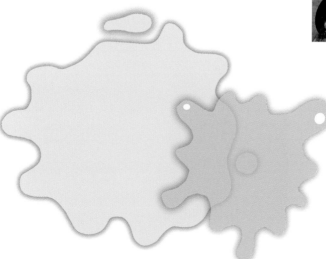

# SKINNY SPIKES (MAKE 1)

*Each spike is approximately 0.5 in/1.5 cm wide and 1 in/2.5 cm tall*

*Accent Color Yarn: Approximately 20 yd/18.25 m worsted/medium weight yarn (this will vary depending on the length of the scale piece)*

1. Starting with a long enough yarn tail to weave in later, Ch 5, starting in the second Ch from hook, Sl St, SC 3, Ch 5, Turn [4]

2. Starting in the second Ch from hook, Sl St, SC 3, Ch 5, Turn [4]

Repeat Row 2 until you have created a line of spikes long enough for your Monster. Leave off the "Ch 5" on the final repeat.

Fasten off with a 24 in/61 cm yarn tail.

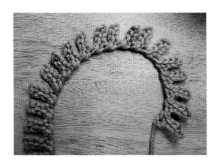

## Assembly

1. Pin the scales in place on the Body of the Monster.

2. Once you are satisfied with placement, sew to the Body using the yarn tail; weave in ends.

Cylinder with Open Mouth and Legs, Open Mouth with Four Pointed Teeth (Lower), Thin Arms with Two Fingers, Skinny Spikes, Long Reptile Tail, Long Slightly Curved Horns

# TAILS

## OPTIONS

Curved Dragon/Dinosaur Tail...242

Long Rounded
Striped Tail...243

Straight Dragon/Dinosaur Tail...245

Cat Tail...246

Long Reptile Tail...246

Tail with Hair Puff ...249

# CURVED DRAGON/DINOSAUR TAIL (MAKE 1)

*Approximately 7.5 in/19 cm long from base to tip, 4 in/10 cm wide at the base*

*Main Body Color Yarn: Approximately 35 yd/32 m worsted/medium weight yarn*

1. SC 6 in Magic Circle, Sl St to beginning stitch, Ch 1 [6]

2. SC 6, Sl St to beginning stitch, Ch 1 [6]

3. SC 5, Inc, Sl St to beginning stitch, Ch 1 [7]

4. SC 7, Sl St to beginning stitch, Ch 1 [7]

5. SC, HDC 4, SC 2, Sl St to beginning stitch, Ch 1 [7]

6. SC 6, <Dec>, SC, Sl St to beginning stitch, Ch 1 [8]

"<Dec>" is a stitch that is defined in the Glossary.

7. HDC 5, SC 3, Sl St to beginning stitch, Ch 1 [8]

8. SC 5, Inc, SC, Inc, Sl St to beginning stitch, Ch 1 [10]

9. SC, 2 Dec in 3 SC, SC 3, Inc, SC 2, Sl St to beginning stitch Ch 1 [10]

10. HDC 6, Inc, SC, Inc, HDC, Sl St to beginning stitch, Ch 1 [12]

11. SC 12, Sl St to beginning stitch, Ch 1 [12]

12. SC 7, Inc, SC, Inc, SC 2, Sl St to beginning stitch, Ch 1 [14]

13. HDC 8, Inc, SC, Inc, HDC 3, Sl St to beginning stitch, Ch 1 [16]

14. SC 2, Dec, SC 7, <Dec>, SC 5, Sl St to beginning stitch, Ch 1 [16]

15. SC 9, Inc, SC, Inc, SC 4, Sl St to beginning stitch, Ch 1 [18]

16. SC 18, Sl St to beginning stitch, Ch 1 [18]

17. HDC 10, Inc, SC, Inc, HDC 5, Sl St to beginning stitch, Ch 1 [20]

18. SC 11, Inc, SC, Inc, SC 6, Sl St to beginning stitch, Ch 1 [22]

19. HDC 12, Inc, SC, Inc, HDC 7, Sl St to beginning stitch, Ch 1 [24]

20. SC 12, Inc, SC, Inc, SC, Inc, SC 7, Sl St to beginning stitch, Ch 1 [27]

21. HDC 14, Inc, SC, <Dec>, SC, Inc, HDC 9, Sl St to beginning stitch, Ch 1 [30]

Egg Shape with Open Mouth and No Legs, Open Mouth with Buck Teeth (Lower), Small Short Rounded Limbs, Large Rounded Feet, Triangular Scales, Curved Dragon/Dinosaur Tail, Fin Ears, Large Ridged Belly

**22.** SC 15, Inc, SC, Inc, SC, Inc, SC 10, Sl St to beginning stitch, Ch 1 [33]

**23.** HDC 17, Inc, SC, <Dec>, SC, Inc, HDC 12, Sl St to beginning stitch, Ch 1 [36]

**24.** (SC 4, Inc, SC 4) x 4, Sl St to beginning stitch, Ch 1 [40]

**25.** (SC 9, Inc) x 4, Sl St to beginning stitch, Ch 1 [44]

**26.** (SC 5, Inc, SC 5) x 4, Sl St to beginning stitch [48]

Fasten off with a 24 in/61 cm yarn tail.

## Assembly

**1.** Stuff the tail medium-firm with fiberfill.

**2.** Pin the tail in position on the back of the Monster's Body.

**3.** Once you are satisfied with placement, sew to the Body using yarn tails and weave in ends.

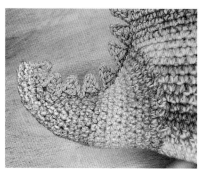

# LONG ROUNDED STRIPED TAIL (MAKE 1)

*Approximately 17 in/43 cm long, 1 in/2.5 cm wide at the base (though this is variable, and you can make a longer or shorter tail as desired)*

*Main Body Color Yarn: Approximately 32 yd/29.25 m worsted/medium weight yarn (this will vary depending on the length of the tail piece)*

*Accent Color Yarn: Approximately 25 yd/22.75 m worsted/medium weight yarn (this will vary depending on the length of the tail piece)*

**1.** Starting with the Main Body Color Yarn, SC 6 in Magic Circle, Sl St to beginning stitch, Ch 1 [6]

**2.** Inc x 6, Sl St to beginning stitch, Ch 1 [12]

**3.** (SC, Inc) x 6, Sl St to beginning stitch, Ch 1 [18]

**4–9.** (6 rows of) SC 18, Sl St to beginning stitch, Ch 1 [18]

**10.** (SC 2, Dec, SC 2) x 3, Sl St to beginning stitch, Ch 1 [15]

**11.** SC 15, Sl St to beginning stitch, Ch 1 [15]

**12.** SC 15, Sl St to beginning stitch, fasten off the Main Body Color Yarn and switch to the Accent Color [15]

> When changing colors in this section, you will fasten off after completing the row entirely. You will attach the new yarn color to the first stitch of the previous row with a "Sl St, Ch 1," and then work the first stitch of the row into the same stitch you slip stitched to attach to.

**13.** Working with the Accent Color Yarn, SC 15, Sl St to beginning stitch, Ch 1 [15]

**14.** (SC 3, Dec) x 3, Sl St to beginning stitch, Ch 1 [12]

**15.** SC 12, Sl St to beginning stitch, fasten off the Accent Color Yarn and switch to the Main Body Color Yarn [12]

**16.** Working with the Main Body Color Yarn, SC 12, Sl St to beginning stitch, Ch 1 [12]

**17.** SC 12, Sl St to beginning stitch, Ch 1 [12]

**18.** (SC 2, Dec, SC 2) x 2, Sl St to beginning stitch, fasten off Main Body Color Yarn and switch to the Accent Color [10]

**19.** Working with the Accent Color Yarn, SC 10, Sl St to beginning stitch, Ch 1 [10]

**20.** SC 10, Sl St to beginning stitch, Ch 1 [10]

**21.** SC 10, Sl St to beginning stitch, fasten off the Accent Color Yarn and switch to the Main Body Color Yarn [10]

> Stuff the end of the tail medium-firm with fiberfill. Do not stuff the rest of the tail as you crochet.

**22.** Working with the Main Body Color Yarn, (SC 3, Dec) x 2, Sl St to beginning stitch, Ch 1 [8]

**23.** SC 8, Sl St to beginning stitch, Ch 1 [8]

**24.** SC 8, Sl St to beginning stitch, fasten off Main Body Color Yarn and switch to the Accent Color [8]

**25.** Working with the Accent Color Yarn, SC 8, Sl St to beginning stitch, Ch 1 [8]

**26.** SC 8, Sl St to beginning stitch, Ch 1 [8]

**27.** SC 8, Sl St to beginning stitch, fasten off Accent Color Yarn and switch to the Main Body Color Yarn [8]

**28–30.** Work 3 rows of SC 8 in the Main Body Color Yarn; then fasten off and switch to the Accent Color Yarn [8]

**31–33.** Work 3 rows of SC 8 in the Accent Color Yarn; then fasten off and switch to the Main Body Color Yarn [8]

**34–?** Repeat the pattern of 3 rows of SC 8 per color, alternating, until the tail has reached the desired length.

Fasten off with a 24 in/61 cm yarn tail.

## Assembly

**1.** Pin the tail in position on the back of the Monster's Body.

**2.** Once you are satisfied with placement, sew to attach using yarn tails and weave in ends.

**Egg Shape with Open Mouth and No Legs, Open Mouth with Short Row of Small Teeth, Three-fingered Wide Limbs, Nubbin Footed Limbs, Long Rounded Striped Tail, Medium Slight Curved Striped Horns, Large Ridged Belly**

# STRAIGHT DRAGON/DINOSAUR TAIL (MAKE 1)

***Approximately 5 in/13 cm long, 3 in/7.5 cm wide at the base***

***Main Body Color Yarn: Approximately 24 yd/22 m worsted/medium weight yarn***

1. SC 6 in Magic Circle, continue in spiral [6]
2. Inc, SC 5 [7]
3. SC, Triple SC Inc, SC 5 [9]

> To make a Triple SC Inc, work 3 SC stitches into 1 stitch.

4. SC 2, Triple SC Inc, SC 6 [11]
5. SC 11 [11]
6. SC 4, Triple SC Inc, SC 6 [13]
7. SC 5, Triple SC Inc, SC 7 [15]
8. SC 15 [15]
9. SC 7, Triple SC Inc, SC 7 [17]
10. SC 8, Triple SC Inc, SC 8 [19]
11. SC 19 [19]
12. SC 10, Triple SC Inc, SC 8 [21]
13. SC 11, Triple SC Inc, SC 9 [23]
14. SC 23 [23]
15. SC 12, Triple SC Inc, SC 10 [25]
16. SC 13, Triple SC Inc, SC 11 [27]
17. SC 27 [27]
18. SC 15, Triple SC Inc, SC 11 [29]
19. SC 16, Triple SC Inc, SC 12 [31]
20. SC 31 [31]
21. SC 18, Triple SC Inc, SC 12 [33]
22. SC 19, Triple SC Inc, SC 13 [35]

Fasten off with a 24 in/61 cm yarn tail.

## Assembly

1. Stuff the tail medium-firm with fiberfill.
2. Pin the tail in position on the back of the Monster's Body.
3. Once you are satisfied with placement, sew to attach using yarn tails and weave in ends.

Square with Deep Pocket Underbite and No Legs, Curved Arms, Crouching Rounded Hind Legs, Rounded Scales, Straight Dragon/Dinosaur Tail, Short Bunny Ears

## CAT TAIL (MAKE 1)

***Approximately 16.5 in/42 cm long, 1 in/2.5 cm wide at base***

***Main Body Color Yarn: Approximately 36 yd/33 m worsted/medium weight yarn***

**1.** SC 6 in Magic Circle, Sl St to beginning stitch, Ch 1 [6]

**2.** (SC, Inc) x 3, Sl St to beginning stitch, Ch 1 [9]

> If you want the tail to be straight and stuffed, it is optional to stuff the tail medium-firm with fiberfill as you go. The tail pictured is unstuffed.

**3–61.** (59 rows of) SC 9, Sl St to beginning stitch, Ch 1 [9]

**62.** SC 9, Sl St to beginning stitch [9]

Fasten off with a 12 in/30.5 cm yarn tail.

### Assembly

**1.** Pin the tail in position on the back of the Monster's Body.

**2.** Once you are satisfied with placement, sew to attach using yarn tails and weave in ends.

Egg Shape with Overbite and No Legs, Short Rounded Limbs, Long Rounded Limbs, Cat Tail, Cat Ears, Two Walrus Tusks, Muzzle for Egg Shape Body (Overbite)

## LONG REPTILE TAIL (MAKE 1)

***Approximately 15 in/38 cm long, 2 in/5 cm wide at base***

***Main Body Color Yarn: Approximately 54 yd/49.5 m worsted/medium weight yarn***

***Optional: Strong wire***

**1.** SC 5 in Magic Circle, Sl St to beginning stitch, Ch 1 [5]

**2–5.** (4 rows of) SC 5, Sl St to beginning stitch, Ch 1 [5]

**6.** SC 4, Inc, Sl St to beginning stitch, Ch 1 [6]

**7–11.** (5 rows of) SC 6, Sl St to beginning stitch, Ch 1 [6]

**12.** (SC, Inc, SC) x 2, Sl St to beginning stitch, Ch 1 [8]

**13–17.** (5 rows of) SC 8, Sl St to beginning stitch, Ch 1 [8]

**18.** (SC 3, Inc) x 2, Sl St to beginning stitch, Ch 1 [10]

**19–23.** (5 rows of) SC 10, Sl St to beginning stitch, Ch 1 [10]

If you want the Tail to be straight and stuffed, it is optional to stuff the Tail medium-firm with fiberfill as you go. You can also use wire in the Tail to make it poseable (this will make it unsafe as a child's toy). If you use wire, take one long wire, bend the end over itself so that the end is not sharp, and secure the wire to itself with a thin strip of duct tape. Insert that end of the wire all the way to the tail tip. Stuff the Tail lightly around the wire. Allow the wire to be several inches longer than the Tail but no longer than what you can fit/hide inside the Body of the Monster. When you pin to attach the Tail, insert the wire into the body of the Monster and then pin the Tail in place.

**24.** (SC 2, Inc, SC 2) x 2, Sl St to beginning stitch, Ch 1 [12]

**25–29.** (5 rows of) SC 12, Sl St to beginning stitch, Ch 1 [12]

**30.** (SC 5, Inc) x 2, Sl St to beginning stitch, Ch 1 [14]

**31–38.** (8 rows of) SC 14, Sl St to beginning stitch, Ch 1 [14]

**39.** (SC 3, Inc, SC 3) x 2, Sl St to beginning stitch, Ch 1 [16]

**40–49.** (10 rows of) SC 16, Sl St to beginning stitch, Ch 1 [16]

**50.** (SC 7, Inc) x 2, Sl St to beginning stitch, Ch 1 [18]

**51–61.** (11 rows of) SC 18, Sl St to beginning stitch, Ch 1 [18]

**62.** SC 18, Sl St to beginning stitch [18]

Fasten off with a 12 in/30.5 cm yarn tail.

## Assembly

**1.** Pin the tail in position on the back of the Monster's Body.

**2.** Once you are satisfied with placement, sew to attach using yarn tails and weave in ends.

Cylinder with Open Mouth and Legs, Open Mouth with Four Pointed Teeth (Lower), Thin Arms with Two Fingers, Skinny Spikes, Long Slightly Curved Horns, Long Reptile Tail

Cylinder with Underbite and No Legs, Wide Flat-ended Short Limbs, Large Cone Limbs, Tail with Hair Puff, Ridged Horns, Pointy Teeth, Embroidered Claws

# TAIL WITH HAIR PUFF (MAKE 1)

*Approximately 10 in/25.5 cm long, 0.75 in/2 cm wide at base*

*Main Body Color Yarn: Approximately 22 yd/20 m worsted/medium weight yarn*

*Accent Color Yarn: Approximately 12 yd/11 m worsted/medium weight yarn*

*Optional: Pet brush*

## Part 1

**1.** With Main Body Color Yarn, SC 6 in Magic Circle, Sl St to beginning stitch, Ch 1 [6]

**2–39.** (38 rows of) SC 6, Sl St to beginning stitch, Ch 1 [6]

**40.** SC 6, Sl St to beginning stitch [6]

Fasten off with an 18 in/45.5 cm yarn tail.

## Part 2

**1.** Cut (at least) 30 pieces of Accent Color Yarn, each about 6–8 in/15–20 cm long.

**2.** Attach in groups of two to three pieces of yarn with a Lark's Head Knot through the stitches of Row 1 and Row 2 on Part 1. If you intend to brush the yarn out, acrylic yarn works well.

**3.** If using multi-ply yarn, unwind the strands for a crazy, curly look or brush it out for a fluffy, fuzzy tail.

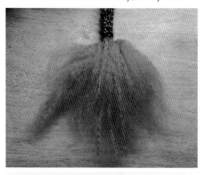

> It is optional to brush out the yarn. I recommend using a pet brush or similar wire brush. You will lose some length and fuzz when brushing; that is normal.

**4.** Pin the tail in place on the Monster's Body; sew in place using the yarn tail. Weave in ends.

**5.** After sewing, feel free to trim the hair to a desired length.

# EARS
## OPTIONS

Pointed Folded Ears...251

Double-layer Pointed
Folded Ears...252

Bugle Ears...253

Axolotl Flaps...255

Big Double-layer
Round Ears...258

Fin Ears...259

Short Bunny Ears...262

Long Bunny Ears...264

Cat Ears...266

Small Half-circle Ears...268

Circle Folded Ears...269

Spiky Ears...270

Double-layer Wedge Folded
Ears...272

Teensy Round
Ears...273

# POINTED FOLDED EARS (MAKE 2)

***Approximately 2.75 in/7 cm long, 2.25 in/5.5 cm wide at the base (unfolded)***

***Main Body Color Yarn: Approximately 7 yd/6.5 m worsted/medium weight yarn per Ear***

**1.** Starting with a short yarn tail, Ch 2, working into the second Ch from hook, SC, Ch 1, Turn [1]

**2.** Inc, Ch 1, Turn [2]

**3.** Inc x 2, Ch 1, Turn [4]

**4.** (SC, Inc) x 2, Ch 1, Turn [6]

**5.** (SC, Inc, SC) x 2, Ch 1, Turn [8]

**6–10.** (5 rows of) SC 8, Ch 1, Turn [8]

**11.** SC 8, Ch 1, do not Turn [8]

**12.** Working along the unfinished edge of the Ear toward the OC/Tip, SC 11, in the OC work the following stitches, SC, Ch 2, Sl St in the second Ch from hook, SC, continuing to crochet down the unfinished edge of the Ear, SC 11 [24]

Fasten off with an 18 in/45.5 cm yarn tail.

## Assembly

**1.** Fold the ear in half lengthwise, as shown.

**2.** Pin to attach on either side of the Monster's head.

**3.** Once you are satisfied with placement, sew to the Monster using the yarn tails.

**4.** Weave in ends.

Cylinder with Overbite and No Legs, Short Rounded Limbs, Long Rounded Limbs, Triangular Spikes of Varying Size, Pointed Folded Ears, Squared Teeth, Circle Belly

# DOUBLE-LAYER POINTED FOLDED EARS (MAKE 2)

*Approximately 3 in/7.5 cm long, 3 in/7.5 cm wide (unfolded)*

*Main Body Color Yarn: Approximately 16 yd/14.75 m worsted/medium weight yarn per Ear*

*Accent Color Yarn: Approximately 13 yd/12 m worsted/medium weight yarn per Ear*

## Part 1 and Part 2 (Make 1 of each Part per Ear)

For Part 1, work Rows 1–12 with the Accent Color Yarn. For Part 2, work Rows 1–12 with the Main Body Color Yarn.

1. Starting with a short yarn tail, Ch 2, working into the second Ch from hook, SC, Ch 1, Turn [1]
2. Inc, Ch 1, Turn [2]
3. Inc x 2, Ch 1, Turn [4]
4. (SC, Inc) x 2, Ch 1, Turn [6]
5. (SC, Inc, SC) x 2, Ch 1, Turn [8]
6–10. (5 rows of) SC 8, Ch 1, Turn [8]
11. SC 8, Ch 1, do not Turn [8]
12. Working along the unfinished edge of the Ear toward the OC/Tip, starting by working around the post of last SC you made in Row 11, SC 11, in the OC work an Inc, continue to crochet down the unfinished edge of the Ear, SC 11 [24]

Fasten off Part 1 with an 18 in/45.5 cm yarn tail.

For Part 2, Ch 1 and continue to Row 13.

13. Hold Part 1 against Part 2, working around the whole edge of the Ear through both pieces at the same time, SC 11, Inc, Ch 2, Sl St in the second Ch from hook, Inc, SC 11 [26]

Fasten off with an 18 in/45.5 cm yarn tail.

## Assembly

1. Fold the ear in half lengthwise, as shown.

2. Pin to attach on either side of the Monster's head.

3. Once you are satisfied with placement, sew to the Monster using the yarn tails.
4. Weave in ends.

Square with Overbite and No Legs, Bulb-ended Short Limbs, Large-footed Bent Limbs, Double-layer Pointed Folded Ears, Small Antlers, Two Long Fangs

If you want to add metal spikes to any part of your Monster, go to page 172 for tips on how to do that.

# BUGLE EARS (MAKE 2)

*Approximately 1.75 in/4.5 cm tall, 1.25 in/3 cm diameter at the top of the bugle, 0.75 in/2 cm wide at the base*

*Main Body Color Yarn: Approximately 6 yd/5.5 m worsted/medium weight yarn per Ear*

**1.** Starting with a long enough yarn tail to weave in later, Ch 12, Sl St to the first Ch, Ch 1

In Row 2, you can capture the starting yarn tail in the stitches as you crochet to weave it in as you go.

**2.** SC 15 around the chain stitches from Row 1 to create a circle of SC, Sl St to beginning stitch, Ch 1 [15]

**3.** (SC 3, Dec) x 3, Sl St to beginning stitch, Ch 1 [12]

**4.** (SC 2, Dec) x 3, Sl St to beginning stitch, Ch 1 [9]

**5.** (SC, Dec) x 3, Sl St to beginning stitch, Ch 1 [6]

**6–7.** (2 rows of) SC 6, Sl St to beginning stitch, Ch 1 [6]

**8.** SC 6, Sl St to beginning stitch [6]

Fasten off with a 12 in/30.5 cm yarn tail.

## Assembly

**1.** Pin to attach on either side of the Monster's head.

**2.** Once you are satisfied with placement, sew to the Monster using the yarn tails.

**3.** Weave in ends.

Blob Body with Open Mouth, Open Mouth with Short Row of Small Teeth (Upper), Bugle Ears, Small Double-pointed Tongue

# AXOLOTL FLAPS (MAKE 4 TO 6)

*Approximately 3.25 in/8.5 cm long, 1.5 in/4 cm wide at base*

*Main Body Color Yarn: Approximately 7 yd/6.5 m worsted/medium weight yarn per Flap*

*Accent Color Yarn: Approximately 4 yd/3.75 m worsted/medium weight yarn per Flap*

### Part 1 (Make 2 per Flap)

**1.** With Main Body Color Yarn, starting with a long enough yarn tail to weave in later, Ch 11, starting in the second Ch from hook, SC 9, Inc, continue to crochet around to the other side of the starting chain, SC 9, Ch 1, Turn [20]

**2.** SC 9, Inc x 2, SC 9 [22]

Fasten off with a 12 in/30.5 cm yarn tail.

### Part 2

**1.** Place two Part 1 pieces back to back. Using Accent Color Yarn, work through both Part 1 pieces at the same time starting through the first stitch on each of the Part 1 pieces, (SC 2, Ch 2, SC in the second Ch from hook) x 5, (Inc, Ch 2, SC in the second Ch from hook) x 2, (SC 2, Ch 2, SC in the second Ch from hook) x 4, SC 2 [24]

> The "Ch 2, SC in the second Ch from hook" are picot stitches and are not included in the stitch count.

Fasten off with a 12 in/30.5 cm yarn tail.

### Assembly

**1.** Pin to attach on either side of the Monster's head.

**2.** Once you are satisfied with placement, sew to the Monster using the yarn tails.

**3.** Weave in ends.

**Blob Body with Open Mouth, Open Mouth with No Teeth, Axolotl Flaps, Big Long Tongue**

Cylinder with
Deep Pocket
Underbite and Legs,
Large Bulb Antennae,
Large Cone Limbs,
Big Double-layer
Round Ears

# BIG DOUBLE-LAYER ROUND EARS (MAKE 2)

*Approximately 3 in/7.5 cm long, 3.25 in/8.5 cm wide, 1 in/2.5 cm wide at folded base*

*Main Body Color Yarn: Approximately 10 yd/9.25 m worsted/medium weight yarn per Ear*

*Accent Color Yarn: Approximately 8 yd/7.25 m worsted/medium weight yarn per Ear*

## Part 1 (Make 1 per Ear)

**1.** With Accent Color Yarn, SC 6 in Magic Circle, Sl St to beginning stitch, Ch 1 [6]

**2.** Inc x 6, Sl St to beginning stitch, Ch 1 [12]

**3.** (SC, Inc) x 6, Sl St to beginning stitch, Ch 1 [18]

**4.** (SC, Inc, SC) x 6, Sl St to beginning stitch, Ch 1 [24]

**5.** (SC 3, Inc) x 6, Sl St to beginning stitch, Ch 1 [30]

**6.** (SC 2, Inc, SC 2) x 6, Sl St to beginning stitch [36]

Fasten off with a 12 in/30.5 cm yarn tail.

## Part 2 (Make 1 per Ear)

**1.** With Main Body Color Yarn, SC 6 in Magic Circle, Sl St to beginning stitch, Ch 1 [6]

**2.** Inc x 6, Sl St to beginning stitch, Ch 1 [12]

**3.** (SC, Inc) x 6, Sl St to beginning stitch, Ch 1 [18]

**4.** (SC, Inc, SC) x 6, Sl St to beginning stitch, Ch 1 [24]

**5.** (SC 3, Inc) x 6, Sl St to beginning stitch, Ch 1 [30]

**6.** (SC 2, Inc, SC 2) x 6, Sl St to beginning stitch, Ch 1 [36]

**7.** Place Part 1 and Part 2 back to back, working through both pieces at the same time, (SC 5, Inc) x 6, Sl St to beginning stitch [42]

Fasten off with an 18 in/45.5 cm yarn tail.

## Assembly

**1.** There are multiple ways to fold or position these ears. You could pin them to attach as big circles. You could fold them in half, pinched together on one side, and pin them to attach that way. Experiment to give your Monster their own personality.

**2.** Pin to attach on either side of the Monster's head.

**3.** Once you are satisfied with placement, sew to the Monster using the yarn tails.

**4.** Weave in ends.

# FIN EARS (MAKE 2)

*Approximately 4.5 in/11.5 cm long from top to bottom at the longest point, 2.5 in/6.5 cm long at base, 1.75 in/4.5 cm wide (from edge of Ear to base of Ear)*

*Main Body Color Yarn (this yarn is used for Part 1/panels/base of the Ear; you could optionally use an Accent Color Yarn): Approximately 4 yd/3.75 m worsted/medium weight yarn per Ear*

*Accent Color Yarn (Part 2/ Edging): Approximately 3 yd/2.75 m worsted/medium weight yarn per Ear*

## Part 1 (Make 1 per Ear)

**1.** With Main Body Color Yarn, starting with a long enough yarn tail to weave in later, Ch 7, starting in the third Ch from hook, HDC Dec, HDC, SC 2, Ch 1, Turn [4]

**2.** SC, HDC, HDC Dec, Ch 2, Turn [3]

> In Rows 2, 4, and 6, the Ch 2 is a turning chain; you will not work into it in the following row.

**3.** HDC Inc, SC 2, Ch 1, Turn [4]

**4.** SC 3, HDC Inc, Ch 2, Turn [5]

**5.** BLO [HDC Dec, HDC, SC 2], Ch 1, Turn [4]

**6.** SC, HDC, HDC Dec, Ch 2, Turn [3]

**7.** HDC Inc, SC 2, Ch 1, Turn [4]

**8.** SC 3, HDC Inc [5]

Fasten off with an 18 in/45.5 cm yarn tail.

## Part 2

**1.** Attach the Accent Color Yarn to the first Ch stitch that you worked in Row 1 of Part 1, starting into that stitch, SC 5 to the end of the ear edge, Ch 3, Turn [5]

**2.** Starting in the second Ch from hook, Sl St 7, rotate the ear to work along the straight unfinished edge of the ear toward the BLO row from Part 1 [7]

**3.** SC 4 along the unfinished edge of the ear up to the BLO row from Part 1 [4]

**4.** Working along the leftover Front Loops from the BLO row in Part 1, SC 5, Ch 3, Turn [5]

**5.** Starting in the second Ch from hook, Sl St 7, rotate the ear to work along the straight unfinished edge of the ear toward the last row from Part 1 [7]

**6.** SC 4 along the unfinished edge of the ear up to the last row from Part 1 [4]

**7.** Working along the last row from Part 1, SC 5, Ch 3, Turn [5]

**8.** Starting in the second Ch from hook, Sl St 7 [7]

Fasten off with a 24 in/61 cm yarn tail.

## Assembly

**1.** Pin in place on either side of the Monster's head.

**2.** Once you are satisfied with placement, use the yarn tails to sew to the Monster.

**3.** Weave in all ends.

Eyeball Monster Main Body/Eye with Crocheted Eye, Eyeball Monster Eyelid, Three-fingered Hand with Elbow and Arm, Two-toed Feet with Knees and Legs, Fin Ears

# SHORT BUNNY EARS (MAKE 2)

*Approximately 4 in/10 cm tall, 1.5 in/4 cm wide at base (slightly folded), 3 in/7.5 cm wide at the widest part*

*Main Body Color Yarn: Approximately 27 yd/24.75 m worsted/medium weight yarn per Ear*

1. SC 6 in Magic Circle, Sl St to beginning stitch, Ch 1 [6]

2. Inc x 6, Sl St to beginning stitch, Ch 1 [12]

3. (SC, Inc) x 6, Sl St to beginning stitch, Ch 1 [18]

4. (SC, Inc, SC) x 6, Sl St to beginning stitch, Ch 1 [24]

5. SC 24, Sl St to beginning stitch, Ch 1 [24]

6. (SC 7, Inc) x 3, Sl St to beginning stitch, Ch 1 [27]

7–14. (8 rows of) SC 27, Sl St to beginning stitch, Ch 1 [27]

15. (SC 7, Dec) x 3, Sl St to beginning stitch, Ch 1 [24]

16–17. (2 rows of) SC 24, Sl St to beginning stitch, Ch 1 [24]

18. (SC 3, Dec, SC 3) x 3, Sl St to beginning stitch, Ch 1 [21]

19–20. (2 rows of) SC 21, Sl St to beginning stitch, Ch 1 [21]

21. (SC 5, Dec) x 3, Sl St to beginning stitch [18]

Fasten off with a 24 in/61 cm yarn tail.

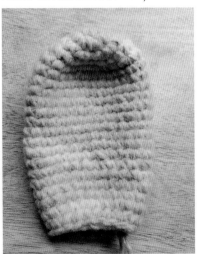

## Assembly

1. Do not stuff with fiberfill. Flatten the ear without stuffing it and then fold the base of the ear in half as shown.

2. Pin in place on either side of the Monster's head.

3. Once you are satisfied with placement, use the yarn tails to sew to the Monster.

4. Weave in all ends.

Cylinder with Open Mouth and Legs, Open Mouth with Short Row of Small Teeth (Bottom), Small Cone Limbs, Short Bunny Ears

# LONG BUNNY EARS (MAKE 2)

*Approximately 10 in/25.5 cm long, 3.5 in/9 cm wide at widest part*

*Main Body Color Yarn: Approximately 50 yd/45.75 m worsted/medium weight yarn per Ear*

**1.** SC 6 in Magic Circle, Sl St to beginning stitch, Ch 1 [6]

**2.** Inc x 6, Sl St to beginning stitch, Ch 1 [12]

**3.** (SC, Inc) x 6, Sl St to beginning stitch, Ch 1 [18]

**4.** (SC, Inc, SC) x 6, Sl St to beginning stitch, Ch 1 [24]

**5.** SC 24, Sl St to beginning stitch, Ch 1 [24]

**6.** (SC 7, Inc) x 3, Sl St to beginning stitch, Ch 1 [27]

**7–14.** (8 rows of) SC 27, Sl St to beginning stitch, Ch 1 [27]

**15.** (SC 7, Dec) x 3, Sl St to beginning stitch, Ch 1 [24]

**16–17.** (2 rows of) SC 24, Sl St to beginning stitch, Ch 1 [24]

**18.** (SC 3, Dec, SC 3) x 3, Sl St to beginning stitch, Ch 1 [21]

**19–20.** (2 rows of) SC 21, Sl St to beginning stitch, Ch 1 [21]

**21.** (SC 5, Dec) x 3, Sl St to beginning stitch, Ch 1 [18]

**22–36.** (15 rows of) SC 18, Sl St to beginning stitch, Ch 1 [18]

**37.** Flatten your work so the first SC of Row 36 is on top of the last SC of Row 36. You will work through 2 stitches at a time in this row to close the top of the ear. SC into both the first and last SC of Row 36 at the same time, SC 8 working through both sides at the same time, Ch 1, Turn [9]

**38.** SC 9, Ch 1, Turn [9]

**39.** SC 9, Ch 1, Turn [9]

**40.** Fold the piece in half so the bulk of the "Sl St, Ch 1" join seam will run down the back of the ear toward the ear tip, insert your hook through the first stitch from Row 39 first and then insert the hook through the last stitch from Row 39 and complete a SC, and then, working through both sides of the row at the same time, SC 3 [4]

Fasten off with a 24 in/61 cm yarn tail.

## Assembly

**1.** Do not stuff with fiberfill. Flatten the ear.

**2.** Pin in place on either side of the Monster's head.

**3.** Once you are satisfied with placement, use the yarn tails to sew to the Monster.

**4.** Weave in all ends.

Square with Overbite and Legs, Small Short Rounded Limbs, Long Bunny Ears, Small Antlers, Medium Tongue

# CAT EARS (MAKE 2)

*Approximately 2.75 in/7 cm wide at the base, 2.5 in/6.5 cm tall*

*Main Body Color Yarn: Approximately 7 yd/6.5 m worsted/medium weight yarn per Ear*

*Accent Color Yarn: Approximately 4 yd/3.75 m worsted/medium weight yarn per Ear*

## Part 1: Inner Ear (Make 1 Per Ear)

1. With Accent Color Yarn, Ch 2, working into the second Ch from hook, SC 3 in that chain, Ch 1, Turn [3]
2. SC, Inc, SC, Ch 1, Turn [4]
3. SC, Inc x 2, SC, Ch 1, Turn [6]
4. SC 6, Ch 1, Turn [6]
5. SC 2, Inc x 2, SC 2, Ch 1, Turn [8]
6. SC 2, Inc, SC 2, Inc, SC 2, Ch 1, Turn [10]
7. SC 10, Ch 1, Turn [10]
8. SC 2, Inc, SC 4, Inc, SC 2 [12]

Fasten off with a 12 in/30.5 cm yarn tail.

## Part 2: Outer Ear (Make 1 per Ear)

1. With Main Body Color Yarn, Ch 2, working into the second Ch from hook, SC 3 in that chain, Ch 1, Turn [3]
2. SC, Inc, SC, Ch 1, Turn [4]
3. SC, Inc x 2, SC, Ch 1, Turn [6]
4. SC 6, Ch 1, Turn [6]
5. SC 2, Inc x 2, SC 2, Ch 1, Turn [8]

6. SC 2, Inc, SC 2, Inc, SC 2, Ch 1, Turn [10]
7. SC 10, Ch 1, Turn [10]
8. SC 2, Inc, SC 4, Inc, SC 2, Ch 1, turn to work back up the edge toward the Row 1 chain [12]

9. Hold Part 1 in front of Part 2, working through both pieces at the same time, SC 8 up one side to the point, Triple SC Inc in the topmost OC stitch, SC 8 down the other side [19]

Fasten off with a 12 in/30.5 cm yarn tail.

## Assembly

1. Curve the bottom of the ear as you pin in position on the head.

2. Once you are satisfied with placement, sew to attach using yarn tails and weave in ends.

Square with No Mouth and No Legs, 2D Open Mouth in Lima Bean Shape with Straight Row of Teeth (Upper) and Tongue (Lower), Small Nubbins Limbs, Nubbin Footed Limbs, Cat Ears, Medium Slight Curved Striped Horns.

# SMALL HALF-CIRCLE EARS (MAKE 2)

***Approximately 1.5 in/4 cm wide at the base, 1 in/2.5 cm tall***

***Main Body Color Yarn: Approximately 3 yd/2.75 m worsted/medium weight yarn per Ear***

**1.** Starting with a long enough yarn tail to weave in later, Ch 2, working into the second Ch from hook, SC 4 in that Chain, Ch 1, Turn [4]

**2.** SC, Inc x 2, SC, Ch 1, Turn [6]

**3.** Inc, SC, Inc x 2, SC, Inc, Ch 1, Turn [10]

**4.** SC 10, Ch 1, Turn [10]

**5.** Sl St 10 [10]

Fasten off with a 12 in/30.5 cm yarn tail.

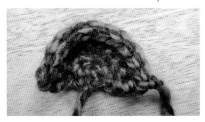

## Assembly

**1.** Pin in desired position on the head of your Monster Body.

**2.** Once you are satisfied with placement, use the yarn tail to sew to attach; weave in ends.

**Egg Shape with Overbite and No Legs, Small Short Limbs, Rounded Feet, Small Half Circle Ears, Mohawk, Small Tongue**

# CIRCLE FOLDED EARS (MAKE 2)

*Approximately 3 in/7.5 cm long from edge to base, 2.5 in/6.5 cm wide from side to side*

*Main Body Color Yarn: Approximately 8 yd/7.25 m worsted/medium weight yarn per Ear*

**1.** Starting with a long enough yarn tail to weave in later, SC 6 in Magic Circle, Sl St to beginning stitch, Ch 1 [6]

**2.** Inc x 6, Ch 1, Turn [12]

**3.** (SC, Inc) x 6, Ch 1, Turn [18]

**4.** (SC, Inc, SC) x 6, Ch 1, Turn [24]

**5.** (SC 3, Inc) x 6, Ch 1, Turn [30]

**6.** Sl St 30 [30]

Fasten off with a 12 in/30.5 cm yarn tail.

## Assembly

**1.** Fold the ear in half along the opening notch, as shown.

**2.** Pin in desired position on the head of your Monster Body.

**3.** Once you are satisfied with placement, use the yarn tail to sew in place; weave in ends.

Square with Overbite and Legs, Wide Flat-ended Short Limbs, Circle Folded Ear, Curly Spritz, Squared Teeth

# SPIKY EARS (MAKE 2)

*Approximately 3 in/7.5 cm long from base to tip, 2.5 in/6.5 cm wide at base (folded)*

*Main Body Color Yarn: Approximately 8 yd/7.25 m worsted/medium weight yarn per Ear*

**1.** Starting with a long enough yarn tail to weave in later, SC 6 in Magic Circle, Sl St to beginning stitch, Ch 1 [6]

**2.** Inc x 5, Ch 1, Turn [10]

> There will be 1 unworked stitch from Row 1 at the end of Row 2.

**3.** (SC, Inc) x 5, Ch 1, Turn [15]

**4.** SC 3, (SC, Inc, SC) x 3, SC 3, Ch 1, Turn [18]

**5.** SC 10, Inc, SC 7, Turn [19]

**6.** Ch 5, starting in the second Ch from hook, HDC 4, Skip the first available stitch on the ear from Row 5, Sl St into the next available stitch, Sl St, (Ch 5, starting in the second Ch from hook, HDC 4, Sl St 2) x 4, Sl St 8 [38]

Fasten off with a 12 in/30.5 cm yarn tail.

## Assembly

**1.** Fold the ear in half as shown.

**2.** Pin in position on the head of your Monster Body.

**3.** Once you are satisfied with placement, use the yarn tail to sew to attach; weave in ends.

Eyeball Monster Main Body/Eye with Crocheted Eye, Eyeball Monster Eyelid, Three-fingered Hand with Elbow and Arm, Two-toed Feet with Knees and Legs, Spiky Ears, Tiny Pointed Claws

Square with Deep Pocket Underbite and Legs, Small Nubbins Limbs, Double-layer Wedge Folded Ears, Tiny Curved Horns

# DOUBLE-LAYER WEDGE FOLDED EARS (MAKE 2)

*Approximately 2.5 in/6.5 cm wide from edge to base, 2.5 in/6.5 cm wide from side to side*

*Main Body Color Yarn: Approximately 12 yd/11 m worsted/medium weight yarn per Ear*

*Accent Color Yarn: Approximately 9 yd/8.25 m worsted/medium weight yarn per Ear*

## Part 1 and Part 2 (Make 1 of each per Ear)

For Part 1, work Rows 1 through 9 in Accent Color Yarn and fasten off with a long enough yarn tail to weave in later. For Part 2, work Rows 1 through 10 with Main Body Color Yarn.

**1.** Starting with a long enough yarn tail to weave in later, Ch 2, working into the second Ch from hook, Inc, Ch 1, Turn [2]

**2.** Inc x 2, Ch 1, Turn [4]

**3.** (SC, Inc) x 2, Ch 1, Turn [6]

**4.** (SC, Inc, SC) x 2, Ch 1, Turn [8]

**5.** (SC 3, Inc) x 2, Ch 1, Turn [10]

**6.** (SC 2, Inc, SC 2) x 2, Ch 1, Turn [12]

**7.** (SC 5, Inc) x 2, Ch 1, Turn [14]

**8.** (SC 3, Inc, SC 3) x 2, Ch 1, Turn [16]

**9.** SC 7, Inc, HDC 7, HDC Inc, Ch 1, Turn [18]

Fasten off Part 1 Accent Color Yarn with a long enough yarn tail to weave in later.

For Part 2, continue to Row 10.

**10.** Hold Part 1 against Part 2, working into Row 9 through both pieces at the same time, SC 18 [18]

Fasten off with an 18 in/45.5 cm yarn tail.

## Assembly

**1.** Fold the ear in half lengthwise, as shown.

**2.** Pin in position on either side of the Monster's head.

**3.** Once you are satisfied with placement, sew to attach to the Monster using the yarn tails.

**4.** Weave in ends.

# TEENSY ROUND EARS (MAKE 2)

*Approximately 1 in/2.5 cm wide*

*Main Body Color Yarn: Approximately 2 yd/1.75 m worsted/medium weight yarn per Ear*

**1.** Starting with a long enough yarn tail to weave in later, in a Magic Circle work the following stitches: SC, HDC, DC 4, HDC, SC, tighten the Magic Circle [8]

Fasten off with a 12 in/30.5 cm yarn tail.

## Assembly

**1.** Pin in position on either side of the Monster's head.

**2.** Once you are satisfied with placement, sew onto the Monster using the yarn tails.

**3.** Weave in ends.

Cylinder with Open Mouth and No Legs, Open Mouth with Humanlike Teeth, Thinner Eyelid/Eyebrow for 30 mm Safety Eyes, Cute Mitten Limbs, Cute Footed Limbs, Teensy Round Ears, Ridged Spiral Horns with Accent Color, Circle Belly

# ANTENNAE

## OPTIONS

Small Bulb Antennae...276

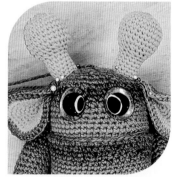

Large Bulb Antennae...276

Thin Curved Antennae...278

Thick Curved Antennae...279

# SMALL BULB ANTENNAE (MAKE 2)

*Approximately 2 in/5 cm long, 1 in/2.5 cm wide at the widest part, 0.75 in/2 cm wide at the base*

*Main Body Color Yarn: Approximately 5 yd/4.5 m worsted/medium weight yarn per Antenna*

1. SC 6 in Magic Circle, Sl St to beginning stitch, Ch 1 [6]
2. Inc x 6, Sl St to beginning stitch, Ch 1 [12]
3–4. (2 rows of) SC 12, Sl St to beginning stitch, Ch 1 [12]
5. Dec x 6, Sl St to beginning stitch, Ch 1 [6]

> You can stuff the bulb lightly with fiberfill at this point to keep it well filled out, but this step is optional.

6. FLO [SC 6], Sl St to beginning stitch, Ch 1 [6]

7–8. (2 rows of) SC 6, Sl St to beginning stitch, Ch 1 [6]

> Leave off the "Ch 1" on the final row.

Fasten off with a 12 in/30.5 cm yarn tail.

## Assembly

1. Pin in place on the Monster's head/Body.
2. Use the yarn tail to sew on the Antennae; weave in ends.

# LARGE BULB ANTENNAE (MAKE 2)

*Approximately 3 in/7.5 cm long, 2 in/5 cm wide at the widest part, 1 in/2.5 cm wide at base*

*Main Body Color Yarn: Approximately 14 yd/12.75 m worsted/medium weight yarn per Antenna*

1. SC 6 in Magic Circle, Sl St to beginning stitch, Ch 1 [6]
2. Inc x 6, Sl St to beginning stitch, Ch 1 [12]
3. (SC, Inc) x 6, Sl St to beginning stitch, Ch 1 [18]
4. (SC, Inc, SC) x 6, Sl St to beginning, Ch 1 [24]
5–9. (5 rows of) SC 24, Sl St to beginning stitch, Ch 1 [24]
10. (SC, Dec, SC) x 6, Sl St to beginning stitch, Ch 1 [18]
11. (SC, Dec) x 6, Sl St to beginning stitch, Ch 1 [12]

> You can stuff the bulb lightly with fiberfill at this point to keep it well filled out, but this step is optional.

12–17. (6 rows of) SC 12, Sl St to beginning stitch, Ch 1 [12]

> Leave off the "Ch 1" on the final row.

Fasten off with a 24 in/61 cm yarn tail.

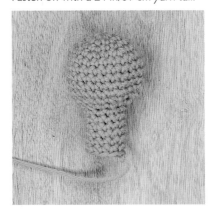

## Assembly

1. Pin in place on the Monster's head/Body.
2. Use the yarn tail to sew the Antennae in place; weave in ends.

Cylinder with Deep Pocket Underbite and Legs, Large Bulb Antennae, Large Cone Arms, Big Double-layer Round Ears

# THIN CURVED ANTENNAE (MAKE 2)

*Approximately 3.5 in/9 cm long, 0.75 in/2 cm wide at the base*

*Main Body Color Yarn: Approximately 15 yd/13.75 m worsted/medium yarn per Antenna*

**1.** SC 6 in Magic Circle, Sl St to beginning stitch, Ch 1 [6]

**2.** (SC, Inc) x 3, Sl St to beginning stitch, Ch 1 [9]

**3–5.** (3 rows of) SC 9, Sl St to beginning stitch, Ch 1 [9]

**6.** (SC, Dec) x 3, Sl St to beginning stitch, Ch 1 [6]

Stuff the end of the Antenna lightly with fiberfill. It is optional to stuff the rest as you go. The Antennae shown are unstuffed below the bulb, but for straighter Antennae, stuffing will help.

**7–16.** (10 rows of) SC 6, Sl St to beginning stitch, Ch 1 [6]

**17.** (SC, Inc) x 3, Sl St to beginning stitch, Ch 1 [9]

**18.** (SC, Inc, SC) x 3, Sl St to beginning stitch [12]

Fasten off with a 12 in/30.5 cm yarn tail.

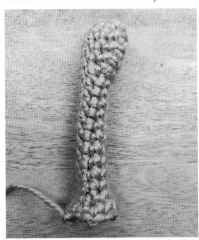

## Assembly

**1.** Pin in place on the Monster's head/Body.

**2.** Use the yarn tail to sew the Antennae in place; weave in ends.

**Cylinder with Deep Pocket Underbite and No Legs, Three-fingered Wide Limbs, Small Feet with Tiny Nubbin Toes, Thin Curved Antennae**

# THICK CURVED ANTENNAE (MAKE 2)

*Approximately 4 in/10 cm long, 0.75 in/2 cm wide at base*

*Main Body Color Yarn: Approximately 8 yd/7.25 m worsted/medium weight yarn per Antenna*

**1.** SC 6 in Magic Circle, Sl St to beginning stitch, Ch 1 [6]

**2.** (SC, Inc) x 3, Sl St to beginning stitch, Ch 1 [9]

**3–4.** (2 rows of) SC 9, Sl St to beginning stitch, Ch 1 [9]

**5.** SC 7, Dec, Sl St to beginning stitch, Ch 1 [8]

**6–8.** (3 rows of) SC 8, Sl St to beginning stitch, Ch 1 [8]

**9.** SC 6, Dec, Sl St to beginning stitch, Ch 1 [7]

**10–12.** (3 rows of) SC 7, Sl St to beginning stitch, Ch 1 [7]

**13.** SC 5, Dec, Sl St to beginning stitch, Ch 1 [6]

**14–15.** (2 rows of) SC 6, Sl St to beginning stitch, Ch 1 [6]

**16.** SC 6, Sl St to beginning stitch [6]

Fasten off with a 12 in/30.5 cm yarn tail.

## Assembly

**1.** Pin in place on the Monster's head/Body.

**2.** Use the yarn tail to sew the Antennae in place; weave in ends.

**Eyeball Monster Main Body/Eye with Crocheted Iris and Pupil, Eyeball Monster Eyelid, Thick Curved Antennae, Spider Legs, Hair Puff**

# HORNS

## OPTIONS

Medium Curved Horns...283

Tiny Curved Horns...283

Skinny Curved Horns...285

Big Round Horns...285

Thin L-shaped Horns...286

S-shaped Horns...289

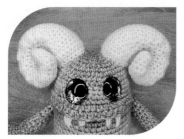

Ram Horns...291

Large Antlers...295

Large Curved Horns...297

Medium Pointy Antlers...297

Small Antlers...300

Ridged Horns...302

Spiral-shaped Horns...302

Rounded Segmented Horns...303

Long Slightly Curved Horns...304

Medium to the Side Curved Horns...305

Medium Slightly Curved Striped Horns...306

Ridged Spiral Horns with Accent Color...308

Eyeball Monster Main Body/Eye with Crocheted Iris and Pupil, Eyeball Monster Eyelid, Two-toed Feet with Knees and Legs, Medium Curved Horns

## MEDIUM CURVED HORNS (MAKE 2)

*Approximately 3 in/7.5 cm tall, 1.5 in/4 cm wide at base*

*Accent Color Yarn: Approximately 8 yd/7.25 m worsted/medium weight yarn total per Horn*

**I.** SC 4 in Magic Circle, Sl St to beginning stitch, Ch 1 [4]

**2.** SC 4, Sl St to beginning stitch, Ch 1 [4]

**3.** Inc, SC 3, Sl St to beginning stitch, Ch 1 [5]

**4.** Inc, SC 4, Sl St to beginning stitch, Ch 1 [6]

**5.** Inc, SC 5, Sl St to beginning stitch, Ch 1 [7]

**6.** Inc, SC 6, Sl St to beginning stitch, Ch 1 [8]

**7.** Inc, SC 7, Sl St to beginning stitch, Ch 1 [9]

**8.** SC 2, Inc, SC 6, Sl St to beginning stitch, Ch 1 [10]

**9.** SC 2, Inc, SC 7, Sl St to beginning stitch, Ch 1 [11]

**10.** SC 3, Inc, SC 7, Sl St to beginning stitch, Ch 1 [12]

**11.** SC 3, Inc, SC 8, Sl St to beginning stitch, Ch 1 [13]

**12.** SC 3, Inc, SC 9, Sl St to beginning stitch, Ch 1 [14]

**13.** SC 4, Inc, SC 9, Sl St to beginning stitch [15]

Fasten off with a 12 in/30.5 cm yarn tail.

For small Horns, leave off the "Ch 1" at the end of Row 9 and fasten off here with an 18 in/45.5 cm yarn tail. For medium Horns, continue to Row 10.

### Assembly

**I.** Stuff the Horn lightly with fiberfill.

**2.** Pin in place to the head of your Monster Body.

**3.** Once you are satisfied with placement, use the yarn tail to sew to attach the Horn; weave in end.

## TINY CURVED HORNS (MAKE 2)

*Approximately 1.25 in/3 cm tall, 1 in/2.5 cm wide at base*

*Accent Color Yarn: Approximately 3 yd/2.75 m worsted/medium weight yarn per Horn*

**I.** SC 4 in Magic Circle, Sl St to beginning stitch, Ch 1 [4]

**2.** SC 4, Sl St to beginning stitch, Ch 1 [4]

**3.** Inc, SC, Inc, SC, Sl St to beginning stitch, Ch 1 [6]

**4.** SC 2, Inc, SC 2, Inc, Sl St to beginning stitch, Ch 1 [8]

**5.** SC 8, Sl St to beginning stitch, Ch 1 [8]

**6.** Inc, SC 7, Sl St to beginning stitch [9]

Fasten off with an 18 in/45.5 cm yarn tail.

### Assembly

**I.** Stuff the Horn lightly with fiberfill.

**2.** Pin to attach to the head of your Monster Body.

**3.** Once you are satisfied with placement, use the yarn tail to sew on the Horn; weave in end.

Eyeball Monster Main Body/Eye with Safety Eye, Eyeball Monster Eyelid, Small Feet with Tiny Nubbin Toes, Tiny Curved Horns

Eyeball Monster Main Body/Eye with Safety Eye, Eyeball Monster Eyelid, Short Arms with Two Fingers, Two-toed Feet with Knees and Legs, Skinny Curved Horns

## SKINNY CURVED HORNS (MAKE 2)

*Approximately 2.5 in/6.5 cm tall, 1 in/2.5 cm wide at base*

*Accent Color Yarn: Approximately 6 yd/5.5 m worsted/medium weight yarn per Horn*

1. SC 5 in Magic Circle, Sl St to beginning stitch, Ch 1 [5]
2. SC 5, Sl St to beginning stitch, Ch 1 [5]
3. Inc, SC, Dec, SC, Sl St to beginning stitch, Ch 1 [5]
4. Inc, SC 4, Sl St to beginning stitch, Ch 1 [6]
5. SC 6, Sl St to beginning stitch, Ch 1 [6]
6. Inc, SC 5, Sl St to beginning stitch, Ch 1 [7]
7. Inc, SC 2, Dec, SC 2, Sl St to beginning stitch, Ch 1 [7]

8. Inc, SC 6, Sl St to beginning stitch, Ch 1 [8]
9. Inc, SC 7, Sl St to beginning stitch, Ch 1 [9]
10. Inc, SC 8, Sl St to beginning stitch, Ch 1 [10]
11. Inc, SC 9, Sl St to beginning stitch [11]

Fasten off with a 12 in/30.5 cm yarn tail.

### Assembly

1. Stuff the Horn lightly with fiberfill.
2. Pin to attach to the head of your Monster Body.

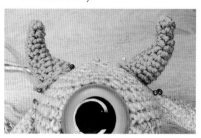

3. Once you are satisfied with placement, use the yarn tail to sew on the Horn; weave in end.

## BIG ROUND HORNS (MAKE 2)

*Approximately 5 in/13 cm long along the length of the horn, 4 in/10 cm wide (from base to tip extending from the Monster's head), 2.5 in/6.5 cm wide at base of Horn*

*Accent Color Yarn: Approximately 20 yd/18.25 m worsted/medium weight yarn per Horn*

1. SC 4 in Magic Circle, Sl St to beginning stitch, Ch 1 [4]
2. BLO [Inc, HDC 3], Sl St to beginning stitch, Ch 1 [5]
3. BLO [SC, <Dec>, SC, HDC 3], Sl St to beginning stitch, Ch 1 [6]

> "<Dec>" is a stitch that is defined in the Glossary.

4. BLO [SC, Inc, SC, HDC 3], Sl St to beginning stitch, Ch 1 [7]
5. BLO [HDC, SC, <Dec>, SC, HDC 4], Sl St to beginning stitch, Ch 1 [8]

6. BLO [HDC, SC, Inc, SC, HDC 4], Sl St to beginning stitch, Ch 1 [9]
7. BLO [HDC 2, SC, <Dec>, SC, HDC 5], Sl St to beginning stitch, Ch 1 [10]
8. BLO [HDC 2, SC, Inc, SC, HDC 5], Sl St to beginning stitch, Ch 1 [11]
9. BLO [HDC 3, SC, <Dec>, SC, HDC 6], Sl St to beginning stitch, Ch 1 [12]
10. BLO [HDC 3, SC, Inc, SC, HDC 6], Sl St to beginning stitch, Ch 1 [13]
11. BLO [HDC 4, SC, <Dec>, SC, HDC 7], Sl St to beginning stitch, Ch 1 [14]

12. BLO [HDC 4, SC, Inc, SC, HDC 7], Sl St to beginning stitch, Ch 1 [15]

13. BLO [HDC 5, Inc x 2, HDC 8], Sl St to beginning stitch, Ch 1 [17]
14. BLO [HDC 5, SC, Inc x 2, SC, HDC 8], Sl St to beginning stitch, Ch 1 [19]

**15.** BLO [HDC 6, SC, Inc x 2, SC, HDC 9], Sl St to beginning stitch, Ch 1 [21]

**16.** BLO [HDC 7, SC, Inc x 2, SC, HDC 10], Sl St to beginning stitch, Ch 1 [23]

**17.** BLO [DC 3, HDC 5, SC, Inc x 2, SC, HDC 5, DC 6], Sl St to beginning stitch [25]

Fasten off with an 18 in/45.5 cm yarn tail.

## Assembly

**1.** Stuff the Horn lightly with fiberfill.

**2.** Pin to attach to the head of your Monster Body.

**3.** Once you are satisfied with placement, use the yarn tail to sew on the Horn; weave in end.

# THIN L-SHAPED HORNS (MAKE 2)

*Approximately 4.5 in/11.5 cm wide (from base to tip, extending from the Monster's head), 1.5 in/4 cm wide at base*

*Accent Color Yarn: Approximately 11 yd/10 m, worsted/medium weight yarn per Horn*

**1.** SC 4 in Magic Circle, Sl St to beginning stitch, Ch 1 [4]

**2.** SC 3, Inc, Sl St to beginning stitch, Ch 1 [5]

**3.** SC 5, Sl St to beginning stitch, Ch 1 [5]

**4.** SC 2, Inc, SC 2, Sl St to beginning stitch, Ch 1 [6]

**5–6.** (2 rows of) SC 6, Sl St to beginning stitch, Ch 1 [6]

**7.** SC 5, Inc, Sl St to beginning stitch, Ch 1 [7]

**8–9.** (2 rows of) SC 7, Sl St to beginning stitch, Ch 1 [7]

**10.** SC 3, Inc, SC 3, Sl St to beginning stitch, Ch 1 [8]

**11–13.** (3 rows of) SC 8, Sl St to beginning stitch, Ch 1 [8]

**14.** (SC 3, Inc) x 2, Sl St to beginning stitch, Ch 1 [10]

**15.** SC 10, Sl St to beginning stitch, Ch 1 [10]

**16–17.** (2 rows of) Inc, SC 2, HDC Dec x 2, SC 2, Inc, Sl St to beginning stitch, Ch 1 [10]

**18.** SC, Inc, SC, HDC 4, SC, Inc, SC, Sl St to beginning stitch, Ch 1 [12]

**19.** SC 4, HDC 4, SC 4, Sl St to beginning stitch, Ch 1 [12]

**20.** SC 2, Inc, HDC 6, Inc, SC 2, Sl St to beginning stitch, Ch 1 [14]

**21.** SC 4, HDC 6, SC 4, Sl St to beginning stitch [14]

Fasten off with a 12 in/30.5 cm yarn tail.

## Assembly

**1.** Stuff the Horn lightly with fiberfill.

**2.** Pin to attach to the head of your Monster Body.

**3.** Once you are satisfied with placement, use the yarn tail to sew on the Horn; weave in end.

Blob Body with Underbite, Big Round Horns, Individual Medium Fangs

Eyeball Monster Main Body/Eye with Crocheted Iris and Pupil, Eyeball Monster Eyelid, Spider Legs, Large Curved Horns

Blob Body with Deep Pocket Underbite, Rounded Segmented Horns

Blob Body with Open Mouth, Open Mouth with Buck Teeth (Upper and Lower), Thin Arms with Two Fingers, Spiral Shaped Horns

Square with
Underbite and Legs,
Short Rounded Limbs,
Long Rounded Striped
Tail, Thin L-shaped Horns,
Hair Puff, Two Medium
Uneven Pointy Fangs

# S-SHAPED HORNS (MAKE 2)

*Approximately 6 in/15 cm wide (from base to tip, extending from the Monster's head), 12 in/30.5 cm long (from base to tip, along the length of the horn), 2 in/5 cm wide at base*

*Accent Color Yarn: Approximately 32 yd/29.25 m worsted/medium weight yarn per Horn*

*Optional: Strong wire*

**1.** SC 6 in Magic Circle, continue in spiral [6]

**2-3.** (2 rows of) SC 6 [6]

**4.** SC 5, Inc [7]

**5.** SC 7 [7]

**6.** SC 6, Inc [8]

**7.** SC 8 [8]

> Short rows are utilized in the following rows.
>
> Follow all sub-steps of each row in order (i.e., 8A, 8B, etc.). These short rows create the curves and shaping. They will sometimes go beyond where the row began; follow the pattern exactly and it will work. Each sub-row will have a stitch count for the number of stitches created in that sub-row indicated by a number that looks like this: [–5]; a final stitch count at the end of the final sub-row to indicate how many stitches are available on the edge of the work once all the sub-rows are complete will be indicated by a number that looks like this: [10].
>
> A video tutorial for how to crochet short rows is available on the Crafty Intentions YouTube channel here: www.youtube .com/watch?v=sh5T -idiwm8&t=159s
>
> Hybrid decreases like the "SC/ HDC Dec & HDC" stitches are defined in the Glossary and demonstrated on the Crafty Intentions YouTube channel here: www.youtube.com/ watch?v=h4wkxMOMqXg &t=5s

**8A.** SC 5, Ch 1, Turn [–5]

**8B.** SC 4, Ch 1, Turn [–4]

**8C.** SC 3, SC/HDC Dec & HDC, SC 2 [–7] [8]

**9.** HDC & HDC/SC Dec, SC 5, Inc [9]

**10.** SC 9 [9]

**11A.** SC 6, Ch 1, Turn [–6]

**11B.** SC 5, Ch 1, Turn [–5]

**11C.** SC 4, SC/HDC Dec & HDC, SC 2 [–8] [9]

**12.** HDC & HDC/SC Dec, SC 6, Inc [10]

**13.** SC 10 [10]

**14A.** SC 6, Ch 1, Turn [–6]

**14B.** SC 4, Ch 1, Turn [–4]

**14C.** SC 3, SC/HDC Dec & HDC, SC 3 [–8] [10]

**15.** SC, HDC & HDC/SC Dec, SC 6, Inc [11]

**16.** SC 11 [11]

**17A.** SC 7, Ch 1, Turn [–7]

**17B.** SC 5, Ch 1, Turn [–5]

**17C.** SC 4, SC/HDC Dec & HDC, SC 3 [–9] [11]

**18.** SC, HDC & HDC/SC Dec, SC 7, Inc [12]

**19.** SC 12 [12]

**20A.** SC 8, Ch 1, Turn [–8]

**20B.** SC 6, Ch 1, Turn [–6]

**20C.** SC 5, SC/HDC Dec & HDC, SC 3 [–10] [12]

**21.** SC, HDC & HDC/SC Dec, SC 8, Inc [13]

**22.** SC 13 [13]

**23A.** SC 9, Ch 1, Turn [–9]

**23B.** SC 6, Ch 1, Turn [–6]

**23C.** SC 5, SC/HDC Dec & HDC, SC 3 [–10] [13]

**24.** SC 2, HDC & HDC/SC Dec, SC 8, Inc [14]

**25.** SC 14 [14]

**26A.** SC 3, Ch 1, Turn [–3]

**26B.** SC 8, Ch 1, Turn [–8]

**26C.** SC 7, SC/HDC Dec & HDC, SC 2, <Dec>, SC 2, HDC & HDC/SC Dec [–16] [15]

"<Dec>" is a stitch that is defined in the Glossary.

**27A.** SC 8, Ch 1, Turn [–8]

**27B.** SC 9, Ch 1, Turn [–9]

**27C.** SC 8, SC/HDC Dec & HDC, SC 2, <Dec>, SC 2, HDC & HDC/SC Dec [–17] [16]

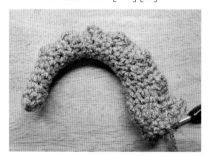

**28A.** SC 9, Ch 1, Turn [–9]

**28B.** SC 10, Ch 1, Turn [–10]

**28C.** SC 9, SC/HDC Dec & HDC, SC 2, <Dec>, SC 2, HDC & HDC/SC Dec [–18] [17]

**29A.** SC 9, Ch 1, Turn [–9]

**29B.** SC 10, Ch 1, Turn [–10]

**29C.** SC 9, SC/HDC Dec & HDC, SC 2, Inc, SC 2, HDC & HDC/SC Dec [–19] [18]

**30A.** SC 10, Ch 1, Turn [–10]

**30B.** SC 12, Ch 1, Turn [–12]

**30C.** SC 11, SC/HDC Dec & HDC, SC 2, <Dec>, SC 2, HDC & HDC/SC Dec [–20] [19]

**31A.** SC 12, Ch 1, Turn [–12]

**31B.** SC 13, Ch 1, Turn [–13]

**31C.** SC 12, SC/HDC Dec & HDC, SC 2, <Dec>, SC 2, HDC & HDC/SC Dec [–21] [20]

**32A.** SC 12, Ch 1, Turn [–12]

**32B.** SC 13, Ch 1, Turn [–13]

**32C.** SC 12, SC/HDC Dec & HDC, SC 2, Inc, SC 2, HDC & HDC/SC Dec [–22] [21]

**33.** SC 21 [21]

Fasten off with a 24 in/61 cm yarn tail.

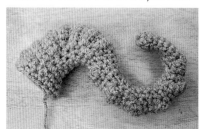

## Assembly

**1.** It is optional to use wire inside these Horns. If you want to be able to shape the Horns to be even tighter on the curves, take one piece of wire, bend over the end of it so that the end is not sharp, secure the bent wire to itself with a thin strip of duct tape, and insert the wire into the Horn. Shape the wire to match or accentuate the curves of the Horn. The wire should extend 2 to 3 in/5 to 7.5 cm beyond the base of the Horn. (Please note that adding wire will make the piece unsafe for children.)

**2.** Stuff the Horn lightly with fiberfill to smooth out the Horn and fill out the shape. Use the process of stuffing the Horns to shape them. You can encourage the Horn to curve one way or the other to create a right Horn and a left Horn as you stuff them.

**3.** Pin the Horns in place on the Monster's head. If you are using wire, insert the wire into the Monster's head/body and then pin the Horn in place.

**4.** Using the yarn tails, sew the Horns to the Monster; weave in ends.

Egg Shape with Open Mouth and Legs, Open Mouth with Four Pointed Teeth (Upper), Thick Short Arms with Claws, S-shaped Horns, Pointed Tongue

## RAM HORNS (MAKE 2)

*Approximately 3.5 in/9 cm wide (from base to edge extending from the Monster's head), 10 in/25.5 cm long (from base to tip, along the length of the horn), 2 in/5 cm wide at base*

*Accent Color Yarn: Approximately 27 yd/24.75 m worsted/medium weight yarn per Horn*

*Optional: Strong wire*

1. SC 6 in Magic Circle, continue in spiral [6]
2. SC 5, Inc [7]
3. SC 7 [7]
4. SC 6, Inc [8]

Short rows are utilized in the following rows.

Follow all sub-steps of each row in order (i.e., 5A, 5B, etc.). These short rows create the curves and shaping. They will sometimes go beyond where the row began; follow the pattern exactly and it will work. Each sub-row will have a stitch count for the number of stitches created in that sub-row indicated by a number that looks like this: [–5]; a final stitch count at the end of the final sub-row to indicate how many stitches are available on the edge of the work once all the sub-rows are complete will be indicated by a number that looks like this: [10].

A video tutorial for how to crochet short rows is available on the Crafty Intentions YouTube channel here: www.youtube.com/watch?v=sh5T-idiwm8&t=159s

Hybrid decreases like the "SC/HDC Dec & HDC" stitches are defined in the Glossary and demonstrated on the Crafty Intentions YouTube channel here: www.youtube.com/watch?v=h4wkxMOMqXg&t=5s

**5A.** SC 5, Ch 1, Turn [–5]

**5B.** SC 4, Ch 1, Turn [–4]

**5C.** SC 3, SC/HDC Dec & HDC, SC 2 [–7] [8]

**6.** HDC & HDC/SC Dec, SC 5, Inc [9]

**7A.** SC 6, Ch 1, Turn [–6]

**7B.** SC 5, Ch 1, Turn [–5]

**7C.** SC 4, SC/HDC Dec & HDC, SC 2 [–8] [9]

**8.** HDC & HDC/SC Dec, SC 6, Inc [10]

You can begin to stuff the piece with fiberfill here and continue to stuff as you crochet.

**9A.** SC 6, Ch 1, Turn [–6]

**9B.** SC 4, Ch 1, Turn [–4]

**9C.** SC 3, SC/HDC Dec & HDC, SC 3 [–8] [10]

**10.** SC, HDC & HDC/SC Dec, SC 6, Inc [11]

**11A.** SC 7, Ch 1, Turn [–7]

**11B.** SC 5, Ch 1, Turn [–5]

**11C.** SC 4, SC/HDC Dec & HDC, SC 3 [–9] [11]

**12.** SC, HDC & HDC/SC Dec, SC 7, Inc [12]

**13A.** SC 8, Ch 1, Turn [–8]

**13B.** SC 6, Ch 1, Turn [–6]

**13C.** SC 5, SC/HDC Dec & HDC, SC 3 [–10] [12]

**14.** SC, HDC & HDC/SC Dec, SC 8, Inc [13]

**15A.** SC 9, Ch 1, Turn [–9]

**15B.** SC 6, Ch 1, Turn [–6]

**15C.** SC 5, SC/HDC Dec & HDC, SC 3 [–10] [13]

**16.** SC 2, HDC & HDC/SC Dec, SC 8, Inc [14]

**17A.** SC 10, Ch 1, Turn [–10]

**17B.** SC 8, Ch 1, Turn [–8]

**17C.** SC 7, SC/HDC Dec & HDC, SC 2, <Dec>, SC 2, HDC & HDC/SC Dec [–16] [15]

"<Dec>" is a stitch that is defined in the Glossary.

**18A.** SC 8, Ch 1, Turn [–8]

**18B.** SC 9, Ch 1, Turn [–9]

**18C.** SC 8, SC/HDC Dec & HDC, SC 2, <Dec>, SC 2, HDC & HDC/SC Dec [–17] [16]

**19A.** SC 9, Ch 1, Turn [–9]

**19B.** SC 10, Ch 1, Turn [–10]

**19C.** SC 9, SC/HDC Dec & HDC, SC 2, <Dec>, SC 2, HDC & HDC/SC Dec [–18] [17]

**20A.** SC 9, Ch 1, Turn [–9]

**20B.** SC 10, Ch 1, Turn [–10]

**20C.** SC 9, SC/HDC Dec & HDC, SC 2, Inc, SC 2, HDC & HDC/SC Dec [–19] [18]

**21A.** SC 10, Ch 1, Turn [–10]

**21B.** SC 12, Ch 1, Turn [–12]

**21C.** SC 11, SC/HDC Dec & HDC, SC 2, <Dec>, SC 2, HDC & HDC/SC Dec [–20] [19]

**22A.** SC 12, Ch 1, Turn [–12]

**22B.** SC 13, Ch 1, Turn [–13]

**22C.** SC 12, SC/HDC Dec & HDC, SC 2, <Dec>, SC 2, HDC & HDC/SC Dec [–21] [20]

**23A.** SC 12, Ch 1, Turn [–12]

**23B.** SC 13, Ch 1, Turn [–13]

**23C.** SC 12, SC/HDC Dec & HDC, SC 2, Inc, SC 2, HDC & HDC/SC Dec [–22] [21]

**24.** SC 21 [21]

Fasten off with a 24 in/61 cm yarn tail.

## Assembly

**1.** It is optional to use wire inside these Horns. If you want to be able to shape the Horns to be even tighter on the curves take one piece of wire, bend over the end of it so that the end is not sharp, secure the bent wire to itself with a thin strip of duct tape, and insert the wire into the Horn. Shape the wire to match or accentuate the curves of the Horn. The wire should extend 2 to 3 in/5 to 7.5 cm beyond the base of the Horn. (Please note that adding wire will make the piece unsafe for children.)

**2.** If you haven't already, stuff the Horn lightly with fiberfill to smooth it out and fill out the shape. Use the process of stuffing the Horns to shape them. You can encourage the Horn to curve one way or the other to create a right Horn and a left Horn as you stuff them.

**3.** Pin the Horn in place on the Monster's head. If you are using wire, insert the wire into the Monster's head/Body and then pin the Horn in place.

**4.** Using the yarn tail, sew the Horn onto the Monster; weave in the end.

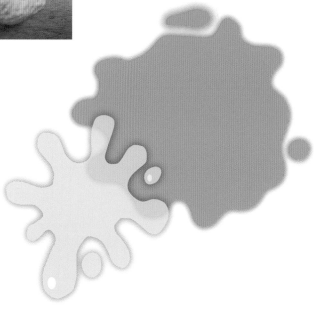

Cylinder with Overbite and No Legs, Bulb-ended Short Limbs, Bulb-ended Long Limbs, Ram Horns, Pointy Teeth, Large Ridged Belly

# LARGE ANTLERS (MAKE 2)

*Approximately 5.75 in/14.5 cm tall, 1.5 in/4 cm wide at base*

*Accent Color Yarn: Approximately 26 yd/23.75 m worsted/medium weight yarn per Antler*

*Optional: Strong wire*

## Part 1 (Make 1 per Antler)

> Make Part 1 first and set aside for use once you reach Part 3.

**1.** SC 6 in Magic Circle, Sl St to beginning stitch, Ch 1 [6]

**2.** (SC, Inc) x 3, Sl St to beginning stitch, Ch 1 [9]

**3–4.** (2 rows of) SC 9, Sl St to beginning stitch, Ch 1 [9]

**5.** SC 7, Dec, Sl St to beginning stitch, Ch 1 [8]

**6.** SC 8, Sl St to beginning stitch, Ch 1 [8]

**7.** SC 3, Dec, SC 3, Sl St to beginning stitch, Ch 1 [7]

**8.** SC 7, Sl St to beginning stitch [7]

Fasten off with a short yarn tail.

## Part 2 (Make 1 per Antler)

> Make Part 2 and set aside for use once you reach Part 3.

**1.** SC 6 in Magic Circle, Sl St to beginning stitch, Ch 1 [6]

**2.** (SC, Inc) x 3, Sl St to beginning stitch, Ch 1 [9]

**3–4.** (2 rows of) SC 9, Sl St to beginning stitch, Ch 1 [9]

**5.** SC 7, Dec, Sl St to beginning stitch, Ch 1 [8]

**6.** SC 8, Sl St to beginning stitch, Ch 1 [8]

**7.** SC 3, Dec, SC 3, Sl St to beginning stitch, Ch 1 [7]

**8.** SC 7, Sl St to beginning stitch, Ch 1 [7]

**9.** SC 7, Sl St to beginning stitch [7]

Fasten off with a short yarn tail.

## Part 3 (Make 1 per Antler)

**1.** SC 6 in Magic Circle, Sl St to beginning stitch, Ch 1 [6]

**2.** (SC, Inc) x 3, Sl St to beginning stitch, Ch 1 [9]

**3–4.** (2 rows of) SC 9, Sl St to beginning stitch, Ch 1 [9]

**5.** SC 7, Dec, Sl St to beginning stitch, Ch 1 [8]

**6.** SC 8, Sl St to beginning stitch, Ch 1 [8]

**7.** SC 3, Dec, SC 3, Sl St to beginning stitch, Ch 1 [7]

**8–11.** (4 rows of) SC 7, Sl St to beginning stitch, Ch 1 [7]

**12.** SC 4, starting in the first stitch of the final row on Part 1, SC 7 around Part 1, SC in *same* stitch as the last SC on Part 3, continuing around Part 3, SC 3, Sl St to beginning stitch, Ch 1 [15]

> Stuff the antler medium-firm and continue to stuff with fiberfill as you go.

> Be careful not to work into the "Sl St, Ch 1" join on Part 1.

**13.** SC 3, Dec, SC 5, Dec, SC 3, Sl St to beginning stitch, Ch 1 [13]

**14.** SC 2, Dec, SC 5, Dec, SC 2, Sl St to beginning stitch, Ch 1 [11]

**15.** SC 2, Dec, SC 3, Dec, SC 2, Sl St to beginning stitch, Ch 1 [9]

**16–17.** (2 rows of) SC 9, Sl St to beginning stitch, Ch 1 [9]

**18.** SC, starting into the first stitch of the final Row on Part 2, SC 7 around Part 2, SC in the *same* stitch as the last SC on Part 3, continuing around Part 3, SC 8, Sl St to beginning stitch, Ch 1 [17]

> Be careful not to work into the "Sl St, Ch 1" join on Part 2.

**19.** Dec, SC 5, Dec, SC 8, *do not* "Sl St, Ch 1," continue in spiral [15]

**20.** Dec, SC 3, Dec, SC 8 [13]

**21.** SC 8, Dec, SC 3 [12]

**22–24.** (3 rows of) SC 12 [12]

**25.** (SC 3, Inc) x 3 [15]

**26.** (SC 2, Inc, SC 2) x 3 [18]

Fasten off with a 12 in/30.5 cm yarn tail.

## Assembly

**1.** Pin in place on the Monster's head.

**2.** Once you are satisfied with placement, sew to attach to head; weave in ends.

> If you want to add metal spikes to any part of your Monster, go to page 172 for tips on how to do that.

**Square with No Mouth and No Legs, Medium Rounded Underbite, Cute Mitten Limbs, Cute Footed Limbs, Spiky Ears, Large Antlers, Four Humanlike Teeth**

# LARGE CURVED HORNS (MAKE 2)

*Approximately 5 in/13 cm tall, 2 in/5 cm wide at base*

*Accent Color Yarn: Approximately 20 yd/18.25 m worsted/medium weight yarn per Horn*

**1.** SC 4 in Magic Circle, Sl St to beginning stitch, Ch 1 [4]

**2.** SC 4, Sl St to beginning stitch, Ch 1 [4]

**3.** Inc, SC 3, Sl St to beginning stitch, Ch 1 [5]

**4.** SC 5, Sl St to beginning stitch, Ch 1 [5]

**5.** SC, Inc, SC 3, Sl St to beginning stitch, Ch 1 [6]

**6.** SC 6, Sl St to beginning stitch, Ch 1 [6]

**7.** SC, Inc, SC 4, Sl St to beginning stitch, Ch 1 [7]

**8.** SC 7, Sl St to beginning stitch, Ch 1 [7]

**9.** SC 2, Inc, SC 4, Sl St to beginning stitch, Ch 1 [8]

**10.** SC 3, Inc, SC 4, Sl St to beginning stitch, Ch 1 [9]

**11.** SC 3, Inc, SC 5, Sl St to beginning stitch, Ch 1 [10]

**12.** SC 4, Inc, SC 5, Sl St to beginning stitch, Ch 1 [11]

**13.** SC 5, Inc, SC 5, Sl St to beginning stitch, Ch 1 [12]

**14.** SC 5, Inc, SC 6, Sl St to beginning stitch, Ch 1 [13]

**15.** SC 6, Inc, SC 6, Sl St to beginning stitch, Ch 1 [14]

**16.** SC 7, Inc, SC 6, Sl St to beginning stitch, Ch 1 [15]

**17.** SC 7, Inc, SC 7, Sl St to beginning stitch, Ch 1 [16]

**18.** SC 8, Inc, SC 7, Sl St to beginning stitch, Ch 1 [17]

**19.** SC 9, Inc, SC 7, Sl St to beginning stitch, Ch 1 [18]

**20.** SC 9, Inc, SC 8, Sl St to beginning stitch, Ch 1 [19]

**21.** SC 10, Inc, SC 8, Sl St to beginning stitch, Ch 1 [20]

**22.** HDC 5, SC 6, Inc, SC 6, HDC 2, Sl St to beginning stitch, Ch 1 [21]

**23.** HDC 5, SC 6, Inc, SC 6, HDC 3, Sl St to beginning stitch, Ch 1 [22]

**24.** HDC 5, SC 7, Inc, SC 7, HDC 2, Sl St to beginning stitch, Ch 1 [23]

**25.** HDC 6, SC 7, Inc, SC 7, HDC 2, Sl St to beginning stitch [24]

Fasten off with a 12 in/30.5 cm yarn tail.

## Assembly

**1.** Stuff the Horn lightly with fiberfill.

**2.** Pin to desired position on the head of your Monster's Body.

**3.** Once you are satisfied with placement, use the yarn tail to sew to attach to head; weave in ends.

# MEDIUM POINTY ANTLERS (MAKE 2)

*Approximately 5.75 in/14.5 cm tall, 1.25 in/3 cm wide at base*

*Any Color Yarn: Approximately 16 yd/14.75 m worsted/medium weight yarn per Antler*

## Part 1 (Make 1 per Antler)

**1.** SC 4 in Magic Circle, Sl St to beginning stitch, Ch 1 [4]

**2.** SC 4, Sl St to beginning stitch, Ch 1 [4]

**3.** SC 3, Inc, Sl St to beginning stitch, Ch 1 [5]

**4.** SC 5, Sl St to beginning stitch, Ch 1 [5]

**5.** SC 4, Inc, Sl St to beginning stitch, Ch 1 [6]

**6.** SC 6, Sl St to beginning stitch, Ch 1 [6]

**7.** SC 5, Inc, Sl St to beginning stitch, Ch 1 [7]

**8.** SC 7, Sl St to beginning stitch, Ch 1 [7]

**9.** SC 3, Inc, SC 3, Sl St to beginning stitch [8]

Fasten off with a short yarn tail.

### Part 2 (Make 1 per Antler)

1. SC 4 in Magic Circle, Sl St to beginning stitch, Ch 1 [4]

2. SC 4, Sl St to beginning stitch, Ch 1 [4]

3. SC 3, Inc, Sl St to beginning stitch, Ch 1 [5]

4. SC 5, Sl St to beginning stitch, Ch 1 [5]

5. SC 4, Inc, Sl St to beginning stitch, Ch 1 [6]

6. SC 6, Sl St to beginning stitch, Ch 1 [6]

7. SC 5, Inc, Sl St to beginning stitch, Ch 1 [7]

8. SC 7, Sl St to beginning stitch, Ch 1 [7]

9. SC 3, Inc, SC 3, Sl St to beginning stitch, Ch 1 [8]

10–11. (2 rows of) SC 8, Sl St to beginning stitch, Ch 1 [8]

12. SC 7, Inc, Sl St to beginning stitch, Ch 1 [9]

13–14. (2 rows of) SC 9, Sl St to beginning stitch, Ch 1 [9]

15. SC 4, Inc, SC 4, Sl St to beginning stitch, Ch 1 [10]

16. SC 4, start a decrease into the next available stitch, complete the decrease into the first stitch of the final row on Part 1, continuing around Part 1, SC 6, start a decrease in the last stitch on Part 1, complete the decrease into the next available stitch on Part 2, SC 4 along the remaining stitches on Part 2, Sl St to beginning stitch, Ch 1 [16]

> Stuff the antler medium-firm and continue to stuff with fiberfill as you go.

> Be careful not to work into the "Sl St, Ch 1" join on Part 1.

17. (SC 3, Dec, SC 3) x 2, Sl St to beginning stitch, Ch 1 [14]

18. (SC 5, Dec) x 2, Sl St to beginning stitch, Ch 1 [12]

19. (SC 2, Dec, SC 2) x 2, Sl St to beginning stitch, Ch 1 [10]

20–22. (3 rows of) SC 10, Sl St to beginning stitch, Ch 1 [10]

23. (SC 2, Inc) x 3, SC, Sl St to beginning stitch [13]

Fasten off with a 12 in/30.5 cm yarn tail.

### Assembly

1. Pin in place on the Monster's head.

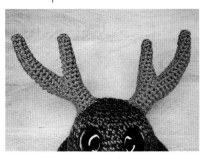

2. Once you are satisfied with placement, sew to attach to head; weave in ends.

Cylinder with Underbite and Legs, Small Cone Limbs, Medium Pointy Antlers, Two Close Together Rounded Teeth

# SMALL ANTLERS (MAKE 2)

*Approximately 3 in/7.5 cm tall, 1 in/2.5 cm wide at base*

*Any Color Yarn: Approximately 10 yd/9.25 m worsted/medium weight yarn per Antler*

## Part 1 (Make 1 per Antler)

1. SC 5 in Magic Circle, Sl St to beginning stitch, Ch 1 [5]
2. SC 5, Sl St to beginning stitch, Ch 1 [5]
3. SC 2, Inc, SC 2, Sl St to beginning stitch, Ch 1 [6]
4. SC 6, Sl St to beginning stitch, Ch 1 [6]
5. Inc, SC 5, Sl St to beginning stitch, Ch 1 [7]
6. SC 3, Inc, SC 3, Sl St to beginning stitch [8]

Fasten off with a short yarn tail.

## Part 2 (Make 1 per Antler)

1. SC 5 in Magic Circle, Sl St to beginning stitch, Ch 1 [5]
2. SC 5, Sl St to beginning stitch, Ch 1 [5]
3. SC 2, Inc, SC 2, Sl St to beginning stitch, Ch 1 [6]
4. SC 6, Sl St to beginning stitch, Ch 1 [6]
5. Inc, SC 5, Sl St to beginning stitch, Ch 1 [7]

6. SC 3, Inc, SC 3, Sl St to beginning stitch, Ch 1 [8]

7. SC 3, start a decrease into the next available stitch, complete the decrease into the first stitch of the final row on Part 1, continuing around Part 1, SC 6, start a decrease in the last stitch on Part 1, complete the decrease into the next available stitch on Part 2, SC 3 along the remaining stitches on Part 2, Sl St to beginning stitch, Ch 1 [14]

> Stuff the antler medium-firm and continue to stuff with fiberfill as you go.

> Be careful not to work into the "Sl St, Ch 1" join on Part 1.

8. SC 2, Dec, SC 6, Dec, SC 2, Sl St to beginning stitch, Ch 1 [12]
9. (SC 2, Dec, SC 2) x 2, Sl St to beginning stitch, Ch 1 [10]
10. (SC 3, Dec) x 2, Sl St to beginning stitch, Ch 1 [8]

11–13. (3 rows of) SC 8, Sl St to beginning stitch, Ch 1 [8]
14. (SC, Inc) x 4, Sl St to beginning stitch [12]

Fasten off with a 12 in/30.5 cm yarn tail.

## Assembly

1. Pin in place on the Monster's head.

2. Once you are satisfied with placement, sew to attach to head and weave in ends.

**Eyeball Monster Main Body/Eye with Safety Eye, Eyeball Monster Eyelid, Wide Flat-ended Short Limbs, Wide Flat-ended Long Limbs, Small Antlers**

**Sphere with Overbite, Spider Legs, Ridged Horns, Two Curved Saber Teeth**

# RIDGED HORNS (MAKE 2)

***Approximately 3.75 in/9.5 cm tall, 1.75 in/4.5 cm wide at base***

***Any Color Yarn: Approximately 15 yd/13.75 m worsted/medium weight yarn per Horn***

1. SC 6 in Magic Circle, Sl St to beginning stitch, Ch 1 [6]
2. BLO [SC 6], Sl St to beginning stitch, Ch 1 [6]
3. FLO [SC 5, Inc], Sl St to beginning stitch, Ch 1 [7]
4. BLO [SC 7], Sl St to beginning stitch, Ch 1 [7]
5. FLO [SC 6, Inc], Sl St to beginning stitch, Ch 1 [8]
6. BLO [SC 8], Sl St to beginning stitch, Ch 1 [8]
7. FLO [Inc, SC 6, Inc], Sl St to beginning stitch, Ch 1 [10]
8. BLO [SC 10], Sl St to beginning stitch, Ch 1 [10]
9. FLO [Inc, SC 8, Inc], Sl St to beginning stitch, Ch 1 [12]
10. BLO [SC 12], Sl St to beginning stitch, Ch 1 [12]
11. FLO [Inc, SC 10, Inc], Sl St to beginning stitch, Ch 1 [14]
12. BLO [SC 14], Sl St to beginning stitch, Ch 1 [14]
13. FLO [Inc, SC 12, Inc], Sl St to beginning stitch, Ch 1 [16]
14. BLO [SC 16], Sl St to beginning stitch, Ch 1 [16]
15. FLO [Inc, SC 14, Inc], Sl St to beginning stitch, Ch 1 [18]
16. BLO [SC 18], Sl St to beginning stitch [18]

Fasten off with an 18 in/45.5 cm yarn tail.

## Assembly

1. Stuff the Horns medium-light with fiberfill.
2. Pin in place on the Monster's head.

3. Once you are satisfied with placement, sew to attach to head; weave in ends.

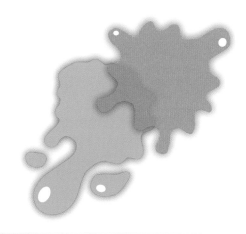

# SPIRAL-SHAPED HORNS (MAKE 2)

***Approximately 4.5 in/11.5 cm long, 1.5 in/4 cm wide at base***

***Any Color Yarn: Approximately 13 yd/12 m worsted/medium weight yarn per Horn***

1. SC 4 in Magic Circle, continue in spiral for the whole piece [4]
2. SC 4 [4]
3. Inc x 2, SC 2 [6]
4. SC 4, Dec [5]
5. Inc x 2, SC 3 [7]
6. SC 5, Dec [6]
7. Inc x 2, SC 4 [8]
8. SC 5, Dec, SC [7]
9. Inc x 2, SC 5 [9]
10. SC 6, Dec, SC [8]
11. Inc x 2, SC 6 [10]
12. SC 7, Dec, SC [9]

13. Inc x 2, SC 7 [11]
14. SC 8, Dec, SC [10]
15. Inc x 2, SC 8 [12]
16. SC 8, Dec, SC 2 [11]
17. Inc x 2, SC 9 [13]
18. SC 9, Dec, SC 2 [12]
19. Inc x 2, SC 10 [14]
20. SC 10, Dec, SC 2 [13]
21. Inc x 2, SC 11 [15]
22. SC 11, Dec, SC 2 [14]
23. Inc x 2, SC 12 [16]
24. SC 12, Dec, SC 2 [15]
25. Inc x 2, SC 13 [17]

Fasten off with an 18 in/45.5 cm yarn tail.

## Assembly

1. Stuff the Horns medium-light with fiberfill.
2. Pin in place on the Monster's head.

3. Once you are satisfied with placement, sew to attach to head; weave in ends.

# ROUNDED SEGMENTED HORNS (MAKE 2)

***Approximately 4 in/10 cm long, 1.5 in/4 cm wide at base***

***Any Color Yarn: Approximately 17 yd/15.5 m worsted/medium weight yarn per Horn***

1. SC 6 in Magic Circle, Sl St to beginning stitch, Ch 1 [6]
2. SC 6, Sl St to beginning stitch, Ch 1 [6]
3. (SC, Inc) x 3, Sl St to beginning stitch, Ch 1 [9]
4. SC 9, Sl St to beginning stitch, Ch 1 [9]
5. (SC, Dec) x 3, Sl St to beginning stitch, Ch 1 [6]
6. FLO [(SC, Inc) x 3], Sl St to beginning stitch, Ch 1 [9]
7. SC 9, Sl St to beginning stitch, Ch 1 [9]
8. (SC, Inc, SC) x 3, Sl St to beginning stitch, Ch 1 [12]
9. (SC, Dec, SC) x 3, Sl St to beginning stitch, Ch 1 [9]
10. FLO [(SC, Inc, SC) x 3], Sl St to beginning stitch, Ch 1 [12]
11. SC 12, Sl St to beginning stitch, Ch 1 [12]
12. (SC 3, Inc) x 3, Sl St to beginning stitch, Ch 1 [15]
13. (SC 3, Dec) x 3, Sl St to beginning stitch, Ch 1 [12]
14. FLO [(SC 3, Inc) x 3], Sl St to beginning stitch, Ch 1 [15]
15. SC 15, Sl St to beginning stitch, Ch 1 [15]
16. (SC 2, Inc, SC 2) x 3, Sl St to beginning stitch, Ch 1 [18]
17. (SC 2, Dec, SC 2) x 3, Sl St to beginning stitch, Ch 1 [15]
18. FLO [(SC 2, Inc, SC 2) x 3], Sl St to beginning stitch, Ch 1 [18]
19. SC 18, Sl St to beginning stitch, Ch 1 [18]
20. (SC 5, Inc) x 3, Sl St to beginning stitch, Ch 1 [21]
21. (SC 5, Dec) x 3, Sl St to beginning stitch [18]

Fasten off with an 18 in/45.5 cm yarn tail.

## Assembly

1. Stuff the Horns medium-light with fiberfill.
2. Pin in place on the Monster's head.

3. Once you are satisfied with placement, sew to attach to head; weave in ends.

# LONG SLIGHTLY CURVED HORNS (MAKE 2)

**Approximately 5.5 in/14 cm long, 1.5 in/4 cm wide at base**

**Any Color Yarn: Approximately 16 yd/14.75 m worsted/medium weight yarn per Horn**

1. SC 5 in Magic Circle, continue in Spiral [5]
2. SC 4, Inc [6]
3. SC 6 [6]
4. SC 5, Inc [7]
5. SC 7 [7]
6. SC 6, Inc [8]
7. SC 8 [8]
8. SC 7, Inc [9]
9. SC 9 [9]
10. SC 3, Dec, SC 2, Inc x 2 [10]
11. SC 10 [10]
12. SC 3, Dec, SC 3, Inc x 2 [11]
13. SC 11 [11]
14. SC 4, Dec, SC 3, Inc x 2 [12]
15. SC 12 [12]
16. SC 4, Dec, SC 4, Inc x 2 [13]
17. SC 13 [13]
18. SC 5, Dec, SC 4, Inc x 2 [14]
19. SC 14 [14]
20. SC 5, Dec, SC 5, Inc x 2 [15]
21. SC 15 [15]
22. SC 6, Dec, SC 5, Inc x 2 [16]
23. SC 16 [16]
24. SC 6, Dec, SC 6, Inc x 2 [17]
25. SC 17 [17]
26. SC 7, Dec, SC 6, Inc x 2 [18]
27. SC 18 [18]

Fasten off with an 18 in/45.5 cm yarn tail.

## Assembly

1. Stuff the Horns medium-light with fiberfill.
2. Pin in place on the Monster's head.

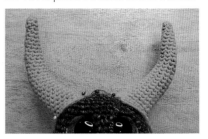

3. Once you are satisfied with placement, sew to attach to head; weave in ends.

**Cylinder with Open Mouth and No Legs, Open Mouth with No Teeth Black Hole, Three-toed Dangling Legs (also used for Arms), Long Slightly Curved Horns**

# MEDIUM TO THE SIDE CURVED HORNS (MAKE 2)

*Approximately 4 in/10 cm wide (from base to tip, extending from the Monster's head), 6 in/15 cm long (from base to tip, along the length of the horn), 1.5 in/4 cm wide at base*

*Any Color Yarn: Approximately 15 yd/13.75 m worsted/medium weight yarn per Horn*

**1.** SC 6 in Magic Circle, Sl St to beginning stitch, Ch 1 [6]

**2.** SC 6, Sl St to beginning stitch, Ch 1 [6]

**3.** SC 6, Sl St to beginning stitch, Ch 1 [6]

**4.** (SC, Inc, SC) x 2, Sl St to beginning stitch, Ch 1 [8]

**5.** SC 8, Sl St to beginning stitch, Ch 1 [8]

Short rows are utilized in this pattern.

Follow all sub-steps of each row in order (i.e., 6A, 6B, etc.). These short rows create the curves and shaping. They will sometimes go beyond where the row began; follow the pattern exactly and it will work. Each sub-row will have a stitch count for the number of stitches created in that sub-row indicated by a number that looks like this: [–5]; a final stitch count at the end of the final sub-row to indicate how many stitches are available on the edge of the work once all the sub-rows are complete will be indicated by a number that looks like this: [10].

A video tutorial for how to crochet short rows is available on the Crafty Intentions YouTube channel here: www.youtube.com/watch?v=sh5T-idiwm8&t=159s

Hybrid decreases like the "SC/HDC Dec & HDC" stitches are defined in the Glossary and demonstrated on the Crafty Intentions YouTube channel here: www.youtube.com/watch?v=h4wkxMOMqXg&t=5s

**6A.** SC 6, Ch 1, Turn [–6]

**6B.** SC 4, Ch 1, Turn [–4]

**6C.** SC 3, SC/HDC Dec & HDC, SC, Sl St to beginning stitch, Ch 1 [–6] [8]

**7A.** SC, HDC & HDC/SC Dec, SC, <Dec>, SC 2, Ch 1, Turn [–7]

"<Dec>" is a stitch that is defined in the Glossary.

**7B.** SC 5, Ch 1, Turn [–5]

**7C.** SC 4, SC/HDC Dec & HDC, SC, Sl St to beginning stitch, Ch 1 [–7] [9]

**8A.** SC, HDC & HDC/SC Dec, SC, Inc, SC 2, Ch 1, Turn [–8]

**8B.** SC 5, Ch 1, Turn [–5]

**8C.** SC 4, SC/HDC Dec & HDC, SC, Sl St to beginning stitch, Ch 1 [–7] [10]

**9A.** SC 2, HDC & HDC/SC Dec, SC 4, Ch 1, Turn [–8]

**9B.** SC 6, Ch 1, Turn [–6]

**9C.** SC 5, SC/HDC Dec & HDC, SC, Sl St to beginning stitch, Ch 1 [–8] [10]

**10.** SC, HDC & HDC/SC Dec, SC 7, Sl St to beginning stitch, Ch 1 [10]

**11.** SC 9, Inc, Sl St to beginning stitch, Ch 1 [11]

**12.** SC 11, Sl St to beginning stitch, Ch 1 [11]

**13.** SC 10, Inc, Sl St to beginning stitch, Ch 1 [12]

**14.** (SC 5, Inc) x 2, DO NOT "Sl St, Ch 1," continue in spiral [14]

**15A.** SC 3, Ch 1, Turn [–3]

**15B.** SC 6, Ch 1, Turn [–6]

**15C.** SC 5, SC/HDC Dec & HDC, SC, Ch 1, Turn [–8]

**15D.** SC 7, SC/HDC Dec & HDC, SC, Ch 1, Turn [–10]

**15E.** SC 9, SC/HDC Dec & HDC, Inc x 2, HDC & HDC/SC Dec [–17] [16]

**16A.** SC 9, Ch 1, Turn [–9]
**16B.** SC 9, Ch 1, Turn [–9]
**16C.** SC 8, SC/HDC Dec & HDC, SC 2, Inc, SC 2, HDC & HDC/SC Dec [–18] [17]

Fasten off with an 18 in/45.5 cm yarn tail.

## Assembly

**1.** Stuff the Horns medium-light with fiberfill.

**2.** Pin in place on the Monster's head.

**3.** Once you are satisfied with placement, sew to attach to head; weave in ends.

## MEDIUM SLIGHTLY CURVED STRIPED HORNS (MAKE 2)

*Approximately 3.5 in/9 cm tall, 1.5 in/4 cm wide at base*

*Any Color Yarn: Approximately 6 yd/5.5 m worsted/medium weight yarn per Horn*

*Second Any Color Yarn: Approximately 6 yd/5.5 m worsted/medium weight yarn per Horn*

**1.** SC 6 in Magic Circle, Sl St to beginning stitch, Ch 1 [6]

**2.** SC 6, Sl St to beginning stitch, Ch 1 [6]

**3.** Inc, SC 4, Inc, Sl St to beginning stitch, fasten off the starting yarn color and switch to the alternate color [8]

**4–5.** (2 rows of) SC 8, Sl St to beginning stitch, Ch 1 [8]

**6.** Inc, SC 6, Inc, Sl St to beginning stitch, fasten off this color, switch back to the original color [10]

**7–8.** (2 rows of) SC 10, Sl St to beginning stitch, Ch 1 [10]

**9.** Inc, SC 8, Inc, Sl St to beginning stitch, fasten off this color, and switch to the alternate color [12]

**10–11.** (2 rows of) SC 12, Sl St to beginning stitch, Ch 1 [12]

**12.** Inc, SC 10, Inc, Sl St to beginning stitch, fasten off this color, switch back to the original color [14]

**13–14.** (2 rows of) SC 14, Sl St to beginning stitch, Ch 1 [14]

**15.** Inc, SC 12, Inc, Sl St to beginning stitch [16]

Fasten off with an 18 in/45.5 cm yarn tail.

## Assembly

**1.** Stuff the Horns medium-light with fiberfill.

**2.** Pin in place on the Monster's head.

**3.** Once you are satisfied with placement, sew to attach to head; weave in ends.

Egg Shape with
No Mouth and Legs,
Small Rounded Overbite,
Small Short Limbs, Medium
to the Side Curved Horns,
Hair Puff, Two Small
Fangs, Nose with Wide
Nostrils

Square
with No Mouth
and No Legs, 2D Open
Mouth in Lima Bean Shape
with Straight Teeth (Upper)
and Tongue (Lower), Small
Nubbins Limbs, Nubbin
Footed Limbs, Cat Ears,
Medium Slightly Curved
Striped Horns

Cylinder with
Open Mouth and No
Legs, Open Mouth with
Humanlike Teeth, Thinner
Eyelid/Eyebrow for 30 mm
Safety Eyes, Cute Mitten Limbs,
Cute Footed Limbs, Teensy
Round Ears, Ridged Spiral
Horns with Accent Color,
Circle Belly

# RIDGED SPIRAL HORNS WITH ACCENT COLOR (MAKE 2)

*Approximately 4 in/10 cm tall, 2 in/5 cm wide at base*

*Any Color Yarn: Approximately 17 yd/15.5 m worsted/medium weight yarn per Horn*

*Second Any Color Yarn: Approximately 8 yd/7.25 m worsted/medium weight yarn per Horn*

## Part 1

**1.** SC 4 in Magic Circle, continue in spiral [4]

**2.** BLO [SC 3, Inc] [5]

**3.** BLO [SC 4, Inc] [6]

**4.** BLO [SC 5, Inc] [7]

**5.** BLO [SC 6, Inc] [8]

**6.** BLO [SC 3, Inc, SC 4] [9]

**7.** BLO [SC 3, Inc x 2, SC 4] [11]

**8.** BLO [SC 5, <Dec>, SC 6] [12]

> "<Dec>" is a stitch that is defined in the Glossary.

**9.** BLO [SC 5, Inc, SC 6] [13]

**10.** BLO [SC 5, Inc x 2, SC 6] [15]

**11.** BLO [SC 14, Inc] [16]

**12.** BLO [SC 14, Inc x 2] [18]

**13.** BLO [SC 15, Inc x 2, SC] [20]

**14.** BLO [SC 16, Inc x 2, SC 2] [22]

**15.** BLO [SC 22] [22]

Fasten off with an 18 in/45.5 cm yarn tail.

## Part 2

**1.** Starting with a long enough yarn tail to weave in later, attach any color yarn to the first leftover front loop at the tip of the horn, as shown, and then Sl St in every leftover front loop down the length of the horn to the last available FLO stitch.

Fasten off with a 12 in/30.5 cm yarn tail.

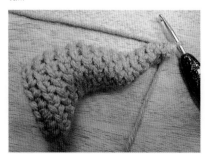

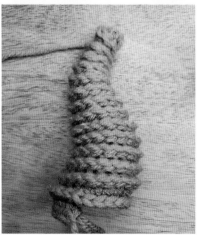

## Assembly

**1.** Stuff the Horns medium-light with fiberfill.

**2.** Pin in place on the Monster's head.

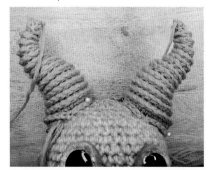

**3.** Once you are satisfied with placement, sew to attach to head; weave in ends.

# HAIR/ HAIRSTYLES

## OPTIONS

Mohawk...310

Curly Spritz...312

Hair Puff...312

Cylinder with Open Mouth and No Legs, Open Mouth with Four Pointed Teeth (Upper and Lower), Large Nubbins Limbs, Nubbin Footed Limbs, Medium Curved Horns, Curly Spritz

Egg Shape with Overbite and No Legs, Small Short Limbs, Rounded Feet, Small Half Circle Ears, Mohawk, Small Tongue

## MOHAWK (MAKE 1)

*Variable in length and height per your preference*

*Body Color Yarn: Approximately 4 yd/3.75 m worsted/medium weight yarn*

*Accent Color Yarn: Approximately 10 yd/9.25 m worsted/medium weight yarn*

*Optional: Pet brush*

### Part 1

1. Starting with a long enough yarn tail to weave in later, using the Body Color Yarn, Ch 31, Turn, starting in the second Ch from hook, SC 30 [30]

Fasten off with an 18 in/45.5 cm yarn tail.

### Part 2

1. Cut (at least) 30 pieces of Accent Color Yarn, each about 4 in/10 cm long.

**2.** Knot them in place, 1 piece of yarn per SC on Part 1. This knot is called a Lark's Head Knot and is defined in the Glossary.

> Add 2 pieces of yarn per stitch for a fuller look.

**3.** If using multi-ply yarn, unwind the strands for a crazy, curly look or brush it out for a fluffy, fuzzy look.

> I recommend using a pet brush or similar wire brush. Acrylic yarn works well for this step. You will lose some length and fuzz when brushing—that is normal.

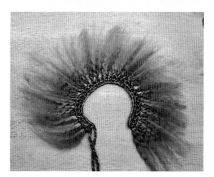

**4.** Pin into position on top of the Monster's head; sew in place.

**5.** After sewing, feel free to trim the Mohawk to a desired length or leave full length.

# CURLY SPRITZ (MAKE 1)

*Approximately 1 in/2.5 cm wide at the base of the hair piece, stretched-out curls reach 3.5 in/9 cm, relaxed curls span 4.5 in/11.5 cm wide*

*Hair Color Yarn: Approximately 18 yd/16.5 m worsted/medium weight yarn*

**1.** Starting with a long enough yarn tail to weave in later, in a Magic Circle, (SC, Ch 16, starting in the second Ch from hook, Inc x 15 along the Ch stitches) x 8, tighten the Magic Circle, Sl St to beginning stitch [8]

The "Ch 16, starting in the second Ch from hook, Inc x 15" are not included in the stitch count. You can crochet more chains to make the spirals longer (and make as many increases as necessary along the length of the chain). You can also create fewer or more sets of "SC, Ch 16, starting in the second Ch from hook, Inc x 15" to create a smaller number or greater number of curls.

Fasten off with a 12 in/30.5 cm yarn tail.

## Assembly

**1.** Pin in place on the Monster's head.

**2.** Use the yarn tail to sew the piece onto the Monster; weave in ends.

# HAIR PUFF (MAKE 1)

*Approximately 1 in/2.5 com wide at base of hair piece, variable in length*

*Hair Color Yarn: Approximately 12 yd/11 m medium/worsted weight yarn*

*Optional: Pet brush*

## Part 1

**1.** Starting with a long enough yarn tail to weave in later, SC 6 in a Magic Circle, Sl St to beginning stitch, Ch 1 [6]

**2.** Inc x 6, Sl St to beginning stitch [12]

Fasten off with a 12 in/30.5 cm yarn tail.

## Part 2

**1.** Cut (at least) 30 pieces of yarn, each about 4 in/10 cm long.

**2.** Knot them in place, one piece of yarn per SC around and on Part 1, anywhere you can fit them, until the piece is as full as possible. This knot is called a Lark's Head Knot and is defined in the Glossary.

Add 2 pieces of yarn per stitch for a fuller look.

**3.** If using multi-ply yarn, unwind the strands for a crazy, curly look or brush it out for a fluffy, fuzzy look.

I recommend using a pet brush or similar wire brush. Acrylic yarn works well for this step. You will lose some length and fuzz when brushing—that is normal.

**4.** Pin in position on top of the Monster's head; sew in place.

**5.** After sewing, feel free to trim the hair to a desired length or leave full length.

**Eyeball Monster Main Body/Eye with Crocheted Iris and Pupil, Eyeball Monster Eyelid, Thick Curved Antennae, Spider Legs, Hair Puff**

# TEETH

## OPTIONS

Pointy Teeth...315

Squared Teeth...316

Two Small Fangs ...318

Individual Medium Fangs...318

Two Medium Uneven Pointy Fangs...320

Two Walrus Tusks...320

Six Sharp Teeth...322

Four Humanlike Teeth...322

Two Close Together Rounded Teeth...323

Two Long Fangs...323

Two Pointed Teeth Two Flat Teeth ...326

Two Small Uneven Pointy Fangs...326

Two Curved Saber Teeth...328

Two Separated Rounded Teeth...329

Individual Small Short Fangs...329

It is optional to use sport weight yarn and a Size D (3.25 mm) hook for a smaller set of teeth for any tooth option.

# POINTY TEETH (MAKE 1)

*Approximately 3 in/7.5 cm wide, 1 in/2.5 cm tall at the tallest tooth*

*White Color Yarn: Approximately 2 yd/1.75 m worsted/medium weight yarn*

1. Starting with a long enough yarn tail to weave in later, Ch 5, starting in the second Ch from hook, Sl St, SC, HDC, DC [4]

2. Ch 5, starting in the second Ch from hook, Sl St, SC, HDC [3]

3. Ch 5, starting in the second Ch from hook, Sl St, SC, HDC [3]

4. Ch 6, starting in the second Ch from hook, Sl St, SC, HDC, DC [4]

Fasten off with an 18 in/45.5cm yarn tail.

## Assembly

1. Tuck the Teeth in place under the underbite or overbite on your Monster Body.

2. Once satisfied with placement, use the yarn tail to sew to attach. Also use the tail to sew down the tip of each of the four teeth to make them look tidy and secure. Weave in ends.

**Cylinder with Overbite and No Legs, Bulb-ended Short Limbs, Bulb-ended Long Limbs, Ram Horns, Pointy Teeth, Circle Belly**

# SQUARED TEETH (MAKE 1)

*Approximately 1 in/2.5 cm tall, 0.5 to 2.5 in/1.5 to 6.5 cm wide (depending on how many teeth you create)*

*White Color Yarn: Approximately 3 yd/2.75 m worsted/medium yarn*

> Before fastening off, you can create more teeth by repeating Row 4. For a shorter set of two teeth, fasten off after Row 2. For a single tooth, fasten off after Row 1.

**I.** Starting with a long enough yarn tail to weave in later, Ch 6, starting in the third Ch from hook, HDC 4 [4]

**2-4.** (3 rows of) Ch 8, starting in the third Ch from hook, HDC 4 [4]

Fasten off with an 18 in/45.5 cm yarn tail.

## Assembly

**I.** Tuck the Teeth in place under the underbite or overbite on your Monster Body.

**2.** Once satisfied with placement, use the yarn tail to sew to attach. Also use the tail to sew down the corners of each of the teeth to make them look tidy and secure; you can also shape them as you sew to be more sharply square. Weave in ends.

Sphere with Underbite, Thinner Eyelids/Eyebrows for 30 mm Safety Eyes, Bulb-ended Short Limbs, Bulb-ended Long Limbs, Thin L-shaped Horns, Squared Teeth

Egg Shape with Underbite and No Legs, Small Short Limbs, Big-toed Feet, Big Round Horns, Two Small Fangs

# TWO SMALL FANGS (MAKE 1)

*Approximately 1 in/2.5 cm long, 2 in/5 cm wide*

*White Color Yarn: Approximately 5 yd/4.5 m worsted/medium weight yarn*

1. Ch 5, starting in the second Ch from hook, Sl St 2, SC 2, Ch 9, starting in the second Ch from hook, Sl St 2, SC 2 [8]

> You can make one single small Fang by fastening off with a 12 in/30.5 cm yarn tail just before the Ch 9 instruction in Row 1.

Fasten off with an 18 in/45.5 cm yarn tail.

## Assembly

1. Tuck the teeth in place under the underbite or overbite on your Monster Body.

2. Once satisfied with placement, use the yarn tail to sew to attach. Also use the tail to sew down the tip of each of the four teeth to make them look tidy and secure. Weave in ends.

# INDIVIDUAL MEDIUM FANGS (MAKE 2)

*Approximately 1.5 in/4 cm tall, 1 in/2.5 cm wide at base*

*White Color Yarn: Approximately 3 yd/2.75 m worsted/medium weight yarn per fang*

1. SC 4 in Magic Circle, Sl St to beginning stitch, Ch 1 [4]

2. Inc, SC 3, Sl St to beginning stitch, Ch 1 [5]

3. Inc, SC 4, Sl St to beginning stitch, Ch 1 [6]

4. Inc, SC 5, Sl St to beginning stitch, Ch 1 [7]

5. Inc, SC 6, Sl St to beginning stitch [8]

Fasten off with a 12 in/30.5 cm yarn tail.

## Assembly

1. Tuck the teeth in place under the underbite or overbite on your Monster Body.

2. Once satisfied with placement, use the yarn tail to sew to attach. Also use the tail to sew down the tip of each fang to make it look tidy and secure. Weave in ends.

Blob
Body with
Underbite, Big
Round Horns,
Individual
Medium Fangs

Square
with Underbite
and Legs, Short
Rounded Limbs, Long
Rounded Striped Tail,
Thin L-shaped Horns,
Hair Puff, Two Medium
Uneven Pointy
Fangs

Egg Shape with
Overbite and No Legs,
Short Rounded Limbs,
Long Rounded Limbs,
Cat Tail, Cat Ears, Two
Walrus Tusks, Muzzle for
Egg Shape Body with
Overbite

Square
with No
Mouth and Legs,
Small Rounded
Overbite, Wide Flat-
ended Long Limbs,
Large Curved Horns,
Four Humanlike
Teeth

## TWO MEDIUM UNEVEN POINTY FANGS (MAKE 1 OR 2)

*Approximately 1 in/2.5 cm from side to side, 1 in/2.5 cm tall for the longest tooth, 0.8 in/2 cm tall for the shortest tooth*

*White Color Yarn: Approximately 5 yd/4.5 m worsted/medium weight yarn per fang*

1. Starting with a long enough yarn tail to weave in later, Ch 5, starting in the second Ch from hook, Sl St, SC, HDC, DC [4]
2. Ch 5, starting in the second Ch from hook, Sl St, SC, HDC [3]

Fasten off with an 18 in/45.5 cm yarn tail.

### Assembly

1. Tuck the teeth in place under the underbite or overbite on your Monster Body.
2. Once satisfied with placement, use the yarn tail to sew to attach. Also use the tail to sew down the tip of each tooth to make it look tidy and secure. Weave in ends.

## TWO WALRUS TUSKS (MAKE 1)

*Approximately 3 in/7.5 cm long, 2 in/5 cm wide*

*White Color Yarn: Approximately 3 yd/2.75 m worsted/medium weight yarn*

1. Ch 13, starting in the second Ch from hook, Sl St 4, SC 4, HDC 4, Ch 17, Turn [12]
2. Starting in the second Ch from hook, Sl St 4, SC 4, HDC 4 [12]

Fasten off with a 12 in/30.5 cm yarn tail.

### Assembly

1. Tuck the teeth in place under the overbite on your Monster Body. These teeth may be difficult to position with an underbite.

2. Once satisfied with placement, use the yarn tail to sew to attach. Also use the tail to sew down the tip of each of the two teeth to make them look tidy and secure. Weave in ends.

Egg Shape with Underbite and Legs, Small Cone Limbs, Medium Curved Horns, Six Sharp Teeth

# SIX SHARP TEETH (MAKE 1)

***Approximately 3 in/7.5 cm wide, 2 in/5 cm tall at the tallest teeth***

***White Color Yarn: Approximately 3 yd/2.75 m worsted/medium weight yarn***

**1.** Ch 3, starting in the second Ch from hook, Sl St, SC, Ch 4, Turn [2]

**2.** Starting in the second Ch from hook, Sl St, SC 2, Ch 5, Turn [3]

**3.** Starting in the second Ch from hook, Sl St, SC 3, Ch 5, Turn [4]

**4.** Starting in the second Ch from hook, Sl St, SC 3, Ch 4, Turn [4]

**5.** Starting in the second Ch from hook, Sl St, SC 2, Ch 3, Turn [3]

**6.** Starting in the second Ch from hook, Sl St, SC [2]

Fasten off with a 12 in/30.5 cm yarn tail.

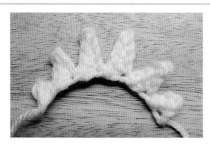

## Assembly

**1.** Tuck the Teeth in place under the overbite or underbite on your Monster Body.

**2.** Once satisfied with placement, use the yarn tail to sew to attach. Also use the tail to sew down the tip of each tooth to make it look tidy and secure. Weave in ends.

# FOUR HUMANLIKE TEETH (MAKE 1)

***Approximately 2 in/5 cm wide, 1 in/2.5 cm tall***

***White Color Yarn: Approximately 3 yd/2.75 m worsted/medium weight yarn***

**1.** Starting with a long enough yarn tail to weave in later, Ch 3, starting in the second Ch from hook, HDC 2, Ch 4, Turn [2]

**2.** Starting in the second Ch from hook, HDC 3, Ch 4, Turn [3]

**3.** Starting in the second Ch from hook, HDC 3, Ch 3, Turn [3]

**4.** Starting in the second Ch from hook, HDC 2 [2]

Fasten off with a 12 in/30.5 cm yarn tail.

## Assembly

**1.** Tuck the Teeth in place under the overbite or underbite on your Monster Body.

**2.** Once satisfied with placement, use the yarn tail to sew to attach. Also use the tail to sew down the tip of each tooth to make it look tidy and secure. Weave in ends.

# TWO CLOSE TOGETHER ROUNDED TEETH (MAKE 1)

*Approximately 1 in/2.5 cm tall, 1.75 in/4.5 cm wide*

*White Color Yarn: Approximately 2 yd/1.75 m worsted/medium weight yarn*

1. Starting with a long enough yarn tail to weave in later, Ch 4, starting in the second Ch from hook, HDC, DC, Half Trip, Ch 4, Turn [3]
2. Starting in the second Ch from hook, HDC, DC, Half Trip [3]

> You can make more teeth in the line of teeth if you want by chaining 4 and repeating Row 2.

Fasten off with a 12 in/30.5 cm yarn tail.

## Assembly

1. Tuck the Teeth in place under the overbite or underbite on your Monster Body.
2. Once satisfied with placement, use the yarn tail to sew to attach. Also use the tail to sew down the tip of each of the two teeth to make them look tidy and secure. Weave in ends.

# TWO LONG FANGS (MAKE 1)

*Approximately 2.25 in/5.5 cm long, 2 in/5 cm wide*

*White Color Yarn: Approximately 3 yd/2.75 m worsted/medium weight yarn*

1. Ch 9, starting in the second Ch from hook, Sl St 2, SC 3, HDC 3, Ch 13, Turn [8]
2. Starting in the second Ch from hook, Sl St 2, SC 3, HDC 3 [8]

Fasten off with a 12 in/30.5 cm yarn tail.

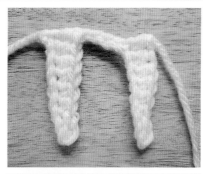

## Assembly

1. Tuck the teeth in place under the overbite on your Monster Body. These teeth may be difficult to position with an underbite.
2. Once satisfied with placement, use the yarn tail to sew to attach. Also use the tail to sew down the tip of each of the two teeth to make them look tidy and secure. Weave in ends.

Square with Overbite and No Legs, Bulb-ended Short Limbs, Large-footed Bent Limbs, Double-layer Pointed Folded Ears, Small Antlers, Two Long Fangs

If you want to add metal spikes to any part of your Monster, go to page 172 for tips on how to do that.

Cylinder with Overbite and Legs, Thick Curved Antennae, Three-fingered Wide Limbs, Two Pointed Teeth Two Flat Teeth

## TWO POINTED TEETH TWO FLAT TEETH (MAKE 1)

*Approximately 2.5 in/6.5 cm wide, 1.5 in/4 cm long*

*White Color Yarn: Approximately 3 yd/2.75 m worsted/medium weight yarn*

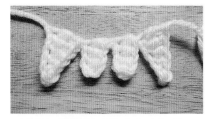

1. Ch 6, starting in the second Ch from hook, Sl St, SC, HDC, DC 2, Ch 5, Turn [5]

2. Starting in the second Ch from hook, HDC 4, Ch 5, Turn [4]

3. Starting in the second Ch from hook, HDC 4, Ch 6, Turn [4]

4. Starting in the second Ch from hook, Sl St, SC, HDC, DC 2 [5]

Fasten off with a 12 in/30.5 cm yarn tail.

### Assembly

1. Tuck the Teeth in place under the overbite or underbite on your Monster Body.

2. Once satisfied with placement, use the yarn tail to sew to attach. Also use the tail to sew down the tip of each tooth to make it look tidy and secure. Weave in ends.

## TWO SMALL UNEVEN POINTY FANGS (MAKE 1 OR 2)

*Approximately 0.75 in/2 cm wide, 1.25 in/3 cm tall for the longer tooth, 1 in/2.5 cm tall for the shorter tooth*

*White Color Yarn: Approximately 2 yd/1.75 m worsted/medium weight yarn*

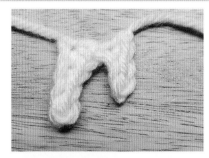

1. Starting with a long enough yarn tail to weave in later, Ch 5, starting in the second Ch from hook, Sl St 2, SC 2 [4]

2. Ch 4, starting in the second Ch from hook, Sl St 2, SC [3]

Fasten off with an 18 in/45.5 cm yarn tail.

### Assembly

1. Tuck the teeth in place under the underbite or overbite on your Monster Body.

2. Once satisfied with placement, use the yarn tail to sew to attach. Also use the tail to sew down the tip of each tooth to make it look tidy and secure. Weave in ends.

Cylinder with Underbite and Legs, Small Cone Limbs, Medium Pointy Antlers, Two Close Together Rounded Teeth

Sphere with Overbite, Pointy-toed Feet, Small Short Limbs, Medium Curved Horns, Two Small Uneven Pointy Fangs (two sets)

If you want to add metal spikes to any part of your Monster, go to page 172 for tips on how to do that.

Square with Underbite and No Legs, Squarish Short Limbs, Squarish Long Limbs, Medium Slightly Curved Striped Horns, Two Separated Rounded Teeth

Sphere with No Mouth, Medium Rounded Underbite, Short Arms with Two Fingers, Tiny Little Footed Legs, Medium Curved Horns, Individual Small Short Fangs, Long Thin Tongue

# TWO CURVED SABER TEETH (MAKE 1)

*Approximately 1.5 in/4 cm long, 2.5 in/6.5 cm wide*

*White Color Yarn: Approximately 3 yd/2.75 m worsted/medium weight yarn*

1. Ch 8, starting in the second Ch from hook, Sl St, SC, Dec, HDC 3, Ch 12, Turn [6]

2. Starting in the second Ch from hook, Sl St, SC, Inc, HDC 3 [7]

Fasten off with a 12 in/30.5 cm yarn tail.

## Assembly

1. Tuck the Teeth in place under the overbite on your Monster Body. These teeth may be difficult to position with an underbite.

2. Once satisfied with placement, use the yarn tail to sew to attach. Also use the tail to sew down the tip of each of the two Teeth to make them look tidy and secure. Weave in ends.

**Sphere with Overbite, Spider Legs, Two Curved Saber Teeth**

## TWO SEPARATED ROUNDED TEETH (MAKE 1)

*Approximately 1 in/2.5 cm tall, 2.5 in/6.5 cm wide*

*White Color Yarn: Approximately 3 yd/2.75 m worsted/medium weight yarn*

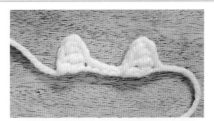

**1.** Starting with a long enough yarn tail to weave in later, Ch 4, starting in the second Ch from hook, HDC, DC, Half Trip, Ch 8, Turn [3]

**2.** Starting in the second Ch from hook, HDC, DC, Half Trip [3]

> You can make more teeth in the line of teeth if you want by chaining 4 and repeating Row 2.

Fasten off with a 12 in/30.5 cm yarn tail.

### Assembly

**1.** Tuck the Teeth in place under the overbite or underbite on your Monster Body.

**2.** Once satisfied with placement, use the yarn tail to sew to attach. Also use the tail to sew down the tip of each of the two Teeth to make them look tidy and secure. Weave in ends.

## INDIVIDUAL SMALL SHORT FANGS (MAKE 1 OR MORE)

*Approximately 0.75 in/2 cm tall, 0.5 in/1.5 cm wide*

*White Color Yarn: Approximately 2 yd/1.75 m worsted/medium weight yarn*

**1.** Starting with a long enough yarn tail to weave in later, Ch 4, starting in the second Ch from hook, SC 2, HDC [3]

Fasten off with a 12 in/30.5 cm yarn tail.

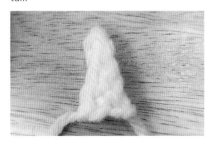

### Assembly

**1.** Tuck the tooth in place under the overbite or underbite on your Monster Body.

**2.** Once satisfied with placement, use the yarn tail to sew to attach. Also use the tail to sew down the tip of each tooth to make it look tidy and secure. Weave in ends.

# BELLIES

## OPTIONS

Large Ridged Belly...332

Medium Pocket Belly...332

Circle Belly...333

Egg Shape with Open Mouth and No Legs, Open Mouth with Short Row of Small Teeth (Upper and Lower), Three-fingered Wide Limbs, Nubbin Footed Limbs, Long Rounded Striped Tail, Medium Slightly Curved Striped Horns, Large Ridged Belly

Cylinder with Overbite and No Legs, Short Rounded Limbs, Long Rounded Limbs, Triangular Spikes of Varying Size, Pointed Folded Ears, Squared Teeth, Circle Belly

Egg Shape with Overbite and Legs, Curved Arms, Long Bunny Ears, Squared Teeth, Medium Pocket Belly

## LARGE RIDGED BELLY (MAKE 1)

*Approximately 4.5 in/11.5 cm tall, 5 in/13 cm wide*

*Belly Color Yarn: Approximately 20 yd/18.25 m worsted/medium weight yarn*

> To make a striped belly as seen on page 332, change colors as often as you prefer (the example shows switching colors every 3 rows).

**1.** Ch 13, starting in the second Ch from hook, SC 12, Ch 1, Turn [12]

**2.** BLO [Inc, SC 10, Inc], Ch 1, Turn [14]

**3.** BLO [Inc, SC 12, Inc], Ch 1, Turn [16]

**4.** BLO [Inc, SC 14, Inc], Ch 1, Turn [18]

**5.** BLO [Inc, SC 16, Inc], Ch 1, Turn [20]

**6–13.** (8 rows of) BLO [SC 20], Ch 1, Turn [20]

**14.** BLO [Dec, SC 16, Dec], Ch 1, Turn [18]

**15.** BLO [Dec, SC 14, Dec], Ch 1, Turn [16]

**16.** BLO [Dec, SC 12, Dec], Ch 1, Turn [14]

**17.** BLO [Dec, SC 10, Dec], DO NOT Ch 1, DO NOT Turn [12]

Continuing Row 17, SC in the same stitch where the last Decreases ended, SC along the unfinished edge of the belly for a total of about 15 SC, continue to crochet along the unused side of the starting chain from Row 1, Inc, SC 10, Inc, continue to SC along the unfinished edge of the Belly for a total of about 15 SC, SC in the same stitch as the first Dec of this row, Sl St to the beginning stitch [~46]

Fasten off with a 36 in/91.5 cm yarn tail.

## Assembly

**1.** Pin in place on the belly of your Monster.

**2.** Once you are satisfied with placement, sew to attach using the yarn tail; weave in ends.

## MEDIUM POCKET BELLY (MAKE 1)

*Approximately 5 in/13 cm wide, 2.5 in/6.5 cm deep*

*Belly Color Yarn: Approximately 11 yd/10 m worsted/medium weight yarn*

**1.** Starting with a long enough yarn tail to weave in later, Ch 2, working into the second Ch from hook, SC 4, Ch 1, Turn [4]

**2.** Inc x 4, Ch 1, Turn [8]

**3.** (SC, Inc) x 4, Ch 1, Turn [12]

**4.** (SC, Inc, SC) x 4, Ch 1, Turn [16]

**5.** (Inc, SC 3) x 4, Ch 1, Turn [20]

**6.** (SC 2, Inc, SC 2) x 4, Ch 1, Turn [24]

**7.** (SC 5, Inc) x 4, Ch 1, Turn [28]

**8.** (SC 3, Inc, SC 3) x 4, Ch 1, reorient to work across the unfinished straight edge [32]

**9.** Starting by working around the side of the last stitch of Row 8, SC about 17 across the edge (it is okay if this is not exact, but it should take about 17 to get across the straight edge) [17]

Fasten off with an 18 in/45.5 cm yarn tail.

## Assembly

**1.** Pin to attach the piece on the belly.

**2.** Once you are satisfied with placement, sew around the curved outer edge of the piece created by Row 8. Do not sew along the straight edge created by Row 9; leave this open to create a pocket. Weave in ends.

# CIRCLE BELLY (MAKE 1)

*Approximately 3 in/7.5 cm diameter*

*Belly Color Yarn: Approximately 12 yd/11 m worsted/medium weight yarn*

It is optional to work this piece in spiral or with the "Sl St, Ch 1" join at the end of each row. If you work it in spiral, it will not have a join seam.

**1.** SC 6 into a Magic Circle, Sl St to beginning stitch, Ch 1 [6]

**2.** Inc x 6, Sl St to beginning stitch, Ch 1 [12]

**3.** (SC, Inc) x 6, Sl St to beginning stitch, Ch 1 [18]

**4.** (SC, Inc, SC) x 6, Sl St to beginning stitch, Ch 1 [24]

**5.** (SC 3, Inc) x 6, Sl St to beginning stitch, Ch 1 [30]

**6.** (SC 2, Inc, SC 2) x 6, Sl St to beginning stitch, Ch 1 [36]

**7.** (SC 5, Inc) x 6, Sl St to beginning stitch [42]

**8.** Optional: Sl St 42 around [42]

Fasten off with a 24 in/61 cm yarn tail.

## Assembly

**1.** Pin to attach the piece on the belly of the Monster.

**2.** Once you are satisfied with placement, sew around the outer edge of the belly piece to attach to the body of the Monster. Weave in ends.

# CLAWS

## OPTIONS

Embroidered Claws...335

Tiny Pointed Claws...336

If you want to add metal spikes to any part of your
Monster, go to page 172 for tips on how to do that.

# EMBROIDERED CLAWS

*Variable width and length*

*Accent Color Yarn: Approximately 2 yd/1.75 m worsted/medium weight yarn total per Limb*

*Darning needle*

1. For a finishing touch, use a contrasting color of yarn and a darning needle. Loop the yarn around several times in 3–4 places on each paw/foot of the Monster to give the indication of claws. Weave in ends.

---

*NOTE: To embroider these embellishments, you can knot the end of your yarn, and then insert the needle between stitches and guide the needle back out of the body part where you want the embroidered accent to start through a crochet stitch (not between stitches) so that the stitch catches the knot; the knot will be hidden inside the work.*

---

**Cylinder with Underbite and No Legs, Wide Flat-ended Short Limbs, Large Cone Limbs, Tail with Hair Puff, Ridged Horns, Pointy Teeth, Embroidered Claws**

# TINY POINTED CLAWS (MAKE AS MANY AS NEEDED)

*Variable width and length, approximately 1 in/2.5 cm long, 0.5 in/1.5 cm wide*

*Accent Color Yarn: Approximately 1 yd/1 m worsted/medium weight yarn per Claw*

**1.** Starting with a long enough yarn tail to weave in later, Ch 4, starting in the second Ch from hook, Sl St, SC, HDC Inc [4]

Fasten off with a long enough yarn tail to sew to attach.

## Assembly

**1.** Pin in place on the end of a limb.

**2.** Once satisfied with placement and the correct number of claws for your Monster, sew to attach using the yarn tail; weave in ends.

**Eyeball Monster**
**Main Body/Eye with Crocheted Eye, Eyeball Monster Eyelid, Three-fingered Hand with Elbow and Arm, Two-toed Feet with Knees and Legs, Spiky Ears, Tiny Pointed Claws**

# TONGUES

## OPTIONS

Small Tongue...338

Medium Tongue...338

Big Long Tongue...339

Pointed Tongue...341

Large Double-pointed
Tongue...342

Small Double-pointed
Tongue...344

Long Thin
Tongue...344

## SMALL TONGUE (MAKE 1)

*Approximately 1.5 in/4 cm long, 1.25 in/3 cm wide*

*Tongue Color Yarn: Approximately 4 yd/3.75 m worsted/medium weight yarn*

1. Starting with a long enough yarn tail to weave in later, Ch 5, starting in the second Ch from hook, SC 3, SC 4 stitches in the last available Ch stitch, keep crocheting around to the other side of the row of chain stitches, SC 3 in each of the next 3 Ch stitches, Ch 2, Turn [10]

2. HDC 3, HDC Inc x 4, HDC 3, Ch 1, Turn [14]

3. Sl St 14 all the way around the edge [14]

Fasten off with a 12 in/30.5 cm yarn tail.

### Assembly

1. Tuck the tongue into an overbite/ underbite or inside an open mouth and pin in place.

2. Use the yarn tail to sew to attach to the Monster; weave in ends.

## MEDIUM TONGUE (MAKE 1)

*Approximately 2.25 in/5.5 cm long, 1.5 in/4 cm wide*

*Tongue Color Yarn: Approximately 5 yd/4.5 m worsted/medium weight yarn*

1. Starting with a long enough yarn tail to weave in later, Ch 9, Turn, starting in the third Ch from hook, HDC 6, HDC 4 stitches in the last available Ch stitch, continue around to the other side of the chain stitches, HDC 6, Ch 1, Turn [16]

2. SC 6, Inc x 4, SC 6 [20]

Fasten off with a 12 in/30.5 cm yarn tail.

### Assembly

1. Tuck the tongue into an overbite/ underbite or inside an open mouth and pin in place.

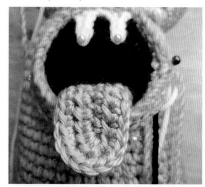

2. Use the yarn tail to sew to attach to the Monster; weave in ends.

# BIG LONG TONGUE (MAKE 1)

*Approximately 5.5 in/14 cm long, 1.75 in/4.5 cm wide at base, 2.75 in/7 cm wide at the widest part*

*Tongue Color Yarn: Approximately 30 yd/27.5 m worsted/medium weight yarn*

**1.** SC 6 in Magic Circle, Sl St to beginning stitch, Ch 1 [6]

**2.** Inc x 6, Sl St to beginning stitch, Ch 1 [12]

**3.** (SC, Inc) x 6, Sl St to beginning stitch, Ch 1 [18]

**4.** (SC, Inc, SC) x 6, Sl St to beginning stitch, Ch 1 [24]

**5–12.** (8 rows of) SC 24, Sl St to beginning stitch, Ch 1 [24]

**13.** (SC 3, Dec, SC 3) x 3, Sl St to beginning stitch, Ch 1 [21]

**14–15.** (2 rows of) SC 21, Sl St to beginning stitch, Ch 1 [21]

**16.** (SC 5, Dec) x 3, Sl St to beginning stitch, Ch 1 [18]

**17–18.** (2 rows of) SC 18, Sl St to beginning stitch, Ch 1 [18]

**19.** (SC 2, Dec, SC 2) x 3, Sl St to beginning stitch, Ch 1 [15]

**20–26.** (7 rows of) SC 15, Sl St to beginning stitch, Ch 1 [15]

**27.** SC 15, Sl St to beginning stitch [15]

Fasten off with a 36 in/91.5 cm yarn tail.

## Assembly

**1.** Stuff the tongue extremely lightly, just enough to have a small, light, puffy cloud inside.

**2.** Flatten the tongue. Using the yarn tail, sew along the center of the tongue from the final row to about Row 5 to create a line down the center of the tongue.

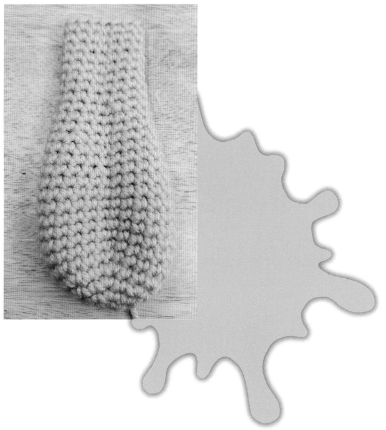

**3.** Use the remaining yarn tail to sew to attach; weave in the end.

**4.** Tuck the tongue into an overbite/underbite or inside an open mouth and pin in place.

**5.** Use the yarn tail to sew to attach to the Monster; weave in ends.

Square with Deep Pocket Underbite and Legs, Small Nubbins Limbs, Double-layer Wedge Folded Ears, Tiny Curved Horns, Small Tongue

Blob Body with Overbite, Small Bulb Antennae, Medium Tongue

Blob Body with Open Mouth, Open Mouth with No Teeth, Axolotl Flaps, Big Long Tongue

Blob Body with Open Mouth, Open Mouth with Short Row of Small Teeth (Upper), Bugle Ears, Small Double-pointed Tongue

# POINTED TONGUE (MAKE 1)

*Approximately 5 in/13 cm long from base to tip, 2.5 in/6.5 cm wide from side to side at base*

*Tongue Color Yarn: Approximately 15 yd/13.75 m worsted/medium weight yarn*

1. SC 5 in Magic Circle, Sl St to beginning stitch, Ch 1 [5]
2. SC 5, Sl St to beginning stitch, Ch 1 [5]
3. SC 2, Inc, SC 2, Sl St to beginning stitch, Ch 1 [6]
4. (SC, Inc, SC) x 2, Sl St to beginning stitch, Ch 1 [8]
5. SC 8, Sl St to beginning stitch, Ch 1 [8]
6. (SC 3, Inc) x 2, Sl St to beginning stitch, Ch 1 [10]
7. SC 10, Sl St to beginning stitch, Ch 1 [10]
8. (SC 2, Inc, SC 2) x 2, Sl St to beginning stitch, Ch 1 [12]
9. SC 12, Sl St to beginning stitch, Ch 1 [12]
10. (SC 5, Inc) x 2, Sl St to beginning stitch, Ch 1 [14]
11. (SC 3, Inc, SC 3) x 2, Sl St to beginning stitch, Ch 1 [16]
12. SC 16, Sl St to beginning stitch, Ch 1 [16]
13. (SC 7, Inc) x 2, Sl St to beginning stitch, Ch 1 [18]
14. SC 18, Sl St to beginning stitch, Ch 1 [18]
15. (SC 4, Inc, SC 4) x 2, Sl St to beginning stitch, Ch 1 [20]
16–19. (4 rows of) SC 20, Sl St to beginning stitch, Ch 1 [20]

**Egg Shape with Open Mouth and Legs, Open Mouth with Four Pointed Teeth (Upper), Thick Short Arms with Claws, S-shaped Horns, Pointed Tongue**

20. SC 20, Sl St to beginning stitch [20]

Fasten off with a 36 in/91.5 cm yarn tail.

## Assembly

1. Stuff the tongue extremely lightly, just enough to have a small, light, puffy cloud inside.
2. Flatten the tongue with the light stuffing inside.
3. It is optional to use the yarn tail and sew along the center of the tongue from the final row to about Row 8 to create a line down the center of the tongue.
4. Tuck the tongue into an overbite/underbite or inside an open mouth and pin in place.

5. Use the yarn tail to sew to attach to the Monster; weave in ends.

# LARGE DOUBLE-POINTED TONGUE (MAKE 1)

*Approximately 5.25 in/13.5 cm long from base to tip, 2 in/5 cm wide at base, 2.5 in/6.5 cm wide at widest point*

*Tongue Color Yarn: Approximately 24 yd/22 m worsted/medium weight yarn*

## Parts 1 and 2

Work Rows 1–10 once for each part.

**1.** SC 5 in Magic Circle, Sl St to beginning stitch, Ch 1 [5]

**2.** SC 5, Sl St to beginning stitch, Ch 1 [5]

**3.** SC 2, Inc, SC 2, Sl St to beginning stitch, Ch 1 [6]

**4.** SC 6, Sl St to beginning stitch, Ch 1 [6]

**5.** (SC, Inc, SC) x 2, Sl St to beginning stitch, Ch 1 [8]

**6.** SC 8, Sl St to beginning stitch, Ch 1 [8]

**7.** SC 7, Inc, Sl St to beginning stitch, Ch 1 [9]

**8.** SC 9, Sl St to beginning stitch, Ch 1 [9]

**9.** SC 8, Inc, Sl St to beginning stitch, Ch 1 [10]

**10.** SC 10, Sl St to beginning stitch [10]

For Part 1, fasten off with a short yarn tail.

For Part 2, continue on to Row 11.

**11.** Ch 1, SC 10, continuing by working into the first stitch from the final row of the Part 1 piece, SC 10 around, Sl St to beginning stitch, Ch 1 [20]

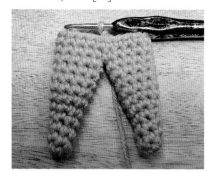

**12–16.** (5 rows of) SC 20, Sl St to beginning stitch, Ch 1 [20]

**17.** (SC 4, Dec, SC 4) x 2, Sl St to beginning stitch, Ch 1 [18]

**18–19.** (2 rows of) SC 18, Sl St to beginning stitch, Ch 1 [18]

**20.** (SC 7, Dec) x 2, Sl St to beginning stitch, Ch 1 [16]

**21–22.** (2 rows of) SC 16, Sl St to beginning stitch, Ch 1 [16]

**23.** (SC 3, Dec, SC 3) x 2, Sl St to beginning stitch, Ch 1 [14]

**24.** SC 14, Sl St to beginning stitch [14]

Fasten off with a 36 in/91.5 cm yarn tail.

## Assembly

**1.** Stuff the tongue extremely lightly, just enough to have a small, light, puffy cloud inside.

**2.** Flatten the tongue. It is optional to use the yarn tail to sew along the center of the tongue from the final row to the split in the tongue to create a line down the center.

**3.** Tuck the tongue into an overbite/underbite or inside an open mouth and pin in place.

**4.** Use the yarn tail to sew to attach to the Monster; weave in ends.

Blob Body with Open Mouth, Open Mouth with Buck Teeth (Upper and Lower), Thin Arms with Two Fingers, Spiral Shaped Horns, Large Double-pointed Tongue

## SMALL DOUBLE-POINTED TONGUE (MAKE 1)

*Approximately 3.5 in/9 cm long, 1.25 in/3 cm wide*

*Tongue Color Yarn: Approximately 5 yd/4.5 m worsted/medium weight yarn*

**1.** Ch 16, starting in the second Ch from hook, Sl St, SC, HDC, DC 12, Ch 1, Turn [15]

**2.** SC 10, Ch 6, Turn [10]

**3.** Starting in the second Ch from hook, Sl St, SC, HDC, DC 12 [15]

Fasten off with a 12 in/30.5 cm yarn tail.

### Assembly

**1.** Tuck the tongue under an overbite or inside an open mouth and pin in place.

**2.** Use the yarn tail to sew to attach to the Monster; weave in ends.

## LONG THIN TONGUE (MAKE 1)

*Approximately 3.5 in/9 cm long, 1 in/2.5 cm wide*

*Tongue Color Yarn: Approximately 5 yd/4.5 m worsted/medium weight yarn*

**1.** Starting with a 12 in/30.5 cm yarn tail, Ch 14, starting in the third Ch from hook, DC 11, work 6 DC stitches into the final Ch, continuing to work along the unworked side of the starting chain stitches, DC 11 [28]

Fasten off with a 12 in/30.5 cm yarn tail.

### Assembly

**1.** Tuck the tongue under an over-bite, underbite, or inside an open mouth and pin in place.

**2.** Use the yarn tail to sew to attach to the Monster; weave in ends.

Sphere with No Mouth, Medium Rounded Underbite, Short Arms with Two Fingers, Tiny Little Footed Legs, Medium Curved Horns, Individual Small Short Fangs, Long Thin Tongue

# EXTRAS/ FACES

## OPTIONS

Muzzle for Egg Shape
Body with Overbite or No
Mouth...347

Row of Spikes...348

Nose with Wide Nostrils...349

Embroidered Eyebrows...350

Embroidered
Sutures...350

*Approximately 3 in/7.5 cm wide, 1.25 in/3 cm tall*

*Main Body Color Yarn: Approximately 5 yd/4.5 m worsted/medium weight yarn*

## Part 1 and Part 2 (Make 2 Rows 1-2)

**1.** Starting with a long enough yarn tail to weave in later, SC 6 in Magic Circle, Sl St to beginning stitch, Ch 1 [6]

**2.** Inc x 6, Sl St to beginning stitch, Ch 1 [12]

Fasten off the first piece with a long enough yarn tail to weave in later. Repeat Rows 1 and 2 for a second piece, and continue to Row 3 without fastening off.

**3.** (SC, Inc) x 3, working into the first stitch on Row 2 of Part 1, (SC, Inc) x 3 [18]

Fasten off with a 24 in/61 cm yarn tail.

**Egg Shape with Overbite and No Legs, Short Rounded Limbs, Long Rounded Limbs, Cat Tail, Cat Ears, Two Walrus Tusks, Muzzle for Egg Shape Body with Overbite, Tiny Pointed Claws**

## Assembly

**1.** After you have sewn in place any desired teeth that you are using with this Monster, pin the muzzle just above/covering the Monster's mouth area.

**2.** Sew in place across the top of the muzzle, across the stitches from Row 3 of Part 2.

**3.** Weave in ends.

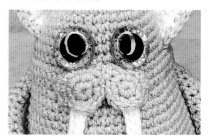

**4.** It is optional to use another length of nose-color yarn to embroider a triangular nose in the center of the muzzle pieces.

# ROW OF SPIKES (MAKE 1 OR MORE)

**Approximately 1.5 in/4 cm tall, 2 in/5 cm wide at base**

**Main Body Color Yarn: Approximately 3 yd/2.75 m worsted/medium weight yarn**

1. Starting with a long enough yarn tail to weave in later, Ch 6, starting in the second Ch from hook, Sl St 2, SC 3, Ch 6, Turn [5]

2. Starting in the second Ch from hook, Sl St 2, SC 3, Ch 6, Turn [5]

3. Starting in the second Ch from hook, Sl St 2, SC 3, Ch 6, Turn [5]

4. Starting in the second Ch from hook, Sl St 2, SC 3 [5]

> Row 4 can be repeated to create a longer row of spikes, as desired.

Fasten off with a 12 in/30.5 cm yarn tail.

## Assembly

1. Pin in place on your Monster anywhere you want.

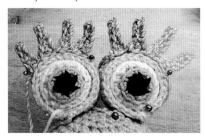

2. Once you are satisfied with placement, sew to attach to the Monster using the yarn tails; weave in ends.

Blob Body with No Mouth, 2D Open Mouth in Round Shape with Fangs, Eye Bumps, Medium Tongue, Row of Spikes

# NOSE WITH WIDE NOSTRILS (MAKE 1)

**Approximately 2.25 in/5.5 cm wide, 1.25 in/3 cm tall**

**Main Body Color Yarn: Approximately 4 yd/3.75 m worsted/medium weight yarn**

**1.** Starting with a long enough yarn tail to weave in later, SC 6 in a Magic Circle, Sl St to beginning stitch, Ch 1 [6]

**2.** SC, Ch 6, SC, Inc x 2, SC, Ch 6, SC, Sl St to beginning stitch, Ch 1 [8]

> Do not work into the Ch 6 stitches in this row. All stitches in Row 2 are worked into the stitches from Row 1.

**3.** SC, working around the next Ch 6 space work the following stitches: SC 5, HDC, continuing into the next available stitch, HDC, HDC Dec x 2, HDC, working around the next Ch 6 space, work the following stitches: HDC, SC 5, continuing into the next available stitch, SC, Sl St to beginning stitch [18]

Fasten off with a 12 in/30.5 cm yarn tail.

## Assembly

**1.** Pin in place on your Monster in the nose area.

**2.** Once you are satisfied with placement, sew to attach to the Monster using the yarn tails and small whipstitches around the outer edge of the stitches of Row 3 the whole way around the nose piece.

**3.** Weave in ends.

Egg Shape with No Mouth and Legs, Small Rounded Overbite, Small Short Limbs, Medium to the Side Curved Horns, Hair Puff, Two Small Fangs, Nose with Wide Nostrils

> If you want to add metal spikes to any part of your Monster, go to page 172 for tips on how to do that.

## EMBROIDERED EYEBROWS

***Contrasting Color Yarn: Approximately 2 yd/1.75 m worsted/medium weight yarn***

**I.** Attach a contrasting color of yarn in the area of the Monster's eyebrow and loop the yarn around several times above each eye to give the Monster an emotive expression (anger, surprise, etc.). Weave in ends.

## EMBROIDERED SUTURES

***Contrasting Color Yarn: Approximately 2 yd/1.75 m worsted/medium weight yarn***

**I.** Attach a contrasting color of yarn on any spot on the Monster's Body, loop the yarn in one long line, and then create several perpendicular stitches across the long line to mimic sutures. Weave in ends.

> Long stitches like these sutures are not suited for young children, who can get fingers stuck inside the stitches. If this Monster is meant for a young child, you can get a similar look using small, slightly overlapping stitches.

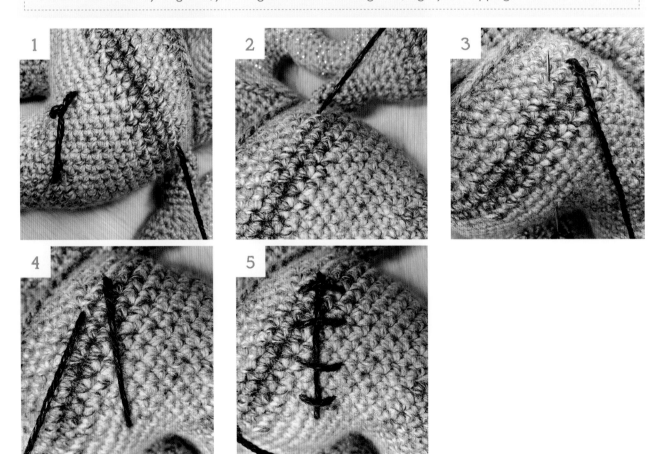

# ACKNOWLEDGMENTS

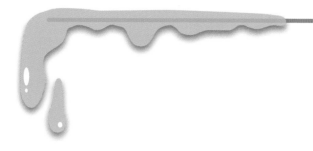

Special thanks to my husband and best friend, Greg, without whom I could not have accomplished all that I have. I love you.

And to my children, Riley and Harper, thank you for being patient with me when I've needed to spend time working. I hope I've made you proud, and I hope you know how much I love you.

Special thanks to my brother, Brendan Conway, who supported me through the process of creating this book, and to my wonderful sister-in-law Grace Conway, and to my new niece, Naomi, just for being you. I love you all dearly.

Thank you to my parents, Velma Conway and Richard Conway, and to my in-laws, Joy Lapp and Jim Lapp, for all of your love and support.

Special thanks to Lauren Lewis for making and photographing the monsters on the cover of this book and taking their individual portraits featured throughout. You are so extremely talented, and I'm glad you are my friend.

Special thanks to Jen Starbird, Sarah Constein, Amie Fournier-Flather, Morgan Carpuski, and Cordia Carlson for helping to check over this book top to bottom, test its patterns, and make it the best it can be. You're amazing.

Thank you to Doug and Barb for allowing me to regularly photograph my work in your magical garden. I love you both, and I'm extremely grateful to be able to photograph in such a stunningly beautiful place that you create and nurture so masterfully.

Extra special thanks to Morgan Carpuski, Sarah Constein, Shawna Dresslar, Amie Fournier-Flather, and Jen Starbird for making extra Monster bodies to be photographed in the step-by-step images in this book.

Special thanks to my FB group moderators and friends:

| | | |
|---|---|---|
| Kat Bifield | Alix Frere | Laura Marshall |
| Morgan Carpuski | Jeremy Leon Guerrero | Stephanie Norby |
| Sarah Constein | Daniel Jagoda | Tammy Simmons |
| Chantal DeFrancesco | Elizabeth Keane | Jennifer Starbird |
| Heather Flint | Lauren Lewis | Jennifer Steyn |
| Amie Fournier-Flather | Ashley Lodge | Jasmine Winston |

Special thanks to my agent, Christi Cardenas. I appreciate you.

# COMING SOON ...